HOLOCAUST HEROINES
JEWISH WOMEN SAVING JEWISH CHILDREN

Beverley Chalmers (DSc (Med); PhD)

and

Dana Solomon (PhD)

Grosvenor House
Publishing Limited

This book is published by
Grosvenor House Publishing Ltd
Link House
140 The Broadway, Tolworth, Surrey, KT6 7HT.
www.grosvenorhousepublishing.co.uk

A CIP record for this book
is available from the British Library

ISBN 978-1-80381-981-5

Dedication

Beverley Chalmers

To the child survivors: Shula, a *Kindertransport* child, and Avraham Werner, who, under the eyes of the *Wehrmacht* passed as Aryan. My heartfelt thanks for offering me a welcoming, accepting, and loving home, and second family.

To my husband Bernie, of over fifty years, who rescued me.

To my ever-enduring daughters who constantly urge me to write of happier things.

To Cecil Hayter and Dana Solomon, who spilled the beans.

Dana Solomon

To Beverley Chalmers, who spent her life protecting mothers and children, and who has always been a heroine.

To my husband, Simon, who saw me when few others did.

To those who fight to protect others from the harms they themselves continue to endure, and who are seldom seen, acknowledged, or honoured.

Acknowledgements

From Bev

My sincere thanks to the many who have contributed in so many ways to this book, but especially to my husband of over fifty years, Bernie, who has unselfishly supported me in my single-minded dedication to my research, academic life, and books. I could not have done this without his unwavering support and love.

To Dana, who despite her own challenges, helps me enormously. Her critical thinking, knowledgeable and insightful criticisms, editing and publishing skills, surpass all others.

From Dana

To Bev, who wrote this book and did not get angry when I ripped it to shreds – a few times. Thank you for inviting me to work with you on this and so many other books and for your patience and endless support over the last few difficult years. Your exceptional career is still the standard against which I measure all my achievements.

To my husband, Simon, who stands by me no matter how difficult life gets. You are my everything.

From Both Authors

To the archivists, colleagues and friends who helped Bev find Jewish women who saved children, including Shula and the late Avraham Werner, Israel; Noam Rachmilevitch of the Ghetto Fighters

House Archives, Israel (who scrutinized the penultimate draft, providing us with invaluable and critical insights); Ron Valdinger of Moreshet, Israel; Stephen Walton, Jessica Talarico and Lucy May Maxwell of the Imperial War Museum in London; Noa Gidron, and Judy Tydor-Baumel Schwartz, colleagues in Israel, and Ettie Zilber, Bev's colleague and "informal research assistant," in the USA. We are also immensely grateful to Les Glassman who helped Bev find stories of Jewish children saved by Jewish women, amongst his hundreds of invaluable interviews of Holocaust survivors.

To Margalit Shlain who connected Bev with Beit Theresienstadt in Israel, which then kindly granted Bev permission to use Friedl Dicker-Brandies' remarkable painting of a girl's face, created while in that ghetto, for the cover of this book.

This book honours over one hundred Jewish women, who despite their own danger, helped rescue or save large groups of Jewish children during the Shoah. It is dedicated to all those who care for children in war and in peace, and in whatever capacity they can.

Authors' Note

Holocaust Heroines emerged out of Bev's research on the sexual and reproductive lives of women in the Holocaust, and on children's experiences of sexual abuse during the Holocaust.

Bev's research examines the birth experiences of women in difficult religious, social, political, and economic situations. These settings reveal challenging circumstances ranging from political and economic repression in Apartheid South Africa and in the former Soviet Union; religiously inspired cruelty of female genital mutilation; over-medicalization of birth in the technologically developed world; and the horrors experienced by those whom the Nazi regime targeted for reproductive and sexual manipulation, and, in the case of Jewish women and children, extermination. This book is the next to address the horrors experienced by Jewish women and children during the Nazi era.

While writing *Birth, Sex and Abuse,* and *Betrayed*, Bev encountered many stories of women who had accomplished remarkable things, including Jewish women rescuing Jewish children, despite the dangers they were facing. She realised that these stories were rarely put together, published, or acknowledged. Even the situations, difficulties, and contexts in which Jewish women rescued children were seldom examined. She chose to honour their memory by focusing her next book on their stories and astonishing achievements.

Bev's professional collaboration with Dana began twenty-five years ago, while Dana was in high school and Bev was an international health consultant – and Dana's mother. Bev observed Dana editing one of her own high school term papers, and recognizing her skill, asked if Dana could do the same thing to one of her books. Thus began a twenty-five-year partnership. While Dana initially provided proofreading and editing, and eventually formatting and e-book publishing, over the years, Dana has also developed her own academic credentials and expertise to the point where she is now comfortable telling her mother to rewrite, rethink, and start again.

Dana's academic career started with her research on the use of Theatre and ParaTheatre during the Holocaust. Her work eventually expanded to include genocide and conflict studies more broadly, and focused on conflicts with significant ideological components. This led to her work on the Arab-Israeli conflict and to pioneering the development of entertainment-based approaches to combatting divisive ideologies. She is an academic, advocate, entrepreneur, and an artist, working on developing innovative and effective strategies to combat prejudice and advocate for equity.

With this complementary expertise, Dana has, over the years, provided increasing levels of conceptual and critical content development to Bev's books. During the work on *Holocaust Heroines*, Dana's contributions to the critical analysis and conceptual understanding of the work were invaluable. She made significant contributions to the content development, structure, and conceptual clarity of the book, while highlighting inconsistencies in the historical record regarding these women. Bev and Dana's frequent debates on the many ethical and moral choices represented in this book defined how they were discussed and how *Holocaust Heroines* engaged with them. With these contributions, Dana's work transitioned from that of a highly valued editor to that of a co-author.

While Bev wrote *Holocaust Heroines*, Dana's conceptual challenges and critical scrutiny have been invaluable and have extended Bev's own knowledge of, and engagement with this work.

About the Cover

Friedl Dicker-Brandeis' work with children in Theresienstadt inspired the cover image of this book, reprinted with permission of Beit Theresienstadt in Israel. She was an artist who was imprisoned in Theresienstadt in 1942. She created very little art in this part ghetto/part camp, as she spent most of her time teaching children and saved her scarce art materials for them. She did not always sign the art she created in Theresienstadt.[1] Three of the last artworks she created in Theresienstadt are images of wild flowers that some older girls gave her for her 45th birthday in the summer of 1943. The girls had smuggled the flowers into the camp under their shirts from the gardens in which they worked. This gift inspired Dicker-Brandeis to paint again. Her last picture, unlike the radiant and seemingly alive flowers, "is an apparently unfinished, lightly delineated aquarelle of a girl's face whose direct gaze seems to turn to us with an appeal and a message."[2] This haunting image reflects the cry of all children who sought help to survive the Nazi destruction of their families, homes, lives, hopes, dreams, and happiness. Although Friedl Dicker-Brandeis did not survive, her care for children helped them find an emotional escape from their surroundings.

Foreword

"Anyone who rescues one person is seemingly elevated as someone who has rescued the whole world" (Mishnah, Sanhedrin 4:5).

The issue of Jews saving Jews, has been quite neglected in Holocaust studies and research, with little or no mention of Jewish women saving Jewish children. Much has been written about non-Jews saving Jews, and the tremendous danger they put themselves and their families in, to do so. Yad Vashem has special awards to honour them, as the "Righteous Among Nations." Since 1958, 28,000 non-Jewish rescuers have received this prestigious title for risking their own lives to save a Jewish person's life, without getting any payment or material benefits for doing so, but only 600 Jewish rescuers have been awarded the honor of "Jewish Rescuers Citation" by the Jewish organization B'nai B'rith.

There might be many reasons why history and historical research has overlooked this issue, such as a psychological blind spot, but the most logical reason is that it seemed obvious that Jews had to help their fellow Jews. Women, above all, were expected to do so, in the same way that they were expected to share their meager portion of bread with the rest of the family, or not to flee from burning Europe while it was still possible to do so if an elderly or sick member of the family needed their aid or care. Thus, we can see that women were the last to be rescued and were left behind many times.

For example, there were no women, no mothers, daughters, sisters, or wives on the trains that rescued the Rebbe of Belz and his *Hasidim* (disciples) in 1939, or the Rebbe of Ger in 1940, or the Rebbe of

Satmar in 1944: all the men were saved, but the women were slaughtered by the Nazis. There might be some excuse for not saving the women in 1939-1940, when the fate of those who were left behind was perhaps unknown to most Jews, but there could have been no doubt about the fate of women left behind during the escapes in 1944. Yet all the trains in 1944 were reserved for men: no women were on them. Female lives were cheaper, since women could not serve as slaughterers (*Shohet*), *Mohels* (circumcisers), or adjudicators (Jewish lawyers). Women were expected to save others, not to be saved, and yet, women were the first to stand up in times of hardship and rescue others, in this case, children.

While early Holocaust studies focused on Jews as victims, Jews as resistors or saviours are only a recent focus of Holocaust study. Gender issues in both these areas of study – as resistors and as saviours – are largely ignored with the focus being on men: Jewish women as resistors were usually included in the study of all resistors, and simply included with their fellow men. As rescuers, women were taken for granted: this is what women should do, it was their duty, as has been said many times by Yad Vashem. An interesting example that is shown in this book is the one of Nicholas Winton, the man portrayed as behind the great rescue of the *Kindertransport*, who achieved far greater recognition than Marie Schmolka, the Czech woman who initiated the whole project, or Recha Freier, who worked in Germany, and created the Youth Aliyah movement. Freier saved thousands of Jewish children that found their home in Aliyat Hano'ar – the Youth Aliyah movement. At least 180,000 Jewish children from Europe, prewar, during the war and post war, were saved and educated thanks to Recha's initiative. Many of them (more than 7,000) were smuggled out during the war from Europe and settled in various *kibbutzim* in British Mandatory Palestine, and later on in Israel. Most of these children were in the age groups of ten to fifteen, many of them were orphans. Recha brought them to *kibbutzim*, to live and learn and find a warm community within a clear Zionist ideology, until they reached the age of eighteen. Many of them stayed for their whole lives. Unfortunately, Recha's initiative was honoured in Israel and elsewhere too late and too little, and not before 1981 when the president awarded her the Israel Reward for a "life mission."

In their book *Holocaust Heroines: Jewish Women Saving Jewish Children*, Dr. Beverley Chalmers and Dr. Dana Solomon (mother and daughter) co-worked on telling the stories of 108 Jewish women who accomplished, in the inferno of the Holocaust, what they were trained to do in their prewar lives: to save others, this time Jewish children, even if it meant endangering their own lives, families and often, even their own children. The book leads readers through different types of rescues: before the war, when Jews tried to escape from Europe, during the war, and during the very first years after the war, when thousands of Jewish orphans needed to find new homes.

Children were rescued in several ways, as we can learn from Chalmers' and Solomon's book. Some of them were saved by women who collaborated with larger organizations and provided false documents for the children and sometimes for their families. Others were helped to cross borders, to reach new and safer places, and then to find escape routes toward new identities. In the ghettos, women that worked in offices warned families with children before an *Aktion* (deportation), so that the families could hide. Often women risked their own lives by smuggling young children out of the ghetto and placing them in Christian institutions or families. In most cases only women were involved in the whole rescue operation. Jewish women provided warm clothing and sometimes food and shelter to the ghetto's orphans. In many cases, that meant sharing their own small portion of food with the children and fighting other members of their own hungry families to do so.

In the concentration camps, female prisoners helped each other, but special help was offered to young prisoners or children who somehow managed to pass the selection and be admitted to the camp. Female kitchen workers smuggled food to their block mates, with special attention given to young prisoners and children.

Another interesting way of rescuing, which is extensively discussed in the book, is children or children's groups that saved other children, or partisan groups, such as the Bielski family, that saved about 1,200 Jewish families, and kept them together in the forests.

The book delves into the awful dilemmas faced by children, their parents, and their rescuers. Dr. Chalmers, with doctorates in both

Obstetrics and Psychology herself, gives many examples of female doctors and nurses that did the impossible, to save the lives of children and their mothers. But, as a psychologist she does not spare her readers the dilemmas that some of the doctors, nurses and mothers had to face when they had to kill children, especially infants, to save other inmates, or to spare them from horrible deaths in the gas chambers or from famine in the ghettos or camps. At this point we must bear in mind that most children under the age of thirteen were killed when they arrived at the camps. If they happened to be strong, they might be sent to work, until they died of hard labour and starvation. Many times, killing them before this journey started, although horrific, was a decision of bravery and strength taken by the female doctors.

One of the dilemmas discussed extensively in the book focuses on the parents, who foresaw the danger of the Nazi regime and yet, could not separate from their children. Hence, the saviours had to convince the parents that staying with their children, especially the young infants, meant death for the parent and for the child, unless they tried to save the child by parting from them. Yet, many parents preferred to face the future together with their child/ren, for better or worse, life or death.

This dilemma has hardly been touched in previous works because the issue of parting with children was and still is too sensitive to be discussed. One of the many names mentioned in the book is Vladka Meed, who co-worked with two other Jewish women Marysia Bronka and Adina Blady. Their mission was first to persuade the Jewish mothers to let them take the children away from the families in the Ghetto, and then to find the children hiding places, mainly in the Aryan side of Warsaw.

Euthanasia and suicide, forbidden in the three dominant monotheistic religions, are thoroughly discussed in the book, on the one hand as a solution to saving young children from starvation, deportation, or other forms of agony, and on the other hand, to save others hiding with infants who cried, and whose cry might endanger the rest of the Jews in that hiding place. One particular story broke my heart while reading Chalmers' and Solomon's book. It was the story of Henry Friedman, a fifteen-year-old boy, who was hiding with his family and another group of people. Henry's mother gave birth to a baby girl, but the newborn had to be suffocated immediately after her birth, before the first cry, in order not to reveal all the other people in the hiding place to the Germans. Many parents could not live with what they did, and committed suicide after killing their child.

Another unbearable decision that parents often had to make was to choose among their children as to which should be saved and which one/s they would give up, or leave to die or be deported with the family, with the clear knowledge that staying in the ghetto meant deportation and death. The chosen child to be saved, however, might have a chance to live. The older and stronger children were usually chosen to be saved, because they had better chances to survive hardships on the one hand and keep the secret of their identity on the other.

Those women who succeeded in rescuing a child or a number of children had to struggle with Jew hunters, who turned in Jews for money, food or for any other reason. Hiding a Jewish child or family put the whole family of the rescuers in danger, thus many times, when the Jew had no more money or goods to offer, and the danger of being caught increased, the rescuer turned over the hidden Jew to the Germans. On the other hand, many rescuers paid with their lives because of informers. Some women rescuers were ready to pay Polish blackmailers with their bodies, just to be saved with their child or children. Although they could hide more easily if they were alone, they insisted on rescuing the child or children they had with them, who were very often not their own biological family. Often the children themselves had been sexually abused, as a part of the rescuing deal.

One interesting point that is made in Chalmers' and Solomon's book, is that among 56,252 testimonies recorded in the Shoah Foundation archives, they could not find even one given by Jewish women who saved Jewish children. The question, of course, is why, and the answer returns us to the beginning of this Foreword. Jews were expected to save other Jews, and above all, Jewish women were expected to save Jews in general, and children in particular. In Jewish tradition, as mentioned, women were the last to be saved and the first to be expected to be saviours. The heroism of Jewish women has, consequently, been overlooked for years.

Chalmers and Solomon are very thorough in their book when in the eighth chapter they outline rescuers from different Nazi occupied countries, with their names and place of activities. Chalmers' and Solomon's book is innovative as they expose 108 cases of Jewish women who rescued Jewish children and arrange them in an Appendix in a user-friendly list which is easy to access and understand. This leads the reader to the sad figures that out of 1.5 million Jewish children, fewer than 150,000 survived, many of them thanks to a brave woman or a group of brave women who rescued them.

So why has so little been written about these acts of heroism and why has it taken so long to do so? How is it that so little is taught in the school system about the glory of the Jewish women that risked their lives to save and rescue Jewish children?

The answer is easy: Women were the last to be rescued, but first to be expected to rescue others, as a part of their traditional upbringing and traditional domestic duties.

The answer brings us back to the patriarchal order in Europe at the second half of the 20th century on the one hand, and Jewish tradition on the other. As is said in the Mishna,

> The man precedes the woman when there is uncertainty with regards to which of them to rescue, or to return a lost item to, first. And the woman precedes the man regarding which of them to provide with a garment first, because her humiliation is great, or release from captivity first, due to the concern that she will be raped… (Mishnah, Horayot 3:7).

Prof. Lily Halpert Zamir
David Yellin Academic College of Education, Jerusalem
Director: WHISC: Women in the
Holocaust International Study Centre
Givat Haviva, Israel
1 February 2024

Table of Contents

Chapter 1: Rescuing Children

In the years building up to and during the Holocaust, some Jewish women went to extraordinary lengths to attempt to save the lives of Jewish children. Few of these women have been recognized or honoured. This book challenges this omission by sharing the stories of 108 Jewish women who saved large numbers of Jewish children. It considers the value of recognizing Jewish rescuers, and reveals the remarkable roles that Jewish women played in rescuing Jewish children. "Large groups" is not easily defined: most of the rescuers described in this book rescued dozens, if not hundreds of children. Some of these attempts were not successful. It is also possible that without survivors of unsuccessful attempts, these attempts have not been reported. Some women saved groups of children but lost their own lives in the attempt. Yet others were successful in rescuing multiple children. With death as their likely punishment should they be caught, both as Jews and as rescuers, these women's actions were courageous and astounding, and long overdue for recognition.

This book also considers the issues surrounding the recognition offered by Yad Vashem to award the honour of Righteous Among Nations to Gentile rescuers and not Jewish ones. Over 28,000 Gentiles have been recognized by Yad Vashem as "Righteous Among Nations."[3] Of these more than half are women.[4] In contrast, only about 600 Jewish rescuers, both men and women, have been awarded a "Jewish Rescuers Citation" by a joint program of the B'nai B'rith World Centre and the Committee to Recognize the Heroism of Jewish Rescuers During the Holocaust.[5]

1

While male rescuers, Gentile or Jewish, are not the focus of this book, some of the most frequently acknowledged Gentiles and Jewish men who rescued children are noted in the text. The focus of the book is, however, Jewish women during the Nazi era and their efforts to save large groups of Jewish children.

How Many Rescuers Were There?

There is no certain answer to this question other than "far too few."[6] Estimates vary from 0 to 0.25% or, at most, to 0.5%. Some have used these numbers to assert that, if correct, this means that 99.5% of approximately 700 million non-Jews in Nazi occupied Europe, did not help rescue Jews.[7] It should be noted, however, that these estimates cannot include people who helped individuals in comparably small ways, such as providing food or choosing not to disclose their hiding places; nor would it account for people who died while trying to help others, or who helped Jews who subsequently died and could not share their stories, to name only a few possible examples. The history of the Holocaust makes it clear that, in many Nazi occupied countries, with a few exceptions, the majority of the population were either active perpetrators or complicit bystanders. We cannot know how many committed small, yet significant acts to help Jews, that have not been recorded.

How Were Children Rescued?

Children were rescued in a variety of ways depending on the country, type of government in place, the duration of German occupation, the legal status of Jews in the country, the relationship of the Jews to local populations, and the attitudes of the government towards Jews.[8] Each and every one of these rescue activities involved danger, fear, bravery, daring, and potential death. Many rescue attempts were successful, but some were not. Many of the rescues were facilitated through major helping organizations. Others were undertaken and accomplished by a person working independently or by a couple who collaborated to rescue children. Some activities helped children to survive for a while, even if their lives were ultimately lost. Other attempts helped to improve the quality of children's lives, and to provide them with moments of happiness, even though they could not be rescued. Rescue efforts varied and involved multiple activities. These included:

- Providing false documents for Jews, including for children, was a central aspect of saving Jews. This involved forging papers, stealing documents and equipment to make documents, obtaining valid or false papers, such as Red Cross papers, traffic documents, food stamps, etc. to modify or adjust. This also involved distributing these papers to Jews wherever they were living or in hiding.

- Jews were helped to cross borders, both as immigrating refugees and as escaping citizens. Assistance also involved helping them find escape routes, pass border controls, adjust to a new country, or settle in a new place.

- Saving Jews involved providing warnings or other communications to Jews in hiding or those about to be deported. In ghettos, changes were made to deportation lists, people were hidden during an *Aktion*, or they were smuggled out of the ghetto. Couriers who travelled between ghettos and even across borders, transferred food, papers, news and weapons.

- Inside concentration camps, prisoners helped others, including sick Jews, by transferring them to work in better conditions, getting food for them and, for children, assisting with hygiene, avoiding them being sent to their deaths, and accompanying them for years, sometimes even to their deaths. Kitchen workers in camps smuggled food to their block companions, and to children's groups' co-ordinators.

- Some rescuers set up partisan camps in forests: some of these provided shelter for Jewish families including children. For example, the Bielski brothers established one of the most recognized partisan groups in the forest near Novogrudok in western Belarus, that saved 1,200 Jewish family members including children.[9]

3

- Underground groups made enormous efforts to free their fellow underground activists who had been caught and were incarcerated in prisons.

- Spiritual leadership was provided by many Rabbis at many stages of the rescue process sometimes at the cost of their own lives.

- Medical assistance was given by many in ghettos and camps as well as partisan units. This included treating the sick, hiding sick Jews, performing abortions, and treating the victims of medical experiments, including children.

- Community leaders exploited contacts, fundraised to assist rescue attempts, provided buildings to shelter Jews, concealed names and addresses of Jews from local authorities, and hid children in their homes. Some tried negotiating with authorities, often with little success. They frequently paid with their lives for offering such help.

- Others created children's homes: In France a network of children's shelters were established that saved tens of thousands of children. In Budapest, Hungary, fifty children's homes were established after October 1944. Within the stifling restrictions imposed on them by Nazis, and minimal chances of success, Jews managed to find courageous means of rescuing each other and particularly their children.

- Some were unable to save the lives of children but were able to offer them emotional or psychological respite from the horrors of the ghettos and camps, for example, through friendship, support, or involvement in activities such as art. These are recognized in this book as having endeavoured to save the quality of life of the children.

Who is a Child?

What ages are regarded as children varies across reports. Global definitions of children often include children under eighteen as defined by the United Nations.[10] Some, such as Deborah Dwork have studied children under sixteen.[11] Many other academics have used thirteen or fourteen as a cut off point.[12] To complicate matters further, most reports of children's rescues do not specify the ages of the children that were saved. In this book, I have regarded children as any whom the rescuing agencies have included in their reports as "children," acknowledging that while most of these were children under around fourteen, some were teenagers. The majority of children hidden with families or in religious institutions were usually much younger children ranging from virtual newborns to teenagers.

How Many Children Survived?

While about a third of Europe's Jews escaped the Nazi net, only about 10% of Jewish children did so.[13] The precise number of children who survived the war is unknown, although approximately 1.5 million were murdered.[14] Children were particularly vulnerable during the Nazi era. Many were killed as part of the Eugenics and Euthanasia programs; others died of starvation and disease in ghettos, camps or elsewhere, or were murdered at birth. Children under thirteen were murdered on arrival at camps such as Auschwitz, although those over this age might be saved to work until they died in labour camps; some were killed in medical experiments. The *Einsatzgruppen* (killing squads that accompanied the *Wehrmacht* murdered thousands in villages, towns, and cities, as the German army invaded the Soviet Union. Children were targeted by the Nazi regime to prevent them growing up and taking revenge.[15]

Sources

This book has relied heavily on academic publications examining rescue efforts and specifically those that addressed the rescue of children. Significant among these are the works of Mordecai Paldiel who served for many years as the director of the Righteous Among Nations Department at Yad Vashem[16] as well as the works of many of his colleagues such as Nathan Stoltzfus, Judy Baumel-Schwartz, and Chana Arnon.[17] The fifteen volume collection of Holocaust rescuers, and specifically those referring to women rescuers, published by Moshe Gromb, a member of this group for some time, are particularly helpful.[18] Other writings about individual major rescue attempts include texts focussing on, for example, the Tehran children,[19] the Buchenwald Boys,[20] the Windermere Children,[21] the American Krauses' rescue of fifty children,[22] the Marcel Network,[23] the *Kindertransport*,[24] and the emigration of about 1,000 Jews who were settled in Oswego in the USA.[25] In addition there are multiple books revealing the amazing stories of rescue, hiding, and caring for children that provided a rich background to assist in understanding the experiences of the children, their rescuers, their families, and the organizations that contributed so magnanimously in so many ways to the children's survival: many of these are referred to throughout this book.[26]

A search of 56,252 testimonies recorded in the Shoah Foundation archives, the Visual History Archives, yeilded twenty-one women with interviews recorded in English and thirty-six with interviews in any other language including Polish, Ukrainian, Russian, German, Lithuanian, Dutch, Hungarian, Slovak, and Czech, who were involved in rescue activities or giving aid to Jews. All of these women belonged to Christian faiths, primarily Catholic, Protestant and Eastern or Russian Orthodox denominations. No testimonies were given by Jewish women rescuers in any language, reflecting the relative paucity of awareness of such brave women. Moshe Gromb's fifteen book collection of Jews who assisted Jews provided a valuable source: some of those mentioned in these books saved Jewish children, but only two of the books focus on Jewish women rescuers. David Boder's remarkable early use of a tape recording device in 1946 enabled him to record the testimony, in Polish, of one Jewish woman, Lena Küchler-Silberman, who rescued large numbers of Jewish children and whose story is included here.[27]

Other archives that were consulted were able to refer me to some female rescuers of children. The Imperial War Museum archives in London, and the Ghetto Fighters House archives in Israel, were particularly helpful in guiding me to texts or reports on Jewish women of valour. In-depth reading about such women and their activities was able to provide me with further links to other women who had worked with them or with whom they had some contact.

Rescuers, both Gentile and Jewish, are hard to locate. Those who hid Jewish children are themselves hidden.[28] Many rescuers have died since the end of World War II. Many of the rescuers who survived chose not to tell their stories, but wanted to move on with their lives, not always thinking that they had done anything remarkable. Indeed, for some the regret at not being able to save more children (or adults) worried them considerably, leading to regret rather than feelings of pride about their activities. For some, and particularly Gentile rescuers, acknowledging their rescue efforts was dangerous due to ongoing antisemitism in Europe after the war. They feared repercussions for their actions. Many did not even want their extended family to know about their wartime actions that could have endangered these family members' lives if they had been discovered.[29] Many of the non-Jewish women rescuers who were honoured as Righteous Among Nations were reported to Yad Vashem by those they saved. Yet children who were rescued rarely knew their rescuer's name: if they did, such names were likely code names, used to protect both the rescuer and the children. For their own safety and for the safety of the children and their parents, rescuers did not tell the parents their own names or where they were taking the children.[30] Not only were the children hidden during the war, but so too were their rescuers, both during and after the war's end. For some rescuers, and some children, only the emergence of Holocaust deniers years later, led to the realization that it was important to speak out and tell their stories.

Ultimately, 108 women who rescued large numbers of Jewish children during the Shoah were identified and their stories included in this book. An appendix lists their names for ease of reference. For some, there is extensive information available about their activities: for others little is now known about them or their rescue missions. A search of the Visual History Archives for each of these women's oral testimonies revealed that only two of the 108 women recorded their stories: Sarah Shner Nishmit and Marysia Bronka Feinmesser. The testimonies of two other women who rescued large numbers of Jewish children were not recorded by the Visual History Archives, although the testimonies of their husbands were: those of Hansi Brand and Basia Temkin-Berman, whose fake name, Barbara Biernacka, was used in Warsaw. It is unknown whether Basia recorded a testimony prior to her death in 1953. A search of the major English language archives did not find any such recording. The extensive omission of Jewish women rescuers' stories raises the question of whether gender bias played a role in determining whether their stories were valued enough to record, either by the researchers and archives, or by the women themselves. No doubt there are more women whose names have yet to be unearthed, but these reports appear to be rare findings. Hopefully this book will stimulate further acknowledgement of such Holocaust heroines.

Types of Rescues

Rescues of children took a variety of paths. Saving children posed challenges from the perspectives of the rescuers, the children, and their families, that are discussed, in general, in Chapter 3. The subsequent chapters of this book consider the types of rescues that were undertaken by Jewish women to save Jewish children in the pre-war years, during the war, and after its end. The challenges facing each of these types of rescues are reviewed at the start of each of these analyses.

Before the war, during the Nazi era, there were few large-scale attempts to save children, as few truly anticipated the horrors that Hitler's ideology was about to unleash on Jews in Germany, or in countries that the Germans later occupied. Germany was a leader in European thinking and was a widely recognized and admired nation. It was virtually inconceivable, especially for German Jews who were deeply imbedded in German society, to consider that such a barbaric and cruel approach to any people, would ever have emerged in a society that was governed by the rule of law, by highly educated citizens qualified in medicine, law, engineering, and civil society in general. Yet it did, allowing little time for those at the receiving end of Nazi vitriol to escape.

After Hitler came to power and started to enact laws restricting Jewish life, people gradually came to see how dangerous the regime was. As often happens, some believed that the latest law was always the last; that things could not get any worse. Others could see that with each new law restricting the lives of certain segments of the population, there was momentum building towards an increasingly restrictive, authoritarian, and violent state. In the early to mid-1930's, Jews tried to get out of Europe through whatever legal or quasi-legal means were available to them, such as obtaining visas. By the later years of the 1930's, programs to facilitate the movement of Jewish children out of Germany were starting to emerge. Such large-scale group escape movements are discussed in Chapter 4.

When war broke out in 1939, and subsequently, as the Nazi decision to implement the "Final Solution" was seriously implemented, the rescue of children became a local and international concern, with rescue attempts varying from country to country, as the Nazis invaded their neighbours. Hiding children became a priority, and subsequently, smuggling them out of Nazi occupied countries to safer neighbours such as Switzerland or Spain, became the primary rescue approach. Jewish women's roles in these activities are discussed in Chapters 5 and 6. When escape for children became impossible, such as when incarcerated in labour and concentration camps, relieving their distress became the only available means of providing emotional or psychological escape from their terrifying living conditions, as detailed in Chapter 7.

At the war's end, a different type of rescue attempt was required, as described in Chapters 8 and 9. Thousands of children from Jewish families were left as orphans, or as hidden children in Christian families or religiously-based institutions. Retrieving these children and facilitating their resumption of a Jewish life became a central concern that was fraught with ethical, religious, and moral considerations.

How, where and when the many women who rescued children during the Holocaust were honoured or recognized for their efforts, remains a concern and consideration today and is discussed in Chapter 2. While the approach of Yad Vashem and more recently, B'nai B'rith, in honouring those who helped Jews, such as Jewish women who saved Jewish children, is outlined in Chapter 2, the national, and

9

particularly international recognition given to such women through media and film is considered in Chapter 10. This chapter also considers the morally ambiguous and sometimes dubious and deceitful decisions and actions that were taken in the honourable process of rescuing Jewish children.

Chapter 2: Honouring Rescuers

The enormity of the horrific events of the Holocaust have dominated study of this era. Early studies of the Holocaust focused on Jews as victims, leading to an erroneous depiction of Jews as being passive or submissive in the face of genocide.[31] The addition of a new perspective of Jews as resistors and as rescuers[32] re-framed this historical representation, transforming the false impression that Jews went to their deaths like "sheep to the slaughter," leading to the perpetuation of that false image becoming a frequently used antisemitic depiction of Jews.[33] The study of Jewish resistance, such as in the Warsaw ghetto uprising and the resistance revolts in concentration camps like Treblinka and Sobibor, have contributed to re-thinking this inaccurate perception, as has the ensuing exposure of heroic Jewish rescuers.[34]

Rescue of Jews, including the rescue of children, was an exceptionally strong form of resistance, but at times, has been a controversial subject to explore. Some might have thought that it was more important to concentrate on the tragedy of the Holocaust than to acknowledge the heroic actions of rescuers. Some were bitter that so few had apparently attempted to rescue Jews: promoting stories of Gentile rescuers might, to their mind, create an exaggerated and misleading image of abundant Gentile heroes. Writing about rescuers may also be seen as an attempt to soften the horror of the Holocaust.[35] Even the Oscar-winning movie *Schindler's List*,[36] which re-focussed the world's attention on the Shoah, is sometimes reviled for acclaiming one Christian rescuer. The academic literature in Israel did not include significant discussion of rescuers until approximately 1990. In 1991, Fogelman reported that an eight-year-old Israeli schoolboy was unable to find even one book in Hebrew about Raoul Wallenberg, a Swedish diplomat who saved the lives of tens of thousands of Jews in Budapest, Hungary, in the second half of 1944.[37] The study, recognition, and knowledge of Jews themselves as rescuers is an even newer area of study, with consequently fewer historical resources and significantly less public awareness.

There are only a handful of organizations around the world that acknowledge and honour those who opposed Nazism and saved Jewish lives during the Holocaust, Yad Vashem being the most prominent among them. To be recognized as "Righteous Among Nations" non-Jews need to have saved one Jew, provided they did not receive payment for their actions.[38] Jewish rescuers, however, have been intentionally excluded from Yad Vashem's Righteous Among Nations program that only acknowledges the heroic actions of non-Jews. Other organizations, such as the B'nai B'rith World Centre and the Committee to Recognize the Heroism of Jewish Rescuers During the Holocaust have started to correct this omission by acknowledging the role that Jews played in rescuing and saving other Jews. The Committee to Recognize the Heroism of Jews who Rescued Fellow Jews during the Holocaust was established in 2000 by Haim Roet who initiated the movement to rectify this omission. The Jewish Rescuer Citation program that emerged from this, established together with the B'nai B'rith World Centre, only started acknowledging the role of Jewish rescuers in 2011.[39] The paucity of Jews cited for their heroic efforts to save fellow Jews, to date, is likely due to many of the same obstacles facing Yad Vashem's program, but carries added challenges. The lack of a system to recognize Jews and the fact that seven decades passed before a program to honour Jewish rescuers emerged, likely plays a major role in preventing the recognition of Jewish saviours. Most Holocaust survivors and their rescuers would have died long before the establishment of this program, and thus been unable to identify these rescuers for recognition. The Committee to Recognize the Heroism of Jews who rescued fellow Jews has identified over 2,000 Jewish rescuers, most of whom remain unrecognized as yet. This project estimates that there are many more, perhaps between 6,000 and 10,000 Jews who may have rescued hundreds, if not thousands, of Jews.[40]

Many Jews who could have tried to escape, in every European centre, chose to remain, sometimes to yield their place to other Jews who might thereby be saved, and in so doing lost their own lives: Chief Rabbi Joseph Carlebach in Hamburg is one example of these.[41] Recognition of these selfless Jews, as well as countless Jews across Europe who engaged in subterfuge, forgery, smuggling, concealing other Jews, or leading them to safety across borders, has yet to be made and their efforts honoured.

There is even less known about those who rescued, or attempted to rescue, people from other groups specifically targeted by the Nazis, such as the Roma and Sinti, LGBTQ+ people, or those with disabilities.

Yad Vashem: Recognizing Gentiles, not Jews

On May 18, 1953, the Israeli Knesset agreed to establish Yad Vashem and its right to acknowledge rescuers as "Righteous Among Nations."[42] The Yad Vashem "Righteous Among Nations" award program subsequently commenced in 1963 as victims wished to honour their rescuers. The acknowledgment of these Gentile rescuers reflects only those rescuers who were reported to Yad Vashem and whose supporting documentation was assessed as meeting the requirements of Yad Vashem for such an honour. There are likely many more who rescued Jews who are not acknowledged for a variety of reasons, for example: those they rescued might not have reported their efforts, especially those living in Soviet countries who were prevented from doing so for decades; or many of the rescued could have died before being able to acknowledge their rescuers; or they lacked the documentation required to prove the valour of these heroes. It is also possible that rescued Jews were unaware of the identities of all those who played a role in saving them, and consequently unable to provide the necessary documentation.

Gentile rescuers living in Israel were largely ignored for decades. Because they were not Jewish, they were not provided with full government benefits or pensions. In 1985, Israeli TV highlighted the plight of these rescuers and, forty years after the end of the war, they

13

were acknowledged. In 1987, rescuers living in Israel were invited to attend a session in the Knesset whose members stood together in their honour. The Jewish Foundation for the Righteous was created to provide financial support for non-Jews who had risked their lives for Jews and were living in poverty. In 2004, the Israeli government offered monthly financial assistance to 1,600 Gentile rescuers in 28 countries living in poverty and gave special grants to rescuers in eastern Europe for the purchase of food for the Holy days.[43]

There are various explanations for the differences between recognizing Gentiles and Jews as rescuers of Jews. The logic provided by Yad Vashem for not recognizing Jewish rescuers is often based on religious conviction and particularly on the *Halakhic* (Jewish law) injunction for Jews to save their brethren.[44] Jews saving Jews was regarded as Jews doing their duty: according to Yad Vashem, this was the expected norm, not the exception, even though this religious injunction does not require one to risk one's own life to do so.[45] Yad Vashem argues that non-Jews had no such obligation or responsibility to their Jewish neighbours, so those who undertook to do so merit special acknowledgement. This, of course, ignores that many, if not most major religions, as well as fundamental principles of secular ethics, include the expectation that people should help others, regardless of background or belief.

On a more pragmatic, rather than ideological or religious level, Yad Vashem has been reluctant to honour Jewish rescuers because they regard Jews as having been in an impossible situation, where rescue of other Jews was virtually unthinkable and almost impossible, making even a perceived judgment of the actions of those who did not, or could not, save others, unfair and unwise.[46] Most Jews tried to save themselves, at least, if not members of their own families, making the honouring of them all an impossible consideration. After lengthy and considerable discussion of this issue, experts at Yad Vashem agreed that naming any single Jew for such an award would "likely create an unhealthy and ultimately divisive atmosphere of competition within Jewish communities and among families of victims and survivors."[47] Further, Yad Vashem considered that such an award "would engender superficial, and essentially unfair, categories of behavior, and risk disparaging the many Jewish victims who had no opportunity to act beyond their own desperate personal battles for survival."[48] To date, multiple attempts to include the recognition of Jews who rescued Jews into the Yad Vashem Act, through the Israeli Knesset, in 2007, 2009, 2010 and 2016, have all failed.[49] The question remains contentious to this day. Yad Vashem has acknowledged the importance and value of Jewish rescuers in recent years through less formal recognition processes, such as honouring Jewish rescuers during the 2020 Holocaust Martyrs' and Heroes' Remembrance Day event.[50]

One consequence of Yad Vashem's opposition to recognizing Jewish rescuers is the creation of significant inconsistencies and disparities in how recognition has been awarded. There are numerous examples of inconsistent and contradictory approaches to recognition as Righteous Among Nations, based solely on religious identity as Jew or Gentile.

One example is provided by Prof. Yair Auron regarding the decision not to grant the title of Righteous Among Nations to the village of Beslenei, a farming town in the Northwestern Caucasus.[51] In 1942 a convoy of Jewish orphans was rescued by Jews from Leningrad, which was under siege. The group travelled for four months on freight trains heading for the Caucasus, where, it was believed, they would be safe. Their escape was interrupted in July, when German bombs targeted the trains and killed many of the children. The remaining convoy travelled on, passing through many towns and villages where local populations refused to help them for fear of Nazi retribution and famine conditions. They eventually reached the village of Beslenei inhabited by Circassian Muslims. In Beslenei, the group of orphans was met by Circassian children between three and fourteen years old whose attempts to communicate with the orphaned Jewish children in the convoy went unanswered. The local children called their mothers who came from the fields to view the convoy. Each mother rescued one child. The villagers went so far as to create false birth records for each hidden child, indicating that the children had all been born in the village. The Nazis arrived shortly afterwards threatening to burn down the village if they found a single Jewish child in it. During the 157 days that the Nazis stayed, no one turned the children over to them. Auron reports that among the thirty-two children who were saved, there were a few non-Jews making the award of the title "Righteous Among Nations" inappropriate, according to Yad Vashem.[52]

Disparities also arise regarding the recognition of the Village of Le Chambon-sur-Lignon as "Righteous Among Nations." Five thousand Jews, including 3,500 children, found shelter in this town and its surrounding villages, rescued by Protestants and local Jews active in the resistance in southern France, Marseille, Nice and elsewhere. The Le Chambon-sur-Lignon rescue story reflects the complexity of efforts involved in saving Jewish children. In this setting, Paster André Trocmé, his wife Magda Trocmé, and co-Paster Édouard Theis, together with thirteen other Protestant ministers and their followers in twelve surrounding parishes, as well as Darbyites, Catholics, Swiss Protestants, American Quakers, Evangelicals, Jewish organizations such as Oeuvre de Secours aux Enfants (Children's Aid Society, OSE), other organizations such as La Cimade (a Protestant youth group) and Secours Suisse aux Enfants (the Swiss Red Cross), nonbelievers, students, scouts, underground railroad workers, farmers, city people, refugees, and other people from all walks of life worked together to save Jews.[53] All the villagers, along with members of these disparate organizations, chose to save Jewish children and adults, who were escorted, over years, to the villages by both Jewish and non-Jewish resistance workers: the villagers never revealed their hidden charges. The Jewish rescuers arranged for forged documents, food cards, and money for endangered Jews. They were essential to this significant, collaborative rescue operation. Despite this, only the Gentiles involved were awarded the honourable rescue title.[54]

Similarly, three hundred Jews, including one hundred children, were rescued in Nieuwlande, in the north-east of the Netherlands, and its nearby villages. Two resistance workers, Johannes Post and Arnold Douwes were recognized as "Righteous Among Nations" but a third rescuer, Max Nico Leons, who was Jewish, worked with them, and who risked his life for years, as had the others, was not granted the award.[55] Such disparities raise questions about distinctions being made between Jewish and Gentile rescuers.

One of the most well-known rescues of children was the *Kindertransport* which took about 10,000 children, predominantly Jewish, in small groups, primarily from Germany and Austria to England, where they survived. It was initiated by a Dutch woman, Gertrude Wijsmuller, who was recognized as "Righteous Among Nations" although her Jewish counterpart Recha Freier, who worked in Germany to rescue large groups of youth, creating the Youth Aliyah movement, was never granted the same honour.[56]

Gender Disparities: Disproportionate Honours

Disparities not only exist between acknowledgement of Gentiles and Jews, but also between the recognition of men and women. The gender imbalance in the study of history in general and the Holocaust in particular is well established. For the first forty or fifty years after World War II, Holocaust scholars concentrated their efforts on exposing the tragedy of the Holocaust as it affected all Jews without much reference to gender differences in this experience. The study of women in the Holocaust was stimulated only in the 1980's with the first conference on this topic being held in New York in 1983, probably emerging from the rise of feminism, and growing women's studies movements, at that time. A further major conference followed, held in Jerusalem in 1995.[57] Since then, the field of study has blossomed.

Despite the emergence of studies of women in the Holocaust, Jewish women rescuers are still seldom acknowledged as major players, or as independent actors in the rescue of large numbers of people. Rescue has been seen as primarily the role of men.[58] When rescue efforts are discussed, prominence is given to male rescuers, even when women played equivalent roles in equivalent rescues. Nicholas Winton has, for example, achieved far greater recognition for his role in the *Kindertransport* than Marie Schmolka, the Jewish Czech woman who initiated, and facilitated, his involvement, or the multiple other men and women who participated in these child transports. Janusz Korczak's heroic actions running the children's orphanage in the Warsaw ghetto and his choice to accompany the children to their deaths when he and 200 children were sent to Treblinka is well known, although the similar actions of his colleague, Stefania Wilczynska, who accompanied him on each step of the way, are hardly ever acknowledged.

Some rescuers, and particularly male rescuers, were credited with far more honour than they would have wished for, or was probably appropriate. For example, multiple people were involved in the organization of the various *Kindertransport* groups. Mary Penman, an experienced Quaker relief worker, Doreen Warriner, a feminist lecturer at the University of London, Beatrice Wellington and Margaret Layton were all instrumental in the initiation, and coordination of the program that brought Czechoslovak children, among others, to the UK as part of the *Kindertansport*. Marie Schmolke, a social worker in Prague was singularly involved in determining which Jewish children would be included in the transports and the list of 500 children that was utilized by Nicholas Winton was based on her work. Trevor Chadwick later took over this work from her. Others such as Tessa Rowntree and her cousin Jean, and the Reverend Waitsell and his wife Martha Sharp escorted children on the transports.[59] Nicholas Winton was only one of many who participated in these actions, but he himself had almost no contact with the children from Czechoslovakia. He was in Prague for only three weeks before the German occupation, he accompanied no trains, made no travel arrangements, never encountered the Gestapo, was never in any personal danger, did not use his own financial resources, and did not act alone. He was a desk-based part of the plan that eventually brought 669 unaccompanied Czech children to the UK alongside many thousands of other children that were rescued by the *Kindertransport*.[60] Winton himself downplayed his role in the children's transports and acknowledged the central roles of Warriner and Chadwick. Both W. R. Chadwick, the son of Trevor Chadwich and Winton's own daughter, Barbara, have written books debunking the myth that Nicholas Winton was so central in organizing the *Kindertransport*.[61] Historians, and particularly the Czech government, however, have continued to perpetuate the myth surrounding Winton's role, with a statue of Winton escorting children onto the trains, which he never did, being erected in Prague's main train station.[62] For his 105th birthday, the Czech President awarded Nicholas Winton the country's highest honour: the Order of the White Lion.[63] By reinforcing the idea that Winton was a Czech hero, the image of the Czech people being victims of Nazism and German aggression is emphasised, rather than acknowledging the role that the Czech government, and particularly activities undertaken under the leadership of the Catholic priest, Jozef Tito, in the Slovakian section of the country, played in persecuting Jews.[64]

The Slovak filmmaker Matej Mináč has made three films about Winton (*All my Loved Ones* (1999); *The Power of Good: Nicholas Winton* (2002) and *Nicky's Family* (2011)) all motivated to tell a positive story about the Holocaust. Mináč has also been behind efforts to nominate Winton for the Nobel Prize. He admits that he uses artistic licence and that he is not a historian, although he markets the films as educational. Mináč claims his films are based on archival documents and historical film footage to tell the story of the 669 children rescued from Czechoslovakia. In each of the films Winton is portrayed as staying in Prague, and working virtually alone. Winton is shown as making all the necessary travel arrangements, escorting the children onto the trains while Gestapo agents watch him suspiciously, and working on a plan that every other refugee agent thought was impossible. The films are misleading and inaccurate.[65] They also write women who worked on the *Kindertransport* operations out of the story. Meeting the children, helping them complete the required paperwork, typing up necessary documents, sheltering them at home and providing counselling, are all roles played by women, that are ignored. Mináč's stories encouraged the children who were saved, who usually did not know who was behind their rescue, to honour this one modest man who did not seek or acknowledge the public acclaim for his work that he received. Winton was the image of an ideal hero: male, British, long-lived, and never politically incorrect. The aggrandizement of his rescue efforts reflects both a need to whitewash the role of Czechoslovakia in the Holocaust and the reluctance of commemorators to recognize women's contributions and, rather, to promote male rescuers. While Winton's contribution should be credited, it should be placed in context.[66]

The subject of Jewish women as rescuers during the Holocaust highlights a number of, if not neglected, then certainly less dominant aspects of Holocaust historiography, including women's experiences, the roles of Jews as rescuers, and specifically the rescue of children. The disproportionate recognition of some male rescuers contrasts sharply with the erasure of women rescuers from history and serves to illustrate the urgent need to address the gender imbalance in this aspect of Holocaust literature.

Righteous or Heroic?

Lang writes that rescuers of Jews who risked their lives could never be expected to do so by any religion, including by Judaism.[67] Consequently, such rescuers are not "Righteous," but "Heroic." They did not simply meet any expectations of them but went beyond the expectations of normal moral conduct. He believes that religions cannot demand that one risks one's own life to save another. Such actions should be honoured but can never be expected.[68] In contrast to Lang's thinking, we note that many who serve in professions such as soldiers, police officers, firefighters, doctors working in dangerous situations, and lifeguards, to name only a few examples, are expected to risk their own lives while saving others. Why should religions hold us to a lower standard? Such heroism is reflected in the inscription on the medal given by Yad Vashem to the "Righteous Among Nations" that "Whoever saves a single life is as one who has saved the entire world."[69] Calling them heroes is certainly appropriate, even if not all are righteous individuals.

In Judaic belief, rescuers of Jews, "represent the *Lamed Vav*, the thirty-six unknown persons whose task it is to do good for their fellow human beings and who, the Talmud says, are required for the survival of the world."[70] This injunction is symbolic of the value placed in Judaism on helping others. Whether such Jews who helped others, often at the risk of their own lives, should be honoured as Righteous or as Heroes, remains controversial. Surely however, whether Gentile or Jewish, responders or initiators, regardless of gender, such rescuers should all be acknowledged.[71]

Chapter 3: Challenges

Extremely difficult moral, ethical, and personal dilemmas faced Jews in Germany as they confronted Nazi threats to their lives. In the pre-war years, some families denied the potential disaster that the Nazis embodied and that for others seemed inevitable. Many believed they would be protected from harm due to their previous history of fighting for Germany in World War I, or their significant social standing in their communities. Some too, could not believe that a socially developed and admired society, such as Germany, could ever commit atrocities on the scale that some anticipated. As Hitler's influence spread across Europe, and World War II began, the reality of the Jews' vulnerability grew increasingly clear, leading to acute anxiety and stress in families across the region. Primary among these was the question of how best to survive and how best to care for their children. Options open to families included trying to save children by hiding them with non-Jewish families or institutions, choosing to stay together and potentially die together, scrambling for rare visas for children to allow them to emigrate, alone, to any foreign country that might accept them, or escaping as a family to other countries that were not yet under Nazi rule.

In January of 1942, the Final Solution of the Jewish problem was established at the Wannsee Conference, held at a comfortable lakeside villa in an affluent Berlin suburb.[72] Fifteen men, many with doctorates, attended this meeting, at which it was agreed to exterminate eleven million Jews of Europe. By this time, however, the killing of Jews by the *Einsatzgruppen* and at the Chelmno death camp was already well underway. By the end of 1940, only around 100,000 Jews had been killed. During 1941, approximately 1.3 million Jews had already been murdered following the invasion of the Soviet Union on 22 June – called Operation Barbarossa – by German troops and their accompanying killing squads, the *Einsatzgruppen*. On 8 December 1941, the day after the Japanese bombing of Pearl Harbour and the entry of the United States into the war, the first large-scale gassing of 700 Jews in trucks, by carbon monoxide poisoning, took place at Chelmno. It became clear that more efficient means of murdering Jews was needed, both to expedite the murder of large numbers of Jews and to protect the German soldiers or SS who found the individual killing of Jews stressful. The Wannsee Conference provided the blueprint for how this could be achieved. By late autumn 1941, the construction of gas chambers at Belzec and Auschwitz was implemented and in early September, experiments with Zyklon B in Auschwitz revealed that this could successfully kill large numbers of Jews simultaneously. In preparation for the mass transport of Jews to such death camps, hundreds of thousands of Jews were moved into ghettos from where they could more easily be rounded up for transportation.[73] The Warsaw ghetto, for example, was established in October-November 1941. Belzec death camp became operational on 16 March 1942, Sobibor on 1 May, and Treblinka on 1 June.[74] As news of mass murders began to spread across Europe, revealed by the few who managed to escape from an *Aktion*, killing sites, or camps, and often transmitted through couriers who smuggled weapons, food and news across borders and between cities, towns and villages, families with children faced increasingly difficult decisions regarding their and their children's safety.

The experiences of parents, rescuers, and the children when facing the questions that arose regarding saving children are discussed in this chapter.

Parting with Children

When parents who foresaw the dangers of the Nazi regime considered how best to protect their children, some were unable or unwilling to consider being separated from them. The prevalence of antisemitism at the time might have led many to fear that others could not be trusted to care for their children. Or they might have preferred to face whatever future was to be theirs, life or death, together. Vladka Meed (Feigele Peltel), who worked as a courier in the Warsaw ghetto and was repeatedly able to cross from inside the ghetto to the Aryan side and return again, reported one such mother's words:

> Manya said: "I can't do it, believe me, I can't part with Artek. My son has no one but me now. I guard him like the apple of my eye. Together we have endured all this misery and misfortune. Without me, he would perish." [...] "No, I cannot do it. [...] Whatever my fate, it shall also be the fate of my son. We've been through so much together. Perhaps we'll succeed in surviving after all. If not, at least we'll perish together." [...] Both of them died in the ghetto.[75]

Vladka Meed, together with two other Jewish women, Marysia Bronka Feinmesser and Adina Blady (Inka) Szwajger, helped to persuade other Jewish women to relinquish their children to rescuers. They saved many children including twins Nellie and Wlodka Blit who were hidden in a house overlooking the ghetto where they could at least see their mother before her deportation and death in Majdanek,[76] six-year-old Olesh Blum, and one-year-old Krysia Klog, whose parents did not survive,[77] six-year-old Else Friedrich and one-year-old Irena Klepfisz who were placed in a Catholic institution and who survived,[78] and two brothers Bolek and Luzeral who were moved to the Aryan side. Bolek stayed and survived, while Luzeral returned to the ghetto voluntarily but was later killed there.[79] Vladka Meed also befriended Juzek, one of a group of Jewish boys who survived in Aryan Warsaw by selling cigarettes on the streets, and sleeping outdoors or wherever they could find cheap accommodation, while passing for Aryan. Yuzik turned down an offer of shelter from Vladka, preferring to live independently outdoors. Vladka was at least able to assist him by providing him with shoes and a warm coat, that facilitated his survival.[80]

It was not only parents who could not part with children but their teachers and caregivers as well. The story of Janusz Korczak's (the pen name of Dr. Henryk Goldszmit[81]) decision to stay with the children in his school as they were transported from the Warsaw ghetto to Treblinka and their deaths is well known. Although he was offered a chance to survive when an *Aktion* took place that rounded up children for deportation from the ghetto, he chose to accompany the children from his school as they were transported to Treblinka where they were all murdered. Stefania Wilczynska and Korczak ran the orphanage together. She too chose to accompany him and the children to Treblinka and to their deaths although Stefania's actions are rarely acknowledged.[82]

Dr. Tola Mintz made a similar choice. She was a physician in the Medem Sanatorium in Miedzeszyn near Warsaw that served as an orphanage for about 200 Jewish children in the ghetto.[83] Dr. Mintz lived at the sanitorium with her son, and served as a paediatrician and dentist. Although she was offered opportunities to escape the ghetto by the Bund (a Jewish socialist organization that resisted the Nazis in Poland) and by friends who arranged false papers for her and a hiding place, she refused to leave. When the ghetto was surrounded in the morning of 20 August 1942, she walked with her patients to the railroad tracks, and boarded the wagons with her nine-year-old son, Oskar. Their transport arrived in Treblinka the same day.

Another example is that of Helena Jockel in Hungary. She was an elementary school teacher in Uzhhorodin Hungary (now in Ukraine but in Hungary during the early 1940's). On March 18, 1944, the first day of Passover, the Jews were rounded up and forced into an old brick factory – a makeshift ghetto. Helena refused to go into hiding, although she had an option to do so, but stayed with the children.[84] As she said, "All over Europe the Nazis were killing children and now my children from the school were about to be rounded up. How could I escape and leave them to their fate? […] No, thank you."[85] Some weeks later they were all sent in cattle cars to Auschwitz where she was sent into the camp, and all the children to the gas chambers. She survived.

Killing Children to Save Them

Dr. Adina Blady Szwajger[86] worked in the Bersohn and Bauman Children's Hospital in the Warsaw ghetto together with Dr. Anna Braude-Heller, a noted, and admired paediatrician who was dedicated to helping mothers and babies, and who established child care centres and orphanages.[87] Within months of the Warsaw ghetto being sealed, children in this hospital were starving to death. Children lay two to three in the few available beds, with no linens, blankets, or sheets. Food rations were so meagre that medical staff gave up portions of their own minute rations to give to the children.[88]

Dr. Szwajger, as well as some nurses, risked their lives to save children both in the hospital and outside it. Dr. Szwajger gathered up children whose mothers had abandoned them, probably hoping to save them in this way, after the last trains had departed from the *Umschlagplatz* on their way to Treblinka. Dr. Szwajger sent these children to the hospital to save them.[89] Ella Golomb-Grynberg hid children who had been taken to the Warsaw ghetto *Umschlagplatz* for deportation to Treblinka under her flowing nurse's cape and hurried them out of the square to safety. She gave them sleeping pills to keep them from crying, knowing that if she were caught, two Jews would be murdered by the Germans for each child saved.[90] She also dressed older children in nurse's uniforms which allowed them to leave the collection area.[91] Ella turned down an opportunity to survive on the Aryan side of Warsaw preferring to stay in the ghetto to help nurse patients. She was captured in January 1943 and sent to the Poniatowa camp. There she took care of children, helping them until both she and the children were murdered together with the remaining 15,000 Jews in the camp.[92] Maria Rotblatt ran an orphanage in the ghetto in Warsaw, where these abandoned children, and others, could be sheltered. She and her son Lutek, served in the resistance. When their bunker at 18 Mila Street was finally threatened by the Germans, Lutek shot Maria at her request, and then took his own life, rather than surrender to the Germans.[93]

In some contentious situations, Jewish women undertook to save children from murder by the Nazis by granting them merciful deaths

25

before they could be transported to extermination camps. In the Warsaw ghetto, in the September 1942 *Aktion*, the Nazis rounded up the last of the hospital patients, and most of the staff of the hospital, for deportation to Treblinka. As a doctor, Dr. Adina Szwajger had a pass, or "ticket" allowing her to be exempt from the transport. She knew she would be forced to give up the children being cared for in the hospital when they were deported. To spare her patients from the death camps, Dr. Szwajger carried out mercy killings of children and adults, by injecting them with morphine.[94] Some have suggested that Szwajger killed the children in order to keep a promise to not abandon them.[95] Some have called her actions heroic, although calling someone who murdered children a "hero" is bizarre. Others have criticized her for killing children, particularly if she did so to keep her promise to not abandon the children, while saving herself and avoiding deportation.[96] However, it appears that Dr. Szwajger was so distraught by her actions that she ingested luminal in an attempt to end her own life on the same day that she murdered the children. Her friend, Dr. Hella Kielson saved her by injecting an antidote.[97] Dr. Swajger survived the Holocaust and served as a paediatrician in Poland until she died in 1993.

Euthanasia and Suicide

The ethical dilemmas surrounding issues of euthanasia, suicide, or even murder in preference to deportation to Nazi death camps or concentration camps were a common experience during the Holocaust. In some contexts, the choice to kill a child (or anybody else) could be, and was, viewed as a way of saving them from far worse tortures and murders. For some, choosing a peaceful, or at least swift death was preferable to the egregious horrors facing those tortured and murdered by the Nazis. Choosing to implement euthanasia for elderly or severely ill patients to help them avoid the tortures of the death camps, was a repeated choice faced by health care providers. Adults also sometimes chose to euthanize their elderly parents, or their children, to spare them the horrors of deportation and the death camps.[98]

In other settings, such as when groups of adults including newborn babies or infants were hiding from Nazis who were searching for Jews, saving the life of a crying baby might risk the lives of all those hidden with the child.[99] The life of the group had to be weighed against the life of the baby and often led to the accidental or even deliberate death of the newborn whose cries were being stifled.[100] Henry Friedman, a fifteen-year-old in hiding with a group, recalls his mother giving birth and the group's decision about the fate of the newborn:

> It came time for Mother to have her baby, and we faced a major crisis. How could Mother give birth? Even if there were a doctor nearby, we could not call him. And how could we control the infant's crying? We argued back and forth what to do. If the baby were allowed to live, our lives would be endangered. Mother had two boys and a third male baby was stillborn in 1938. She desperately wanted to have a girl. We decided to vote, and the decision we made has haunted me ever since. I wake in the middle of the night crying. My brother still denies that he voted. The baby would be suffocated by Sarah, who assisted with the birth [...] Later we learned that the baby was a girl.[101]

Parents were afraid of what appeared to be unfolding as the Nuremberg Laws were announced and enforced from 1935 onwards. Many chose to emigrate if they could, but often found doors closed to them. For some of those that remained, the prospect of Hitler's draconian rule left them only one choice: to commit suicide. In Amsterdam, more than 100 people committed suicide in the early weeks of the German occupation, putting their heads in gas ovens or jumping out of windows.[102] Mary van Itallie's parents were among those who chose to end their lives when the Germans began persecuting Jews in Amsterdam, forcing Mary to seek refuge by hiding in Corrie Ten Boom's home.[103] Within the first ten days of the annexation of Austria, known as the *Anschluss*, nearly 100 suicides were reported to the police in Vienna, almost all of them Jews.[104] Bernard Linhard had

27

once owned a thriving Viennese restaurant: he lost it after Hitler annexed Austria. He had been unsuccessful in getting his family out of Austria. In April 1939, his apartment was ransacked for valuables, with the thieves taking all the family's remaining money. On 20 April, Hitler's birthday, and two days after his son Peter's sixth birthday, he hanged himself with the cord of their venetian blinds.[105] In France, one woman living in the Marais district threw her two young children from her fifth-floor window and leaped after them: all died.[106] In Warsaw, during the Nazi attack on the ghettos, one by one, mothers jumped to their deaths with their small children, amid hails of German bullets.[107]

Parents' Perspectives

Which Children Should be Saved?

Many families tried to find hiding places for their children among the Aryan population. Some families had many children but were often only able to arrange a hiding place for one of them, leading to impossible, agonizing choices. Parents often preferred to give the oldest child a chance for rescue, thinking they would be best able to survive. Those who rescued these children and smuggled them out of ghettos to take them to hiding places, may have used different criteria when choosing which children to save. The rescuers' choices were based on the pragmatic needs of their rescue operations: for example, selecting infants who could be hidden more easily because they would be unable to accidentally betray themselves. Conversely, rescuers would also prefer older adolescents, who understood what was happening, and were more likely to remain silent about their Jewishness.[108] A key consideration was always whether the child would be able to successfully pass as a non-Jew. For boys, this was significantly more difficult, as being circumcised made concealing their Jewishness difficult. Some parents even tried to arrange circumcision reversals: for some this was successful[109] but for others it was not.[110] Children with a more Jewish appearance were also more difficult to hide. Similarly, as most Jewish children were not familiar with Christian practices or

28

prayers, such as how to cross themselves, they could not blend easily into a Christian world, making their rescue more dangerous. The inability to speak fluent Polish (or French or other local language) without any trace of an accent, was also a deterrent to successful concealment.[111]

Irena Sendler, a Polish Gentile who saved about 300 Jewish children by smuggling them out of the Warsaw ghetto,[112] focused on children from assimilated Jewish families, mostly from professional backgrounds, who could speak Polish, otherwise hiding them would have been far more difficult.[113] Irena Sendler discounted the common reports that she saved 2,500 children without acknowledging that she was assisted by many, including Jewish women who worked with her on these missions, such as Ewa Rechtman, Maria Rotblatt and Ella Golomb-Grynberg whose stories remain largely unknown and untold.[114]

Trusting Gentiles

For Jewish parents, there was no guarantee that giving up their children for rescue by non-Jews would help the child survive. A wrong word might give the child away, or the person who sheltered them might go back on their word.[115] Relying on non-Jews to save their children was also difficult for Jewish parents. Jews in Europe had faced millennia of antisemitism, including violent attacks, or pogroms, from the non-Jewish population increasing in frequency and virulence over the previous few centuries. That history, combined with the prevalent acceptance of Nazi ideology and actions in much of Europe, made trusting Gentiles extremely difficult for desperate Jewish families.[116]

With few alternatives, some parents did give their children to whomever they could trust in the hope that the children would be cared for. In some cases, the children's nannies or caretakers were entrusted with their care; often the nannies felt as much loyalty and connection to the families as the families felt towards them.[117] Other families turned to former colleagues asking them to care for their child, or asked strangers to take their children, or even left their children outside ghettos with notes attached, begging for someone to look after the child.[118]

For older children, like Avraham Werner, parents helped their children escape the ghetto, knowing that if they succeeded, their children would have nobody to turn to for assistance. In Avraham Werner's case, as a sixteen-year-old, his father provided him with false Aryan papers and the name of an acquaintance, and sent him from the Sanok ghetto in Poland to Lodz to make his own way, thinking Avraham would be safer in the city than in the ghetto. His father was correct: Avraham's entire family was murdered. Avraham survived, remarkably, while passing for Aryan, even after being recruited into the German army in the engineering corps, with which he travelled into the occupied Soviet Union through Romania, Hungary, Poland and, ultimately, Germany, where he was liberated by the Allies.[119]

Other children, even without their parents' initial help, managed to escape the ghettos and seek their own sources of support, or even learned to live independently. Those who survived found ways to do so by whatever means were available to them. The cigarette sellers of Warsaw were a remarkable example: as children, these approximately twenty teenagers traded cigarettes to scrape together enough on which to survive.[120] At first, they sang on the streets, begged, or offered themselves for causal labour. Later they sold cigarettes on the Three Crosses Square. Some smuggled food and arms into the ghetto and even participated in the uprising in the ghetto in 1943 and the Warsaw uprising in 1944. They learned to defend themselves, fight for their existence, and to help each other. Most survived.[121]

Spiritual Murder

Children rescued from ghettos were often baptised and became Catholic, allowing them to obtain authentic Church records and documents.[122] But many parents were afraid that if they released their children to the care of non-Jews they would be committing spiritual murder – *shmad* – or the loss of their children's Jewish identity and faith.[123] Fear of conversion, or baptism of their children into another faith, was frequently an insurmountable obstacle for these parents.[124] Orthodox religious Rabbis advised "We cannot exile our children from the Jewish nations simply to save them."[125] Jewish families called upon the Rabbis to guide them, some of whom argued that "We must not acquiesce in the spiritual destruction of our children [...] If more than 300,000 Jews are to be annihilated in Warsaw, what is the use of saving several hundred children? Let them perish or survive together with the entire community."[126]

Even if Jews ignored the Rabbis' injunctions not to send their children into Aryan care, fewer children of the more strictly observant Jews were likely rescued compared to those who were already orphans or from less adherent believers, or those who were culturally more assimilated.[127] While we have no figures to support this assertion, Irena Sendler's preference to save less distinctively "Jewish" children (children who were unfamiliar with Christian ways, or who spoke with more distinct Jewish accents), as they would be more easily identified and less easily concealed, is telling.[128] Children in Orthodox religious homes were less likely to be fluent in local languages since these families had less regular contact with the non-Jewish population. If they spoke local languages, such as Polish, they tended to speak a Jewish-inflected version of the language that was interspersed with loosely translated Yiddish expressions, making them more easily identified, and betrayed, as Jews.[129]

Some devout Jews, however, managed to overcome their religious convictions to save their children. Irena Sendler recounts one such story. She rescued a baby girl, born Elżunia but known as Elzbieta or by the nickname Bieta Koppe. The grandfather was told that the child would be baptised, and the family was heartbroken at the thought. Bieta's grandfather was devastated. A few days later, however, a package arrived for Bieta:

> Inside, carefully wrapped, was an exquisite lace christening gown and a bright golden crucifix for the baby, wrapped carefully in tissue paper. There was no note. There didn't need to be, because the message was clear: it was the family's goodbye to a desperately loved child, and it had come, Irena knew, at the cost of everything they must have saved inside the ghetto.[130]

31

Remarkably, this story was independently retold by Bieta herself, in Polish, in 1992, fifty years after Bieta's birth in Warsaw, and translated into English in 1998. The story was re-told by the adult child, now named Elzbieta Ficowska, who was adopted at about six months old, by Stanislawa Bussold, the midwife who helped Bieta's (Elzbieta's) biological mother give birth to her.[131] Stanislawa cooperated with Żegota and Irena Sendler to help deliver babies for Jewish women in hiding. Elzbieta learned as a child that her adopted mother's stepson, (Stanislawa's stepson), a building contractor, had transported her out of the ghetto in a wooden case with holes placed in it, that was hidden among the bricks that he was allowed to take into and out of the ghetto. In addition to her adoptive mother, Stanislawa, the baby was cared for by her parents' faithful nanny, Janina Peciak, who looked after her until her matriculation and who recalled that Elzbieta's biological mother had telephoned periodically and would ask for the receiver to be passed to the baby so that the mother could hear her baby's babbling. In October 1942, her biological Jewish mother called for the last time. It was the nanny who met with the baby's grandfather, Aron Pejsach Rochman, in "Aryan" Warsaw and who received the gift given to the new baby by her parents and family. Aron worked for the Germans outside of the ghetto and was able to meet with the nanny. The nanny informed the grandfather about the pending baptism of the baby Bieta, and he, in turn, gave the nanny the christening dress and small gold cross to be delivered. It was through the nanny's contacts with the family that Bieta learned of her parent's names, Josel Koppel and Henia Koppel, née Rochman. The nickname Bieta Koppe[132] clearly has its origins in the name Elzbieta Koppel given to the child.[133]

Although most parents did not know where their child/ren were taken or who was looking after them if they were hidden, a few Jewish parents confided in a friend that their child was being hidden so that, if the parents did not return, someone would be able to trace the child, identify the child as Jewish, and assist him or her. If they did not do so, then all trace of the child would be lost unless the rescuer willingly reported their actions or brought the child to a Jewish agency after the war.[134] Such was the experience of Leah Hirschman whose mother confided in a policeman about her being hidden, who was then able to testify to this after the war when questions of Leah's identity were raised.[135]

Rescuers' Perspectives

Religious Motivations

Religious affiliation did not appear to be a major motivation for rescuers, although some who rescued children might well have been spiritually inspired. Studies of rescuers have revealed that only about 12-15% of rescuers cite religion as a motivation for their actions,[136] with most of these belonging to particular faiths and nationalities such as Dutch Reformed, French Darbyites, Italian Catholics, Ukrainian Baptists, French Huguenots, and German Lutherans.[137]

While some rescuers, and particularly those rescuers who belonged to religious orders, convents, or other institutions, might have considered religious conviction when acting to rescue Jews, it is likely that many rescuers probably acted primarily on humanitarian grounds – with an often, rapid decision, such as when someone knocked on their door seeking shelter – to help another in dire straits when asked to do so. They did not necessarily see the supplicants of such urgent requests for help as Jews but as simply people in need of help.[138] The agreement to help others may have had religious roots, but not necessarily so. As André Trocmé said, when asked to turn over Jews hiding in Le Chambon-sur-Lignon, "We don't know what a Jew is. We only know men."[139] Likewise, many Jews who rescued other Jews also spontaneously initiated rescue operations.[140]

In contrast, it is estimated that 99.5% of baptised Christians did not help Jews.[141] The Catholic Church was traditionally antisemitic and no Papal decree was issued to encourage Catholics to rescue Jews. While people of other faiths are known to have helped Jews during the Shoah, such as the Muslim community of Beslenei, the predominant religions in Europe at the time were Christian. In pre-war Germany, for instance, almost all (ca 60 million) were Christian, either Protestant (ca 40 million) or Catholic (ca 20 million), with less than 1% of the population being

Jewish. In stark contrast with the lack of any Papal policy directed towards assisting Jews during the Holocaust, in September 2023, the Vatican beatified an entire Polish family for hiding a Jewish family, during the Shoah, for eighteen months. The Polish family were all killed for their actions, including their seven children, all aged under seven, and a newborn baby that was murdered with its mother at the moment of its birth.[142] It is unclear why the Church chose to bestow such a high honour on just this one family, when hundreds of Catholics helped hide or save Jews. It is also intriguing as to why this gesture has been made now, after so many decades.

Conditional Rescues

While religion may not have been a major motivating factor for many rescuers, for some rescuers, religious beliefs sometimes influenced their actions in ways that are contrary to humanitarian values. Jan Dobraczyński, the Director of the Child Care desk at the Warsaw Municipal Social Assistance Department, and a member of the Polish resistance, helped Irena Sendler and other co-workers to rescue thousands of Jewish children and to place them in Polish Gentile homes. He and Jaga Piotrowsak, who collaborated with him, were both ardent Catholics for whom baptism of the children was essential.[143] Jan felt comfortable with the thought that if the parents returned, they could return the child to Judaism. If not, the children could simply stay with their Polish family and choose, for themselves, when adults, whether they would remain as Christians or return to Judaism. The choice to return to Judaism as an adult, after a lifetime of upbringing as a Christian was, however, extremely unlikely to occur. On the other hand, their lives, and from Jan's perspective, likely their souls, would have been saved.[144] When challenged on this issue by a Jewish doctor, Dr. Adolf Berman, who was hiding on the Aryan side of Warsaw, Jan replied:

> Baptism was the price of his assistance and the Jewish community could take it or leave it. [...] If children and their parents want them to return to the Jewish faith when the war is over [...] this will be

the children's decision. Until then the children in
the convent homes [...] would be raised as Catholics
[...] to be Polish.[145]

Conditional rescues such as these can be viewed as yet another form
of attack on Jewish people and on Judaism: by killing the Jewish in the
child the Jew is killed. The intent behind these rescues is one that takes
advantage of Jews by forcibly converting their children. This is different
from the rescuer who places a child in a convent or with a family who
baptises the child to keep their Jewish identity secret, and to protect them,
and who, by not baptising the child would endanger the child's and,
perhaps, their rescuers' lives. The United Nations Genocide Convention
of 1948, Article 2(e), specifically states that "forcibly transferring
children of one group to another" is one of the specified characteristics of
genocide. While Jewish parents were not physically forced to agree to
baptism of their children when seeking their safety, the emotional and
psychological pressure put on them to do so, exerted by rescuers such as
Jan Dobraczyński and Jaga Piotrowsak, raises some serious concerns,
and undermines the integrity of these rescuers' motivations.[146]

Such conversions of the children also raise questions regarding the
spiritual value of these practices. Are conversions to Christianity
performed "under duress" or to effectively camouflage the child under
the guise of Catholic rituals, genuinely spiritually valid conversions? For
some children, and especially older children with deeper understanding,
this might well have been a truly spiritual undertaking, but for others, this
possibly reflected an expedient means of hiding the children rather than
some deeply felt spiritual acknowledgment of faith. The practices of
baptism, communion or confirmation, performed to effectively hide
Jewish children in a Catholic environment, were, however, apparently
regarded by those religious who officiated them, as having honest
spiritual meaning. They could, however, be viewed as spiritually
meaningless, if not dishonest.

Hiding Places

People who hid Jewish children were in serious danger. In much of
German-occupied eastern Europe, those who were caught hiding Jews

were likely to be executed if caught. Public executions of rescuers deterred others from offering to help.[147] In 1942, this injunction extended to those who simply knew a Jew was being hidden and failed to report it. In the Netherlands, Jew hunters were encouraged to reveal hidden Jews and were paid approximately half a week's wage for each Jew they reported to the occupying Nazis.[148] Known as *kopgeld* (head bounty), this was initially 7.5 guilders per person or approximately US $48 today.[149] Some Poles killed Jews in hiding, or took advantage of the situation by extorting or harassing Jews by demanding payments to keep quiet about the Jews' concealment. Sometimes the extortion was repeated multiple times, after which the extorter would denounce the Jew anyway.[150] Some Poles made a livelihood out of these actions: they were known as *szmakownicy* (blackmailers).[151] In consequence, rescuers did not always divulge that they were hiding children, even to their own family members, for fear that their family members might betray them. On one occasion this extended to one Polish man keeping his actions unknown to his wife and his daughters.[152] Some rescuers hid Jewish children while their houses were being searched by Nazis, but were so terrified by this that they then asked the children to leave the house, even though the rescuers stayed in touch with the children and even helped them later.[153]

Many Polish families were reluctant to hide Jewish children as, although they were often better off than their Jewish neighbours, they were also poor and ill able to care for an additional child.[154] Some who hid Jewish children regarded their care of the children simply as a financial transaction and returned the children to the ghettos if the money for their keep ran out – or they simply expelled the children from their homes. Alternatively, they placed the children in an orphanage or handed them over to the Germans.[155] Children told to leave the houses in which they had been hiding often moved to rural areas and usually paid their way through doing farmwork: they did not often reveal their Jewishness although it might have been presumed by the farmers.

In contrast, some Polish rescuers continued to keep the children they were hiding regardless of the dangers, even taking in vagrant children with little or no hope of remuneration. Other rescuers paid dearly for their safeguarding of Jewish children. For instance, one family hid two Jewish children. When their home was raided by the Germans, they hid in the forest with the two Jewish children and their own children. The Germans set their home on fire when they could not find the Jewish children, killing the elderly parents of one of the couple. Despite these enormous losses, the couple continued to care for the two Jewish children.[156]

Children's Perspectives

Challenges

In addition to the trauma of having to leave their own parents, children had to adopt entirely new personalities, names, religions, languages, and backgrounds if they were to be hidden successfully. In addition, they were told by their parents not to have sad faces: they had to pretend to be happy, as looking sad was a giveaway that they might be Jewish.[157] Going to Church was necessary for them to obtain baptismal papers.[158] Complying with these demands was essential for their survival. In many cases the children developed bonds with their hiding families to the extent that, with the children's agreement, some families wanted to formally adopt them, particularly if the children had been taken from an orphanage and both the children and their hiding family were not aware they were Jewish. In most cases adoption was not formalized during the war, as this might have led to their Jewishness being revealed.[159]

On the other hand, not all children who were offered shelter stayed with their hiding families for the duration of the war as these places of refuge were sometimes unhappy places for them. Children's experiences in hiding ranged from the extremely positive to devastating, in addition to being frightened and alone.[160] Some children were regarded as domestic workers who were forced to undertake the most unpleasant or difficult tasks around the house. Some children were physically, emotionally, and/or sexually abused by their hiding families[161] so that they fled, choosing rather to roam the countryside seeking alternate shelter, often by working on farms.[162] For example, one fifteen-year-old girl was placed with a family but her foster father wanted to have sex with her. She was moved to another home where the same thing happened. She was ultimately placed with two old ladies and that solved the problem.[163] Not all cases of abusive foster parenting were as easily resolved.[164]

Chapter 4: Pre-War Escapes

We will likely never learn of the rescue efforts made by all Jewish women who managed to save large numbers of Jewish children. Those Jews who saved one or two or even a few children are even less likely to be acknowledged today. Many of these stories have never been recorded as there was no incentive to record them in a central database dedicated to their retrieval. The few that we know about are, however, stunning examples of heroism.

Some of the most significant group rescue efforts by Jewish women saving children and youth include the endeavours of Gilbert and Eleanor Kraus, Americans, who rescued fifty Jewish children from Vienna before the onset of war, Recha Freier's Youth Aliyah movement in Germany that began during the early Nazi period, as well as the *Kindertransport* which managed to take 10,000 children, of whom 7,500 were Jewish, to the UK just before the start of World War II. Others, like Fela Perlman, Beate Berger and Basia Berman, undertook localized endeavours that helped make the lives of Jewish children a little easier. Fela Perlman, for example, with the mayor's permission, created a school for Jewish children in Brussels when they were forbidden to attend local schools. Her school lasted for a few months before it too was closed down. She then helped to find safe refuges for children, including offering sanctuary in her own home.[165] After the war she established four orphanages for Jewish children.[166] Beate Berger created a home for children escaping the Holocaust to live in British Mandatory Palestine/Israel.[167] Basia Berman, during the first months of Nazi occupation, did not rescue children in the sense of helping them escape, but did manage to improve the quality of their lives considerably by collecting books for refugee children in Warsaw. In 1940 she established a library in the ghetto. She and her husband escaped the ghetto in September 1942 and passed as Aryan to survive. Ultimately, her collection of books included about 120,000 books mostly in Yiddish and Hebrew.[168]

Although there were other endeavours to save children undertaken by non-Jewish women, such as the remarkable rescues of Irena Sendler and her colleagues,[169] the focus of this book is on Jewish women who played a major role in child rescue. Many of the non-Jewish rescuers have been honoured by Yad Vashem as Righteous Among Nations, including Irena Sendler, a social worker who, with many others, saved many children from the Warsaw ghetto;[170] Mary Elmes, an Irish woman from a progressive and wealthy family;[171] Marion Pritchard, a student social worker in the Netherlands who was enraged when she witnessed Germans throwing children onto a truck for deportation and chose instead to rescue children;[172] Suzanne Spaak, who came from a wealthy family and was married with two children but who found the Nazis intolerable and chose to enter the resistance;[173] Lois Gudrun, an American Mennonite woman who was sent to establish a children's home on the Mediterranean;[174] and Jeanne Daman-Scaglione, from Belgium, who was outraged when Jewish children were not allowed to attend schools and chose instead to help them hide from deportation.[175]

There are also many Jewish men who participated in the rescue of Jews, either children or adults, such as Wilfred Israel, whose department store helped equip some of the children on the *Kindertransport*; Walter Suskind, who helped smuggle Jews and Jewish children out of the Nazi holding place in Amsterdam, before their deportation to the camps; Georges Garel and Georges Loinger who helped hide or smuggle children out of France; and Rabbi Schneerson, who moved children from place to place evading their capture by Germans. Some of the children he cared for were captured and all but one of those were killed in Auschwitz. The others, together with the Rabbi, remained in hiding until liberation.[176] The stories of these men are mentioned in this book only to the extent that their activities interacted with Jewish women rescuers of children.

American Jewish Women

While most rescuers worked within Nazi occupied Europe, there were some international efforts to save Jews, particularly from the USA and British Mandatory Palestine. In the USA, those who wanted to rescue Jews out of Europe faced significant opposition from both the American population and the USA government. The USA opposed Jewish immigration, making it difficult to rescue Jews, including Jewish children.

The USA, in addition to other countries such as Canada, is renowned for its reluctance to admit Jewish immigrants before, during and after World War II. In the USA, immigration quotas were set, but rarely filled. In 1933, only 5% of the allocated quota for German immigrants was filled, admitting 1,445 people. In 1936, only 27% of the quota was filled, allowing 6,642 into the country. In 1938, the quota remained two-thirds filled. During the first five years of Hitler's rule, from 1933 to 1937, only 25,930 German Jews were admitted into the USA. The annual quota for German Jews, however, was 25,957 for each of these years (for a total of 129,785 from 1933 to 1937).[177] Following *Kristallnacht*, demand for immigration escalated but senior officials in the State Department deliberately responded slowly fearing that Jews would flood the country.[178]

At about the same time, other groups in the USA were trying to get special permission to bring 20,000 children from Germany to the USA over and above the current quotas allowed, following the example of the *Kindertransport* in the UK.[179] The plan was proposed in congress as the Wagner-Rogers Bill supported by Senator Robert Wagner in the Senate and Edith Rogers, in the House of Representatives. Given the attitudes towards Jews in the United States at the time, the Bill had no chance of success. A Gallup poll soon after *Kristallnacht* revealed that 94% of Americans disapproved of the events of that night, but 72% remained disapproving of admitting any more refugees to the USA.[180] A Roper poll further revealed that 67% of Americans favoured stopping the immigration of ten thousand children from Nazi Germany into the USA including 20% of American Jews who favoured a stricter immigration policy for fear of inflaming antisemitic sentiments.

Polls in the late 1930's showed that 60% of Americans regarded Jews as greedy, dishonest, and pushy. More than 40% felt Jews had too much power, a number that rose to 58% by 1945. As many as 10% of Americans thought that all Jews should be expelled from the country.[181] Antisemitism in the USA was fuelled by Father Charles Coughlin, the so-called radio priest of the 1930's as well as antisemitic diatribes issued by Fritz Kuhn, the German born leader of the German American Bund, a pro-Hitler group popular in the 1930's.[182] Antisemitism was rife in government circles too. At a Washington dinner party, someone asked Laura Delano Houghteling, the wife of the US Immigration Commissioner and President Roosevelt's first cousin, about Jewish immigration. She responded: "Twenty thousand charming children would all too soon grow up into twenty thousand ugly adults."[183]

Not surprisingly the Wagner-Rogers Bill was not supported by Roosevelt. Fewer than 400 Jewish children were admitted to the USA by the end of 1938. They usually arrived only one or two at a time. The Wagner-Rogers Bill was the only Bill proposing increased Jewish refugee admission to the USA to be debated in Congress. In contrast, one year later, when British children were threatened by the bombing of London, President Roosevelt and congress rushed through legislation allowing two thousand British children to be granted temporary shelter in the USA.[184]

Another American organization that tried to bring in children also had minimal success, initially. The German-Jewish Children's Aid, led by Cecilia Razovsky, a Jewish woman, rescued ten Jewish children from Germany in 1934 but was severely criticized for doing so. Although Razovsky continued to fight against the quota system in the USA,[185] she was only able to bring in a few children at a time.[186] Cecilia was an activist social worker who dedicated her life to assisting immigrants and refugees to the USA including Jewish refugees from Nazi occupied regions. Later efforts by Cecilia Razovsky and her various affiliated organizations, the National Coordinating Committee for Aid to Refugees and Emigrants Coming from Germany (NCC), the German-Jewish Children's Aid (GJCA) and the Migration Department of the National Refugee Service, were more successful with about 1,000 children aged two to sixteen, ultimately smuggled clandestinely out of Germany and Austria between 1934 and 1945 and taken to live with Jewish foster families in the USA. Cecilia gave the children personal attention supporting their needs. After World War II she travelled to Displaced Persons camps to find children and to arrange their transfer to British Mandatory Palestine and to the USA. She worked closely with Francis Perkins, Roosevelt's Secretary of Labour, in the USA and Kate Rosenheim who was Head of the Department of Children's Emigration in Germany, to secure the safety of these children. Between the three of them, by fighting the quota laws and through persuasion of their personal and political contacts they managed to rescue 7,250 Jewish children, although only 1,000 of these children were ever admitted to the USA.[187]

Gilbert and Eleanor Kraus in the USA

Given widespread antisemitism in the USA and the reluctance to formally approve the admission of Jews or Jewish children to America, through the formal quota system, the rescue efforts of Gilbert Kraus, an American lawyer, and his wife Eleanor, were notable. They were both affluent secular Jews from Philadelphia. In January 1939, Gilbert was approached by Brith Sholom, a Jewish organization in the USA, to undertake a rescue mission for Jewish children. Gilbert and Eleanor had become increasingly concerned about reports of Nazi atrocities against Jews in Germany and Austria, and Gilbert determined to do what he could to help. The couple were confronted by the difficulty, if not impossibility, of seeking an additional allowance to the existing USA refugee quotas.[188]

The discrepancy between the allocated quota and the actual number of admissions to the USA created an opportunity for Gilbert and Eleanor to undertake an unusual rescue of fifty Jewish children from Germany. Instead of seeking to increase the quotas, as many other potential rescue agencies attempted to do, mostly unsuccessfully, Gilbert explored why the existing quotas had not been filled and discovered that, while visas had been issued to applicants, they had not always been taken up. He learned that some Jews who had applied to the USA for entry had escaped to Shanghai or to Cuba before receiving their USA visa. In other cases, visas had been issued but Jews could no longer afford to get to the USA, having been stripped of their wealth or lost their earning capacity in Germany. Gilbert, with the assistance of some members of congress, requested permission to utilize these unused, but already granted visas, to bring children to the States, before the visas expired. He specified that they would be used for children of families that were already waiting for their visas to be issued. The Jewish organization that was supporting this venture, Brith Sholom, was willing to pay for their boat tickets, but each child would have to have a financial sponsor in the USA who would guarantee the child would not become dependent on any type of public American support.[189]

Gilbert and Eleanor, who had developed their innovative manipulation of the quota system, were required to provide affidavits for each of the fifty children they planned to rescue, from American sponsors.[190] These required extensive disclosure of financial status and assets of sponsors, making them challenging to secure. Eleanor took on this task and after six weeks managed to obtain fifty-four guarantees allowing for four extras in case of need.[191] In April 1939, Gilbert and a friend, a German speaking paediatrician, Dr. Robert Schless, left for Germany via Austria, as it was difficult to travel to Germany at the time. Initially it was decided that it was unsafe for Eleanor to accompany them, but soon after his departure, Gilbert called for Eleanor to join him in Austria to assist with the choice of children.[192] They interviewed the children and families of 1,500 children whose parents wished them to go to the USA.[193]

The children who were rescued came from diverse nationalities: Austrian, Polish, Romanian, and Ukrainian. Some were from poor families, others were better off. All had lived in Nazi occupied Vienna. All the families had intended to leave Austria but lacked sufficient resources to do so. Their parents were from all walks of life: doctors, lawyers, salesmen, merchants, and shop workers.[194] Eleanor found the process of taking the children from their parents difficult, even though this is what their parents wanted. As she said, "To take a child from its mother seemed to be the lowest thing a human being could do."[195] Just before they left Vienna, one of the children, Heinrich Steinberger became ill and another child, Alfred Berg, took his place. Sadly, Heinrich and his mother were sent to Sobibor and were most likely murdered there.[196]

The children were taken from Vienna to Berlin by train where they waited for their visas to be processed by the American embassy. They were then sent by ship from Hamburg to New York and on to a home that Brith Sholom had built outside Philadelphia for their retired members, and where the children could live until finding foster homes or until their parents could join them.[197] Some of the children were later reunited with their families who also made it to the USA. Others were placed in foster families and hoped their parents would escape Europe. Some children's parents did not survive. Gilbert and Eleanor took two of the children, Robert and Johanna Braun, into their own home, together with their own two children, until after the war when they were reunited with their parents.[198]

The rescue efforts of Eleanor and Gilbert Kraus occurred at the same time as the infamous *St. Louis* tragedy. The children rescued by the Kraus's left Hamburg on 25 May 1939 with fifty children on board the SS *President Harding*. Ten days before, 937 Jews left from the same port of Hamburg for New York on the *St. Louis*. The USA refused the passengers on the *St. Louis* permission to disembark on American soil; the ship was forced to return to Europe. Twenty-nine passengers were admitted to Cuba, 288 to Great Britain, 224 to France, 214 to Belgium, and 181 to the Netherlands. Of the 937 original passengers, 254 of those returned to France, Belgium, and the Netherlands, were murdered in the Holocaust.[199]

Overall, the USA admitted between 1,000 and 1,200 unaccompanied children between 1933 and 1945. The fifty children rescued by Gilbert and Eleanor Kraus were the largest single group admitted during this period.[200]

Recha Freier and Youth Aliyah

Recha Freier was married to a Rabbi in Germany and was the mother of four children. She founded Aliyat Hano'ar[201] (Youth Aliyah)

45

and helped thousands of Jewish children emigrate to British Mandatory Palestine.[202] Her activities began in 1932 in response to a request from five sixteen-year-old Jewish boys who had lost their jobs because they were Jewish and could not find employment in Germany. As the Rabbi's wife, she tried to help. Since there were so few opportunities for Jews in Germany, she decided to help them move to British Mandatory Palestine. These actions led her to create a movement to prepare youth for work in British Mandatory Palestine and to help them get there. After exploring a number of sources of assistance to implement her idea, she was advised to consult Henrietta Szold, the head of the social department of the Palestinian Jewish National Council in Palestine. Szold was an American born Zionist leader who had established the Hadassah Women's Organization and had settled in Palestine. For no obvious reason, Szold informed her that Jewish children could not be brought to Palestine.

Freier was not put off by Szold's initial rejection. She contacted Kibbutz Ein Harod directly, one of three *kibbutzim* that she had been informed would take Jewish youth. They agreed to take the boys, as did the Ben Shemen's children's village. Wilfred Israel's department store in Germany provided some equipment for the voyage to British Mandatory Palestine and the aid association of German Jews covered the cost of the journey. A further appeal to Szold for assistance, even after making these arrangements, was also refused. Even though Freier travelled to British Mandatory Palestine to meet with Szold in 1933, they could not agree to collaborate. Although Szold later changed her mind and assumed leadership of the Youth Aliyah program, she simultaneously carried out a vindictive campaign directed against Recha Freier, based on a personal dislike of each other. In the meantime, going ahead without Szold's assistance, Freier established the program and in less than a year helped about 1,000 children emigrate to British Mandatory Palestine. Freier also managed to have children from her Youth Aliyah program included in the *Kindertransport* program.[203]

By late 1933, with the Youth Aliyah program established and proving successful, Szold assumed control over the program. For many years, Szold claimed and was credited with the creation of the Youth Aliyah program, with Recha Freier's role going unrecognized.[204]

By the end of 1938, about 4,000 youth had arrived in British Mandatory Palestine through the Youth Aliyah program, many of them thanks to Recha Freier.[205]

Even after Szold's takeover of the Youth Aliyah program, Freier continued working to help Jewish children escape Nazi Germany. Freier collaborated with Rebecca Sieff, a Jewish women's activist in the UK and the daughter of Michael Marks, the founder of the Marks and Spencer empire. Rebecca was active in promoting women's vocational training, which ultimately resulted in the founding of WIZO: the Women's International Zionist Organization. Freier and Sieff organized 2,000 entry permits for Jewish youth to the UK before war began in 1939.

Ultimately, Adolf Eichmann grew angry with Freier's illegal activities and she was warned of her possible arrest. Towards the end of 1940, she fled Germany with her eleven-year-old daughter Maayan, managing to rescue a further ninety children at the same time. Forty-three children who did not have certificates had, however, to be left in the care of Josef Indig, a member of Hashomer Hatza'ir (a secular Zionist youth movement).[206] He managed to board the last train out in July 1941, with thirty of the children. He moved them illegally through Italy, until its occupation by Germany, and then to Switzerland and finally in 1945, to British Mandatory Palestine. Almost all the children survived the war.[207]

Freier eventually made it to British Mandatory Palestine, where she wanted to continue her work on Youth Aliyah. Unfortunately, her differences with Henrietta Szold proved insurmountable. Instead, she founded an Agricultural Training Centre for Israeli children as well as a fund to encourage musical creativity. She died in 1984. There are no reliable statistics on how many children she managed to save but some claim it was many thousands.[208]

Beate Berger

Beate Berger, a nurse by training, was the Director of the Beith Ahawah Children's home in Berlin. The home housed about 120

Jewish children from Eastern Europe at any one time. The school was Zionist and religious with the children studying Hebrew and Torah while living adjacent to a synagogue.[209]

With the rise of the Nazis, Beate, recognizing the threat, started planning to move the Jewish children in her Berlin home for refugee children out of Germany. Her efforts to raise money to move the children were initially unsuccessful, until she raised the money by auctioning the artwork of two Jewish artists, Max Lieberman and Herman Struck. She then sold her own private property, and travelled to British Mandatory Palestine alone to make arrangements for a new home for the children there. She purchased a large plot on the outskirts of Haifa (later Kiryat Bialik) on which to build the children's home.

The British government made moving the children to Palestine, which was still under British Mandate and unwelcoming of Jews, difficult. The British government demanded that the children be between 15 and 17 years old, have a medical certificate vouching for their health, have parental approval if their parents were living, and attend a Zionist preparation camp (probably to provide agricultural education and preparation for life in Palestine) to ensure they were ready for immigration. They then only approved a few dozen certificates although they did promise, and deliver, additional certificates once the children's home was completed in British Mandatory Palestine. The first group of thirty-five children left Germany for Palestine in April 1934. After this Beate continued to travel between Berlin and Palestine and eventually facilitated the travel to Mandatory Palestine of 100 children from Berlin, seventy-five from Austria, fifteen from Italy, and 100 from Czechoslovakia, Hungary and Poland.[210]

Beate immigrated to British Mandatory Palestine as well. She died suddenly of heart disease in 1940. Some months later, the Nazis took over her Berlin facility and made it the home of the Hitler Youth. Twenty Jewish children under the age of fourteen were still in the home waiting to emigrate. All of them were sent to Auschwitz where they were likely murdered.[211] Beate's foresight, however, allowed her to save around 300 children.

The *Kindertransport* and Marie Schmolka

After the horrors of *Kristallnacht* (the Night of Broken Glass) on 9-10 November 1938, when 1,000 synagogues in Germany had been set alight, 7,500 Jewish businesses smashed and looted, over 90 Jewish men murdered and 3,000 Jewish men forced into concentration camps, some in the western world became increasingly alarmed at the Nazis' treatment of Jews.[212] Consequently, British public opinion added weight to the efforts of refugee and aid committees to rescue Jewish children from Germany and other European countries. Organizations such as the British Committee for the Jews of Germany and the Movement for the Care of Children from Germany capitalized on the public outrage against the actions of *Kristallnacht* and were able to gain permission for Jewish children from Germany to be temporarily allowed into the UK – the start of a process that became known as the *Kindertransport*.[213]

The UK government imposed restrictions on the children and their foster families, and required that refugee groups guarantee that the children would not become a financial burden on the UK. Adoptive UK families were required to have expensive insurance policies to cover their actions. Additionally, the British government did not officially recognize the children as immigrants: they were expected to return to their parents and home countries after the war. Their parents were explicitly excluded from the transports, thus effectively creating orphans. While the *Kindertransport* saved many Jewish children, as well as children of other religious denominations, these rescue efforts could have been far more robust had there not been restrictive rules imposed on them.[214]

While there were significant restrictions in place to protect the UK from the potential "burden" of taking care of refugee children, there were far fewer structures in place to protect the children. Potential foster homes were not always carefully vetted, leading to mistreatment of some of the children.[215] Some foster families viewed the children as domestic workers, others indulged in predatory behaviours towards them, and at least one viewed their foster daughter as a prospective marriage partner for their own errant son.[216] Furthermore, the multi-denominational groups involved in the organization of the transports did not require that the prospective homes for Jewish children be Jewish, often resulting in the loss of Jewish identity and heritage for rescued children. Desperate parents of the *Kindertransport* children often agreed to their children being hosted by Christian families in the UK, in an attempt to ensure they might be rescued. At least twenty-five of these children were brought out by the Barbican Mission, an explicitly conversionist organization. These children were rescued by the Mission, on the clear understanding that they would be baptised.[217] Jewish children were deliberately dispersed to prevent any antisemitic outcry against them by situating a large group of Jews in any one area. Despite these issues, about 10,000 children, mostly Jewish, from Germany, Austria, Poland and Czechoslovakia were included in these transports, which continued until the declaration of war on 1 September 1939.[218]

Of the 10,000 children brought to the UK, 669 were from Czechoslovakia. Marie Schmolka, who was instrumental in assisting Czech children to join the *Kindertransport*, was the Czechoslovakian representative of the JOINT (American Jewish Joint Distribution Committee) and HICEM (a combination of three immigrant aid organizations: HIAS, the Hebrew Sheltering and Immigrant Aid Society, New York, the ICA, the Jewish Colonization Association, Paris, and Emigdirect, Berlin). Marie Schmolka was the sole Czechoslovak representative of the League of Nations Commission for Refugees. She became the President of the National Coordinating Committee for Refugees in Czechoslovakia and was the Czechoslovakian representative at the Evian conference in 1938.[219] While abroad, Marie was repeatedly offered asylum by her colleagues but she chose rather to return to Czechoslovakia to assist other refugees. Marie Schmolka worked with Doreen Warriner, the representative of the British Committee for Refugees from Czechoslovakia to set up a scheme for sending unaccompanied children from Czechoslovakia to the UK as they recognized that seeking admission for child refugees had a greater chance of success than applying for adult refugee admissions to the UK. Warriner and Schmolka tasked Martin Blake and his friend, Nicholas Winton, a British stockbroker and humanitarian to establish the scheme that became known as the *Kindertransport*. Marie and her team provided the majority of the lists of children that were to be rescued including the list of 500 children used by Blake and Winton that included German and Austrian refugee children based in and around Prague.

Germany occupied Czechoslovakia on 15 March 1939. Marie Schmolka and her co-workers from the Committee for Refugees in Czechoslovakia were among the first to be arrested and held in Pankrac prison where she (a diabetic) was subjected to six to eight-hour interrogations by the Gestapo.[220] She was released two months later, in May 1939. Once the war began, Winton had almost no contact with the children from Czechoslovakia.[221]

Marie Schmolka was sent by Eichmann to Paris in August 1939, to demand more efficient Jewish emigration but moved to London where she continued her work assisting refugees. She died on 27 March 1940, in London, of a heart attack at the age of forty-six.[222] Schmolka and her fellow Jewish women organizers are featured in contemporary references but are lost from public memory in later records. Her male compatriots, Felix Waltsch and Max Brod, are remembered with monographs recording their activities, but Marie Schmolka's contributions are neglected.[223] A recent group has been established with the goal of recognizing and honouring her contributions.[224]

Chapter 5: Hiding

With the onset of war in Europe, options for legally, or even quasi-legally, helping Jewish children emigrate out of Nazi occupied Europe were eliminated. Those hoping to save Jewish children had few options available to them: they could hide them, or smuggle them out of Nazi controlled territory. In countries with large expanses of forest land close to urban centres, escape into the partisan forest camps (such as the Bielski brothers' camp) might also have been possible, but these were usually locally organized escapes undertaken by individuals or small groups. Smuggling Jews into safe havens such as Switzerland or Spain was only feasible for countries that bordered these potential places of refuge: escape routes that required crossing multiple borders were usually too difficult to attempt. While a few rescuers were able to smuggle children across borders (discussed in a later chapter), an unknown number were captured or killed trying to escape or smuggle children and adults to safety. Consequently, most attempts to rescue children, particularly in the early years of the war, involved hiding them within Nazi occupied Europe. Some children hid in attics, barns, closets, behind false walls, in basements or even in underground spaces – out of sight of neighbours who might denounce them or those helping them. Others hid "in plain sight," with families, or in convents or church-run institutions. In most cases, this was achieved by manufacturing fake identities. Forged ID cards, ration cards, hiding places, money for food and board, medical supplies, and emotional support, warnings about deportations and danger, all contributed to the survival of rescued children.[225] Dozens of men and women participated in saving the lives of children, with Jews and Gentiles often working in tandem to do so. Many of these efforts were further assisted by non-Jews who helped provide false papers or offered hiding places – although they did not always know they were hiding Jews, and were frequently paid for their contributions.[226] None of the stories are identical: there was no blueprint for successful children's rescues. Imagination, courage, innovation, contacts, and ability, all contributed to the multiple methods of rescue that these stories reveal.

Challenges

Hiding children was particularly fraught with danger. In many situations hiding a Jewish child was punishable by death. In most cases, children hidden with families had to be integrated into the new world of their rescuer without alerting others to their origins. Stories were concocted to explain the sudden appearance of a child in a family, for example, that the child was a niece or nephew whose mother had died. Many children did not speak the language of their rescuers, or if they did, might have spoken with a Yiddish accent, or included Yiddish phrases, or might have included observations of Jewish customs, such as "My father never smoked on Saturdays." Jewish children had to learn and become fluent in not just the language of their rescuers, but with their (usually) Christian religious traditions, prayers, forms of worship and customs. They had to, very quickly, adopt and accept a new persona, name, family background, religion, and history, and to learn to never reveal their Jewish ancestry. While older children might have appreciated the importance of this for their and their rescuers' safety, younger children were less reliably able to safeguard their previous identity. Children who were too young, or who "looked" Jewish or who could not speak French (or the local language) fluently were smuggled across the Swiss or Spanish border whenever possible rather than being hidden with families or in institutions.[227] Boys, in particular, had to avoid being seen naked in change rooms or dormitories, for fear of revealing their circumcision. It was rare for Jewish boys to pass for Aryan and not be discovered, as did Avraham Werner.[228] Leaving their families was almost always traumatic for the children. Younger children, in particular, often perceived these experiences as abandonment, rather than rescue. Obtaining and providing the children with forged identity documents, especially those that would pass scrutiny, remained challenging at all times.

Organizations and Networks

Multiple organizations and networks emerged in Europe that were dedicated, amongst other activities, to saving Jewish children. Some focussed on hiding children, others on smuggling them to safer countries. Many collaborated with each other or with individuals in other networks. Within these major groups, dozens of men and women participated in saving the lives of the children with Jews and Gentiles often working together.

The most well known of the Jewish organizations, as well as the Jewish women who were associated with them in the rescue of children and whose stories are included here, are listed below by country.

France

- The OSE (Oeuvre de Secours aux Enfants or Children's Aid Society), including Vivette Hermann-Samuel, Andrée Salomon and Elizabeth Hirsch. The OSE rescued about 5,000 people. The OSE gave assistance to about 1,300 children by placing them in homes. As the Nazis approached Paris in 1940, all the homes were transferred to the unoccupied zone in southern France. After the Nazis moved into southern France, the OSE went underground but continued to hide children and transfer them to Switzerland when possible.[229]

- The Éclaireurs Israélites de France (EIF) (a Jewish scouting movement) was created in 1923 by Robert Gamzon – including the Garel Network managed by Georges Garel – and created homes for children, hiding places for them, or smuggling them across borders.[230] It was also known as the Sixième (the Sixth). It was led by Robert Gamzon and included his wife, Denise Gamzon, Denise Siekierski-Caraco and Madeleine Dreyfus.

- In 1941 the EIF was forced to join the Union Générale des Israélites de France (UGIF the Union of French Jews). The UGIF was established by the Pétain government to integrate all French Jewish organizations into one.[231] It included Juliette Stern and Rachel Ida Lifchitz.

- The Mouvement des Jeunesses Sionistes (MJS) A Zionist Youth movement, with Mila Racine, Marianne Cohn, and Charlotte Sorkine, was active in smuggling Jewish children in Southern France (except Nice) across borders and collaborated with the OSE and the EIF.[232] The Marcel Network, Odette and Moussa Abadi, saved children primarily from the Nice area.[233]

- The Armée Juive (AJ) also participated in rescuing and smuggling children. This was a secret resistance organization of Jews that was created in January 1942 in the southern French city of Toulouse. It was founded by Zionist activists Abraham Polonski and Lucien Lublin, who created a Jewish militia in response to the German occupation of France. Its members swore their loyalty to the AJ on the Bible and the Zionist flag. Not all Zionist groups supported or trusted them.[234]

Germany

- The German Children's Aid Society in New York established in 1934, brought several hundred children to the United States, despite USA restrictions on immigration.

Poland

- The Council for Aid to Jews, known as Żegota, a Polish-Jewish organization, established a special department dedicated to helping about 2,500 Jewish children by placing them in non-Jewish homes or in institutions.[235] Żegota was established towards the end of 1942, when most of the Jews in Poland had already been killed. A Jewish underground network worked in close cooperation with Żegota comprised of two sections: the Jewish National Committee (ZKN) and the (non-Zionist) Bund.

- Many Polish families, including children, were also able to escape into Russia when Poland was annexed by the Russians: almost 1,000 children who managed to survive the harsh Siberian frozen wastes were later able to migrate to Tehran, and other central Asian regions, and from there to emigrate to British Mandatory Palestine, or later, Israel, aided by Henrietta Szold and the Hadassah movement.[236]

Lithuania

- 2,178 Polish refugees, including children, escaped to East Asia from Lithuania to where they had fled. Organized by Zionist leader Zorah Warhaftig, they were able to obtain transit visas from Chiune Sugihara, the Japanese consul in Kovno who was sympathetic to them, and from Dutch diplomats.[237]

Hungary

- In 1944, Hungarian Zionist activities set up under International Red Cross protection, saved over 6,000 Jewish children.[238] Thousands of other children were rescued in Budapest by Protestant and Catholic Churches, many hidden behind convent walls.[239]

Netherlands

- In the Netherlands, resistance movements saved thousands of Jewish children by hiding them in monasteries, hospitals and schools.[240] In particular, the work of Walter Suskind and his colleagues in the Jewish Theatre[241] and Jewish members of the Westerweel group including Mirjam Waterman[242] were notable.

Belgium

- Jewish women who ran the Gestapo approved orphanages in Belgium saved hundreds of children, including Madame Marie Albert-Blum[243] and Ruth Tiefenbrunner.[244]

France

Rescues that focused on hiding children (and others) took place throughout Nazi occupied Europe. There were common elements to the rescues, such as the challenges involved in hiding children, and idiosyncratic elements that made each rescue attempt unique. Rescues in France were notable as being one country in which the underground movement and rescue operations were highly organised and often conducted by, or in collaboration with, comparatively large, established networks. They were also remarkably successful. At the start of the war, the Jewish population of France was around 300,000. Of these 75,721, including 11,600 Jewish children,[245] were deported with only 2,560 adults, and 300 of the children,[246] surviving the camps.[247] The remaining Jews, who were not deported, about 224,000, survived (75%), largely thanks to the rescue efforts of Jewish organizations.[248] In addition to being hidden in France, many Jewish children were smuggled across the French borders to Switzerland and Spain.[249] Of the 72,400 children who survived the war, about 62,000 remained with their parents in hiding or were placed in homes or institutions. It is estimated that between 850-1,250 children escaped to Switzerland and 88-132 to Spain.[250]

The Mouvement des Jeunesses Sionistes (MJS) collaborated with the Oeuvre de Secours aux Enfants (OSE), and the Scouts movement, the EIF, (later called the Sixth) to smuggle children and adults across the borders to Switzerland and Spain.[251] Georges Garel and his network of helpers in the EIF saved about 16,000 children, either in hiding or by smuggling them out of France: more than any other rescue group.[252]

Approximately 40% of Jewish underground workers in France were women. They supported large underground rescue organizations in various roles, such as counselors in youth movements and paid office employees in offices and social services. One area in which Jewish women took on significant roles and risks was in missions that required travel on public transportation or appearance in public places, to, for example, move hidden children from one place to another. Because circumcision made it easy to identify Jewish men, it was easier for women to disguise themselves as Aryans.[253] Also, women, rather than men, accompanied by children was a socially acknowledged activity that did not arouse suspicion. Despite taking significant risks and being major contributors to rescue organizations in France, women were seldom decision-makers in these larger organizations. One notable exception was Denise Gamzon, who was on the Board of the Jewish Scouts movement in the 1930's and whose husband, Robert Gamzon, was its leader.[254]

Of the numerous women who contributed to the rescue of children through larger organizations in France, there were some Jewish women whose stories are included in this chapter: Andrée Salomon, Vivette Hermann-Samuel, Madeleine Dreyfus, Margot Cohn, and Denise Gamzon.[255] Others, about whom we know less, included Juliette Stern,[256] Sabine Elzon,[257] Fela Botek Izbutsky[258] and Aviva (Ingeborg) Simon (Igael).[259]

Andrée Salomon

Andrée Salomon was active in both the EIF and the OSE at various times in the 1930's and 1940's. Before the war, she worked in the EIF to protect the children of Jewish refugees, many of whom had fled from Germany to France as the Nazis increased their persecutory actions against Germany's Jews. After the accession of the Pétain government in France in 1940, when the OSE was forced to move its children's homes into Southern France, Salomon joined OSE, and was based in the Rivesaltes internment camp,[260] a detention centre for refugees and Jews who had been rounded up, before being sent onwards to concentration camps. Salomon's experiences in Rivesaltes led to her continuing to help children imprisoned in the thirty-one similar internment camps that were created in the South of France. OSE and other aid organizations succeeded in rescuing about 1,300 children from these camps, including about 600 from Rivesaltes, and sheltering them in dormitories and eventually houses operated by the OSE, with approval of the Vichy government.[261] In Rivesaltes, barracks were created for men, women, and children separately: families were not housed together, leading to child neglect.

For example, on 26 February 1941, Salomon was able to move forty-eight children aged four to fourteen from the camp at Gurs who were sent to various Jewish institutions, with their parents' permission, and with approval of authorities, on the grounds that this was better for the children. She was skilled at persuading parents to let their children move to these shelters. She also helped several dozen children emigrate to the United States on the rare occasions when small numbers of children were allowed to emigrate through activities such as those facilitated by Cecilia Razovsky.[262]

Deportations from these internment camps to the east, to concentration camps, began in the summer of 1942 following mass arrests of Jews. When the German army occupied the South of France in November 1942, hundreds of children who had been rescued from internment camps and absorbed into OSE and EIF homes were in danger. The Germans ordered the children in the OSE houses to be reunited with their parents in the internment camps so that they could be deported to the east together. Working underground, Salomon and the members of her teams transferred the children to hiding places in non-Jewish families and institutions rather than reuniting them with their families in the internment camps. She warned parents not to reunite with their children in the camps, but to allow her to hide them. While many granted her this permission, some did not, with, in most cases, tragic outcomes.[263] Some of the children who did not speak French or who came from ultra-Orthodox homes, were smuggled to Switzerland. Salomon also arranged for a group of 85-143 children who had relatives in British Mandatory Palestine to be smuggled to Spain via Andorra and from there to Palestine.[264] Though most of the children never saw their parents again, hundreds of children survived the Holocaust thanks to Andrée Salomon. Many of them regarded Salomon as their second mother.[265]

Vivette Hermann-Samuel

Vivette Samuel (*née* Hermann) was encouraged by a friend of her Zionist father to work as a social worker in Rivesaltes where a kindergarten had been established. There she met Andrée Salomon who persuaded her to work at the camp, to help rescue some of the 5,000 children between four and fifteen held there.[266] Seven months after she arrived, Vivette had moved over 400 children from the camp into OSE housing.[267] Between May 1941 and May 1942, four small groups of children were sent to the USA, a rare opportunity created by OSE's deliberate attempts to facilitate emigration of children across the Atlantic with the necessary documentation, and with the agreement of camp authorities.[268] She assumed responsibility for returning the mothers to the camp, after they had seen their children board the ships. Of the ten mothers at the quay watching one ship leave, only one survived. The remaining nine were sent to their deaths in camps in Poland. When only five children whose parents refused to part from them were left in Rivesaltes, Vivette left to work for OSE in its various centres in Lyon, Marseille, and Montpellier.[269]

In Marseille, Vivette became engaged to Julien Samuel who was responsible for the OSE branch in that city in August 1942[270] and they married on 6 October 1942.[271] Their daughter Francoise was born on 14 July 1943. Julien was arrested by the Gestapo and sent by train to the camps. He jumped off the train and retuned to Vivette, after which time they stayed hidden until liberation.[272]

Madeleine Dreyfus

In 1941 Madeleine Dreyfus' family fled to Lyon, where the director of the local OSE branch, Böszi Hirsch, invited Dreyfus to work with her as part of the Garel network. Madeleine was trained as a psychologist. She was also married with three children, a fact that played a part when she was arrested later. Dreyfus was tasked with searching for families and institutions willing to take in Jewish children and young people, among them the mountain villagers of Le Chambon-sur-Lignon.[273] Remarkably, 5,000 Jews including 3,500 children, found shelter in this town and its surrounding villages, rescued by Protestants and local Jews active in the resistance in southern France, Marseille, Nice and elsewhere. For two years, Madeleine frequently made the round trip between Lyon and Le Chambon-sur-Lignon, accompanying over 100 children aged between eighteen months and sixteen years,[274] with whom she remained in contact, bringing them food, clothing, medicines, and letters from their parents, if these were themselves in hiding or had not yet been deported to camps. Their parents never knew where their children were hidden.[275] The work was risky. As she said, "We live clandestinely under the constant threat of the Gestapo."[276]

On 23 November 1943, Madeleine learned that the Gestapo were planning to raid an institution where one of the rescue children was sheltering. She hurried to attempt to save the child, but the Germans preceded her and arrested her.[277] She begged to be allowed to go home to feed her three-month-old baby but was refused. She asked if she could phone her home to ask for the baby to be fed by bottle. Instead of dialing home, she called the Union Générale des Israélites de France (the National Jewish council created to coordinate Jewish and Social Philanthropic Organizations in France) and managed to say "Madeleine Dreyfus. Would you kindly inform my family that I have been arrested by the Gestapo and will not be home to feed my daughter?"[278] A few hours later she again asked to go home to feed her baby. A Gestapo officer accompanied her. It was clear that her family had fled so she knew they received her message. While there the telephone rang. It was her mother to whom she was able to say "Go away ... Leave ... all of you."[279]

Madeleine was imprisoned, interrogated by the notorious Klaus Barbie, sent first to Drancy, where she managed to save yet more children, and then to Bergen-Belsen, where she remained for eleven months before liberation in April 1945. She was then reunited with her husband and three children. She continued her work with OSE helping counsel children whose parents had not returned, including the Buchenwald boys, who were a very few boys who survived in that camp.[280] She went on to develop a career in psychotherapy. In 1947 she was awarded the *Médaille de la Résistance*.[281]

Margot Cohn

Margot Cohn also worked within the OSE in the Lyon area moving children from internment camps into hiding with French families. She was trained as a librarian but worked as a volunteer in a Jewish youth movement: Yeshurun. In 1942 she was asked by Andrée Salomon to work with Madeleine Dreyfus rescuing children. She spent the next two years working with OSE. During this time, she served as a counselor in an orphanage established by her future husband, Jack Cohn. The house had no running water, no heating, and no food supply. She was tasked with finding foster homes for the children among the local population and in Christian institutions, and to caring for the children who stayed hiding in the orphanage. She encouraged the children and provided them with information about their parents, at least until their parents were deported. In the spring of 1944, she was sent to accompany groups of children from their hiding places with foster families, on a night train to Toulouse, to meet a friend who would smuggle them into Switzerland. Before *Rosh Hashanah* of 1944, a few days after the liberation of Lyon, Margot managed to find a Jewish family in Toulouse who would host all thirty of the children until she could find alternative accommodation. A few days later, she and a friend, Gary Wolff, rented an apartment on their own initiative and took care of all the children so that they would not have to return to the foster families that they had now left. Although Jack Cohn had been arrested earlier, he survived. They married in 1945 and immigrated to Israel in 1952.[282]

Denise Gamzon

Denise Gamzon was a Zionist and a member of the social justice movement in France. She was married to Robert Gamzon, the founder and director of Les Éclaireurs Israélites de France (the EIF), the scouting movement. When World War II broke out, Denise Gamzon coordinated the evacuation from Paris of the children of Jewish refugees. While the French authorities evacuated the children of holders of French citizenship, they did not try to protect those with foreign nationalities. The EIF decided to take responsibility for the fate of the children of Jewish foreigners.

They opened children's homes, establishing technical and educational teams to operate and raise funds for them and acquired several farms. Denise Gamzon took charge of the fundraising work and was appointed the director of the agricultural centre in the village of Lautrec.

In the summer of 1942, the centre took in three Jewish boys and a group of thirty Jewish girls, all from the internment camps. When Denise Gamzon learned of their impending arrest in August 1942, she hid the children in a forest and arranged to smuggle them to Switzerland or to hide them. In December 1942, when she was about to give birth to her third child, she was released from her position as director of the agricultural centre but continued to work as part of the EIF's underground, known as "the Sixth," which engaged primarily in hiding adolescents.[283]

Aviva (Ingeborg) Simon (Igael)

Aviva joined the underground activities of the Jewish Scouts (the Sixth) to rescue Jewish children. She worked as a counselor, in Toulouse, at a shelter for abandoned Jewish children whose parents had been arrested, and was a courier of identity cards and other papers needed by the underground. She also participated in smuggling several groups of Jewish children from France to Switzerland.[284] Her partner was killed on one of these trips. She did not let this interfere with her work. She quickly transferred the children to a collaborating convent nearby, and to other places that would shelter them, saving them. She also kept in touch with children who were in hiding. At the end of the war, she joined the Haganah and helped smuggle Jews to Israel to where she immigrated on an illegal immigrant ship.[285]

Fela Botek (Izbutsky)

Fela worked with the Scouts.[286] Together with two non-Jewish women, Juliette Vidal and Marinette Guy, she rented a hotel in Saint-Étienne and turned it into a shelter for forty-two Jewish children. She was responsible for the girls, and also served as a courier, delivering fake IDs. One of the children who spent two years in this orphanage from the age of thirteen, Nelly Einhorn (later Nurit Reubinoff), reported that the children were treated in "an extraordinary way."[287] The children were not forced to change their religion: they observed *Shabbat* with lighting candles, as well as *Hanukkah* and *Pesach* and were told to never forget they were Jews. In 1944, when the area was liberated, very few of the children could find their parents. Fela helped them to reach OSE orphanages. She also helped children who had been taken to Switzerland, or hidden in monasteries or with non-Jewish families, to move to these homes. She remained in touch with her non-Jewish co-workers, the non-Jewish families that had sheltered children, and with the children. She saved 137 children.

Sabine Elzon

Sabine Elzon served as a courier to hidden families in the Lyon region, bringing forged documents and other necessities, primarily to hidden children. She and her husband lived next to a church and were on friendly terms with the priest. On receiving information about an impending round-up in 1942, they facilitated hiding seventy-five Jews in his church for two days. When the round-up was over, they were able to find more long-term places for the Jews to hide in through the war.[288] She survived the war and moved to Israel, where she worked with Yad Vashem classifying thousands of Pages of Testimonies in the Hall of Names. She retired from volunteer work at Yad Vashem in 2006, at the age of ninety-five.

Juliette Stern

In the 1930's, Juliette Stern visited British Mandatory Palestine and, on her return to France, established a women's club, Kadimah, that studied the history of Zionism. In 1935 the club merged with another small organization, Jewish Women in France for Palestine, to establish a branch of the Women's International Zionist Organization (WIZO). Stern was appointed Director-General.

In January 1942, the Office for Jewish Affairs (Commissariat général aux questions juives, CGQJ) under the Pétain government closed all Jewish community groups and replaced them with the umbrella organization Union Générale des Israélites de France (UGIF), Stern was appointed a member of that organization's leadership. She managed Branch Number 5 of the UGIF.

Some of the children who were imprisoned in the Drancy camp together with their parents were handed over to the UGIF. Branch Number 5 lodged them in one of its dormitories. The UGIF dormitories could house up to four hundred children, but Branch Number 5 had a larger number of children. Stern decided, against German orders, to move the children to non-Jewish families and institutions. Members of the Women's International Zionist Organization (WIZO) and social workers, both Jewish and non-Jewish, in secret and at great risk, found hiding places for the children, ensured their welfare and paid a monthly fee for their board and lodging. One of these Jewish social workers was Rachel Ida Lifchitz, who helped find children left alone after their parents were deported, and found them safe homes in which to hide.[289] Rachel had, prior to the war, worked as a social worker in the Rothschild philanthropic enterprises designed to rescue children. Juliette Stern diverted UGIF funds to cover expenses, in contradiction to orders. Joseph Antignac, the secretary-general of the CGQJ, suspected her and in the spring of 1943, contacted the commander of the Gestapo's Jewish department, Heinz Röthke, asking him to investigate. Instead of doing so, the Gestapo arrested the employees of UGIF's Branch 5, including their manager, Joséphine Getting. All were deported and murdered. Stern was attending a funeral on the day of the arrests, and avoided capture. After this, Stern worked underground continuing to rescue Jewish children. WIZO was responsible for saving more than a thousand children; every child in their care.

Independent Rescuers

In addition to the large networks such as the OSE and EIF in France, one group of Jewish rescuers of Jewish children worked relatively independently. The Marcel Network, as it was called, was operated by Odette Rosenstock and Moussa Abadi.

Odette Rosenstock and Moussa Abadi

Moussa Abadi was inspired to help Jewish children after learning from an Italian priest that Nazis were murdering all Jewish children, and when he witnessed a French policeman stamp on the head of a Jewish woman and kill her while her six-year-old son watched.[290] Odette Rosenstock was a physician in Paris, where she met Moussa, and had grown increasingly concerned about the Nazi movement in Germany. Odette and Moussa fled in 1940 from Paris to Nice. After Italy fell to the Germans in September 1943, Moussa and Odette began to rescue Jewish children whose parents had been deported or were hidden. They became known as the Marcel Network. With the help of the Bishop of Nice, Bishop Rémond, they found hiding places in Catholic institutions and were offered a place in which to forge ID cards and baptismal certificates.[291] They also sought out assistance from Protestant ministers and collaborated with underground organizations such as Georges Garel of OSE[292] and the Joint Distribution Committee (JDC).[293] The Marcel Network saved 527 children ranging in age from babies to teenagers.[294] While Georges Garel's network employed about fifty people, the Marcel Network had only each other.[295]

Bishop Rémond arranged nomination for Abadi as a school inspector, known as Monsieur Marcel, and for Odette as a social worker under the name of Sylvie Delattre. Both these aliases allowed the couple to travel anywhere to check on their hidden children.[296] Of the 527 children they rescued, 300 went to Catholic institutions organized largely by Moussa, with Odette developing Protestant contacts who agreed to hide the remaining children.[297]

Every child had a file card containing their vital information: their real name, date of birth, nationality, last known address, and the name, profession, and whereabouts of the parents. If the parents were known to be deported, then a relative's details were noted. The child's photograph, fingerprints and false name were also included. After the war, these cards were crucial in helping to reunite the children with their families. There were three copies of each card. One was buried in the garden of the bishop's residence in Nice. A second went with the groups that crossed over to Switzerland with instructions for the guides to give the cards to the International Red Cross in Geneva. The third set was for Moussa and Odette. These were hidden between books in the bishop's library. These were dangerous to keep because, if found by the

Gestapo, the children and their parents could be traced.[298] Fortunately they were not.

Hiding the children was challenging. Getting false papers and a safe place to hide was only part of the difficulty. Many had emotional problems. Some children refused to speak or say anything other than "Mama." Odette visited the hidden children monthly to check on them, pay their caregivers, and bring clothing, toys, the occasional chocolate, and comfort and love.[299] The most religious children were more difficult to hide. They were passed on to the Sixth (the Scouts) to be smuggled over the border to Switzerland.

As serious and complex as the rescuers' challenges were in keeping the children safe, they also had to contend with the needs of the children beyond the basics of shelter and food. One six-year-old boy refused to be separated from his four-year-old sister. He had promised his mother he would look after her, so, upon facing the prospect of being separated from his sister, he pushed her onto the floor and sat on her to protect her. Moussa and Odette found another home where the two of them could stay together.[300] Another child, Jeanette Wolgust, while in hiding in a convent, had been given the title role in a school play of Joan of Arc. She was upset that on the night of the production she would have no family members in the audience to support her, unlike all the other children. Odette had given Jeanette the bishop's telephone number to call in case of emergency. She called him a few days before the opening night telling him her problem. He notified Odette who was able to attend the performance. Odette was also able to bring Jeanette's little brother, Jean, with her. Jean was in hiding elsewhere. She also arranged with the Mother Superior of the school to allow the little boy to stay with Jeanette overnight, an unheard-of accommodation in the convent.[301]

Odette and Abadi did not hide the 527 children they rescued at the same time. They usually hid only as many as 140 at any one time, although they never turned a child away. Sometimes children were hidden for only a few days while their parents found alternative accommodation for the whole family. Others were smuggled out of France. Some were not hidden by the Marcel Network but were helped while still living with their parents. Moussa and Odette were able to visit the 140 children at least once a month: often six or more children were hidden nearby each other and could be visited on the same day, making this possible.[302] Only two children being cared for directly by Moussa and Odette were lost to the Germans, Joseph and Theodore Gartner. They had been hidden with a priest named Father Goens in a village. He had boasted about them to villagers, and was informed on. The children were arrested and escorted to Drancy and then to Auschwitz. Odette had seen them on a bus and moved to approach them but was warned away by a gesture from the boys. She realised they were being accompanied by plain-clothed police and moved away. She was, however, arrested three days later, suggesting that her cover had been blown by this incident.[303]

As with any attempt to rescue Jews from the Nazis, the work done by the Marcel Network was dangerous. They were helped for a short while by a twenty-one-year-old Jewish woman, Nicole Weil. Three weeks after joining them, she was denounced, arrested, sent to Drancy and then on to Auschwitz with some of the children she had been trying to rescue. She refused to abandon them and was sent with them to the gas.[304] A second Jewish social worker, Huguette Wahl was sent by Georges Garel to assist Moussa and Odette, but she was arrested a few days later while carrying children's clothing. She was sent to Auschwitz where she was murdered. After that, Odette and Moussa worked alone.[305] Despite taking all possible precautions, Odette was also denounced in April 1944 and was imprisoned and tortured. She admitted to assisting children but did not reveal Abadi. She was sent to Drancy, then to Auschwitz and then to Bergen-Belsen. She survived and was reunited with Abadi, whom she later married, and who had hidden himself for the final three months of the war. They continued to assist the children they had rescued to reunite them with their families when they could: more than half were orphaned.[306]

During the war and for long afterwards almost all the children did not know who had hidden them. Some only knew their cover names of Monsieur Marcel and Sylvie Delattre. Moussa and Odette refused to talk about their wartime actions for fifty years after the war ended.[307] Odette was deeply disturbed by her wartime experiences.

"She was like a dead person." She appeared to carry "a kind of stone inside her after Auschwitz that weighed on her and pained her for the rest of her life."[308]

Rescue in Other Countries

While we know some details of the lives and actions of many French child rescuers, far less is recorded about Jewish women who rescued children in other countries where large-scale, co-ordinated, rescue organizations did not appear to have been established to the same extent as in France. In these settings many rescue attempts were individually organized in local settings. Consequently, the approach taken to rescues varied significantly depending on the idiosyncratic requirements of each context and the people involved. Individual rescuers from Lithuania, the Netherlands, Hungary, Poland, Belgium, Italy, Sweden and British Mandatory Palestine are included here. In addition, some rescues in Belorussia were particularly noteworthy, as they represent an unusual example of children rescuing children.

Lithuania

Rona Rosenthal

Rona Rosenthal organized the rescue of multiple children from the Kaunas ghetto.[309] She was a teacher at a teacher's training college that included nuns, but was forced to move to the Kaunas ghetto in 1941. With the nuns' help she organized hiding places for children in the convent, in orphanages and in Christian homes. Other Jewish women, about whom little is known other than their names, who assisted her included Pesia Karnovsky, Rachela Katz, Sonia Lifshitz-Goldschnidt, Zivia Kapit, Malka Pogetsky-Shamali, Shulamit Lerman, Leah Kozel and Lyuba Schwartz.[310] In 1943, the SS took control of the ghetto and converted it into the Kauen concentration camp. A major effort to save any remaining children was undertaken by partisan rescuers. It began in 1944 after the deportation of children from the ghetto began, but prior to the ghetto's final evacuation on 8 July 1944.[311] Babies and

toddlers were anaesthetised by medical personnel and carried out in a sack or backpack. Older children were hidden in strollers or garbage bags. Adolescents left the ghetto on labour brigades and would slip away from the group once they reached the Aryan side, tearing off their Jewish stars and moving to hiding places. Sometimes a child was thrown across the ghetto fence at night, to a waiting Lithuanian who had offered to help rescue the children. Most of the women who helped with this rescue effort were murdered in extermination camps. Rona Rosenthal died in Stutthof in 1945 just before liberation.[312]

Pesia Kissen

Pesia Kissen also rescued children in and around the Kaunas ghetto while serving as a paediatrician.[313] She saved dozens of children with the help of a local priest and other non-Jews. The children were hidden in a variety of places including in Lithuanian peasant houses. Pesia was later sent to Stutthof camp together with her daughter. After the war she joined an orphanage established in Selvino in northern Italy for child survivors of the Holocaust. She served as an instructor there before moving with her daughter and many of the children to Israel in 1949.

Liza Magon

Liza Magon met with teenagers during the deportations from the Ashmiani ghetto and encouraged them to flee to the forest, thereby saving the lives of many who took her advice. Liza served as a courier in the Vilnius ghetto but was arrested and killed at Ponary on 17 February 1943.[314]

The Netherlands

Jewish Theatre of Amsterdam

During the Nazi deportation of Jews from Amsterdam, Jews were rounded up and collected at deportation centres, or points of assembly,

where they were held until they could be deported to concentration or extermination camps. One of these deportation centres was the Jewish Theatre in Amsterdam, known as the Hollandsche Schouwburg.[315] As was common practice, the Nazis appointed a Jewish "leader" who was forced to take responsibility for ensuring that Nazi orders were followed. In the case of the Jewish Theatre, this dubious responsibility fell to Walter Suskind. Suskind convinced the Nazis to establish a separate point of assembly for children, across the road from the theatre, in a crèche housed in a Protestant religious seminary. The crèche offered a student nurse training program that included both Jewish and non-Jewish women, as part of its normal functions. Henrietta Pimentel, a Jewish woman, managed this crèche, in much the same way that Suskind managed the theatre.

Henrietta, with help from Suskind and several other women working in the crèche, found ways to smuggle children out of the crèche and into hiding in private homes or other places of sanctuary. Rescues were, by necessity, carefully planned, creative and highly dangerous. For example, the entrance to the daycare, through which the children were smuggled, was occasionally hidden by a passing tram, preventing Nazi observers at the Jewish Theatre across the road from viewing the door. As the tram passed, the children were smuggled out of the crèche hidden in laundry bags, rucksacks, baskets, or other bags, or hidden under coats. One newborn was hidden in a cake box.[316] Another method of smuggling the children out of the crèche, was by asking permission from the Nazis to take the children for walks around the daycare centre. The Nazis counted the children when they left the centre and again upon their return. After a group of children had left the crèche, and been counted, an additional, uncounted child or two was passed through windows that were out of sight. They could then join the group going for a walk, hiding in plain sight. During the walk, these uncounted children were then surreptitiously passed on to underground couriers who were waiting in nearby buildings to move them to safe houses. The walk continued with the same number of children returning to the crèche as the Nazis had counted leaving it. Jewish and non-Jewish rescuers risked their lives to save these children. Henrietta Pimental was arrested in July 1943, sent to Auschwitz, and murdered

there.[317] Suskind, as well as Pimental, and her assistants were able to save about 1,000 Jewish children and a similar number of adults during Suskind's eighteen months as director of the theatre. Suskind's activities were hidden behind his apparent fraternization with the Nazi officer in charge of deportations, Ferdinand aus der Fünten.[318] Neither Suskind nor his family survived after deportation to Auschwitz-Birkenau with one report saying he died on the death march from the camp in January 1945 and another reporting he was killed by Dutch inmates of Auschwitz who believed – because of his apparent friendship with a Nazi – that he was a collaborator.[319] Although Suskind is credited with these rescues, it must be remembered that he was assisted by and supported by many others.

Several Jewish women worked with Henrietta Pimental to make these highly complex rescue efforts possible. Betty Odkerk survived and lived to age ninety-six.[320] Rebecca Boas was captured and sent to Sobibor where she was murdered in July 1943 at the age of twenty-two.[321] Sieny Kattenberg, Innese Cohen and Viri Cohen, all worked as student nurses or interns at the crèche and helped rescue the children.[322] Adeline Finkelstein-Salomé was also a member of this underground movement at the crèche. She was born in Germany but moved to the Netherlands after *Kristallnacht* where she joined the underground and helped hide Jewish children. In June of 1943, she was arrested with some of her friends and sent to Ravensbrück. She survived and returned to Amsterdam.[323]

Hilde Jacobsthal, a seventeen-year-old who loved children and dreamed of being a paediatrician, was enrolled at the crèche in the student-nurse program.[324] She helped to comfort children and to cheer them up by singing songs in the various languages that they spoke. She was part of the operations to smuggle children out of the crèche to be sheltered in Christian homes.

Numerous non-Jewish women and men were also involved in rescuing these children, despite the pressures, bribes and threats enforced by the Nazis against those who helped Jews. For example, Hetty Voûte, Gisela Söhnlein and Kees Veenstra helped find safe addresses for the children and then escorted them to those homes.

Hetty Voûte came from a deeply anti-Nazi Dutch family. She was introduced into the underground through her brothers who established the first underground resistance newspaper. Gisela Söhnlein was a law student when the Nazis entered the Netherlands and soon became active in the Nazi resistance movement. Kees Veenstra would ride for dozens of kilometers on his bike taking Jews to safe homes. Clara Dijkstra, who grew up in a Jewish part of Amsterdam, Heiltje Koolstra who took nine Jews into her house in Utrecht and hid them throughout the war, and Janet Kalff, a Quaker, all took Jewish children into their own homes, sometimes at a moment's notice. Mieke Vermeer visited the hiding families, taking them food ration coupons and money. Rut Matthijsen helped to raise the money, and Ted Leenders stole large supplies of ration coupons from government offices for distribution to hidden Jews. Piet Meerburg developed security measures to ensure that the children could not be discovered even if he or other members of the group were arrested.[325]

The work to rescue children in the Netherlands was extensive, with Jews and non-Jews working together. Those mentioned here, and numerous others, saved over 4,000 children.[326] While this is a significant number, it was just a small fraction of the 140,000 people needing help.[327]

Westerweel Group

More than 320 Zionists living in the Netherlands were saved by Mirjam Waterman, Menachem Pinkhof and Joachim Simon, who were Jewish activists working with Joop Westerweel (later named a Righteous Gentile). The Westerweel Group found hiding places for some children and smuggled others from the Netherlands through France to Spain and on to British Mandatory Palestine.[328] Mirjam grew up on a farm, born to pacifist, secular Jewish parents. She became a teacher at a humanistic school and, while there, encountered stories of the German treatment of Jews. She learned of a Jewish immigrant school nearby where she met Menachem Pinkhof, the man she would marry after the war. When the Nazis banned Jews from schools, she founded a school for Jewish children in her parents' home.

Mirjam Waterman helped to pick up babies whose parents had been transported to Westerbork or were destined to be sent there. She would come with a stroller to the train station, collect the children and take them to families or institutions that would hide them.[329] Waterman and Pinkhof were eventually betrayed and sent to Bergen-Belson but survived the camp and later married. They emigrated to British Mandatory Palestine in 1946. Simon and Westerweel lost their lives saving others.[330]

Letty Rudelsheim also worked with the Westerweel group. She had been a teacher in a Talmud-Torah school in Amsterdam until it became unsafe for her, as a Jew, to appear in public. She went into hiding but offered to assist the Westerweel group in any way she could. She hid in a small apartment in Rotterdam where she sheltered a group of youngsters waiting to escape to southern France and then to Spain. She had to obtain food for many, although only two people were registered as living there. With the help of false ID papers, she managed to do so, thereby saving their lives. She was eventually arrested with eight of her friends in the apartment and sent to Auschwitz. She survived.[331]

Paula Kaufman helped the Westerweel group hide children on farms and smuggle them out of the Netherlands.[332] She also helped rescue children from the Jewish Theatre in Amsterdam. In 1944 she escaped from the Netherlands, hiding in a shack in the forest for about a year. She then made her way to Paris where she worked under an assumed name in the Gestapo offices. While there she smuggled Gestapo documents to the French, the British and the Dutch underground movements. She was eventually caught and deported to numerous camps, including Buchenwald and Bergen-Belsen, where she survived.

Alice Cohn

Alice Cohn, born in Lichtenstein, was a German-Jewish master forger with a career in graphic arts. She fled from Germany to the Netherlands and hid for two years in an attic in Utrecht. There she forged documents for her underground group, the Utrecht Children's Committee. They managed to save 350 children from deportation.[333] Her forgeries were some of the only forgeries that would pass Nazi inspection.

Hungary

Hajnalka "Hansi" Brand

Hansi Brand, a Zionist Hungarian activist (and her husband Joel Brand), actively supported refugees, including children, who fled from Nazi occupied countries into Hungary. In 1944 she was appointed the head of the International Division of the Red Cross Economy Division for child migration. In this capacity she helped obtain food for Jewish ghettos, children's homes, and other hiding places where Jews found shelter in the last weeks of the war.[334]

Chava Richer Halevi

Chava Richer Halevi crossed the Hungarian border into Romania together with her sister. There they were caught and imprisoned for more than two months. After her release from prison, Chava joined the underground. She collected orphans and took them to orphanages run by the Zionist youth movements.[335]

Poland

Basia Temkin-Berman

Basia Temkin (later Basia Temkin-Berman) and her husband Adolf Avraham Berman, as well as dozens of other women and men, both Polish and Jewish, saved the lives, or gave assistance to, between 11,000 to 12,000 Jews through the efforts of their organization called CENTOS (Zespół Zwiazek Towarzystw Opieki nad Sierotami). Adolf and Basia were involved in the creation of the Jewish National Committee in the autumn of 1942, a secret umbrella organization of six Zionist parties formed to manage the fighting organization, the ZOB, in the ghetto, and to assist Jews who were in hiding in Warsaw, outside the ghetto. It was aided by the non-Jewish Polish underground Council for Aid to Jews, later named as Żegota, and was secretly funded by the Joint Distribution Committee (JDC) and by other Jewish organizations, one of which was the non-Zionist organization, the Bund. Adolf served as the secretary of Żegota and chairman of the National Jewish Committee. CENTOS took care of children in the ghetto. The Jewish National Committee (the ZKN) together with the (Jewish) Bund and the (Polish) Żegota provided Jews with forged documents, food, shelter, money and medical assistance and cared for orphaned Jewish children.[336] The precise number of children that they helped is unknown.

Basia and Adolf were smuggled out of the Warsaw ghetto and lived as "Aryans" outside the ghetto. Basia pretended to be a poor woman dressed in shabby clothes and shoes but carrying around a double bottomed briefcase, torn on one side, stitched together with grey thread, and bound by a cord rather than a strap, which was missing. Under apples, onions, rolls, potatoes, and cucumbers were forged documents such as marriage and baptismal certificates and ID cards.[337]

On some occasions, Basia had to save Jewish newborns. Some women in hiding occasionally got pregnant. Despite the difficult conditions, the women sometimes chose to give birth anyway in the hope that their child might live to see better times. One woman, for example, had two children murdered by the Germans in 1942. Basia arranged lodgings for both the mother and the child where they could live safely. In other cases, such as when pregnancies resulted from rape, the Bermans managed to arrange, and pay for, abortions.[338]

Basia was a librarian who specialized in Jewish books. After the first Warsaw ghetto *Aktion*, she and her husband fled to the Aryan side and, while in hiding, collected information to document experiences of hiding on the Aryan side of Warsaw. The Ringelblum Archives, the extensive and secret collection of documents describing life in the ghetto, survived.[339] Ringelblum collaborated with the Bermans in documenting Jewish experiences of hiding on the Aryan side.

Belgium

In Belgium the Jewish Defence Committee saved over 3,000 Jewish children under sixteen, and thousands more adults. Hertz and Hava Jospa, both from wealthy families, moved from Bessarabia and

Moldova to Belgium to study. Hava became a social worker. Using forged identity cards in the names of Joseph and Yvonne, they created an underground Jewish movement which they called the Jewish Defense Committee. Working with two non-Jews, Brigette Moons and Yvonne Nèvejearn, they arranged for Christian families and institutions to hide Jewish children. Once a safe place was arranged, others, including Paule Renaud, Claire Murdoch and Andrée Geulen, all non-Jews, were assigned to convince parents to give up their children, and to escort those children to their new homes.[340] The couriers did not tell the parents their real names nor where the children would be taken.

Also in Belgium, but not linked to Hertz and Hava Jospa, Ida Sterno and her non-Jewish partner Andrée Geulen, a teacher from Brussels, collected children for over two years and hid them with Christian families and monasteries.[341] As a non-Jew, Andrée Geulen was able to move around with children more easily than Ida. Ida Sterno had come from a wealthy, non-religious, Jewish family but moved to Belgium where she became a social worker. Ida was eventually imprisoned, although Andrée hid and continued her mission to save Jewish children. Andrée Geulen was honoured by Yad Vashem while Ida Sterno was awarded a Jewish Rescuer Citation.

The administration and planning behind these rescues were in the hands of the Jewish activists Maurice and Ester Heiber, Yvonne/Hava Jospa, and Sophia Werber. Ester Heiber kept track of the hidden children using an elaborate series of five notebooks.[342] One held the child's name and a code number. Another listed the child's false name, birth date and code number. The third had the child's code number and his or her original address. A fourth listed the hiding places of the children with their own code numbers. The fifth listed the false names and the codes of the hiding places. The five books were hidden in five separate places. Only by integrating all five could the children be traced.

Rescuing children was always dangerous, and the children themselves were fully aware of the dangers they faced. For instance, a five-year-old boy had been hidden with a farmer whose eight-year-old daughter had been given a Christmas gift of a nativity scene including a manger, the baby Jesus, and some saintly figures. One evening the little girl noticed that the baby Jesus and some saints were missing. After long questioning, the boy confessed to having taken them. He admitted to the disappearance of the figures but said he had not taken them but had hidden them. When asked why he replied, "the small Jesus and the saintly virgin are Jews, so I hid them. The Gestapo will not have them."[343] While on the surface this story is appealing, it also reflects the need for rescuers to keep children psychologically and emotionally supported as well as physically safe. This five-year-old boy was acutely aware of the danger he was in and was terrified enough of what the Gestapo would do to a Jew, that he kept his actions – of saving the Jewish baby Jesus and his Jewish mother the saintly virgin Mary – safe and secret from his sheltering family.

Orphanages

While many Jewish children were hidden in Christian establishments or private families in Belgium, a unique alternative in the form of Jewish orphanages openly run under the constant supervision of the German occupiers, also saved hundreds of Jewish children.[344] To continue their deception of the Belgian population that concentration camps did not exist, the Nazis allowed Jewish orphanages to be established under Nazi supervision. These orphanages were purportedly for the children of parents who had been deported to labour camps for "employment" or who had died. The German occupiers agreed to allow seven Jewish orphanages to be established. These were the Antwerp Jewish orphanage (later the orphanage at Lasne), the orphanage of Jonas and Ruth Tiefenbrunner in Brussels, Home Wezembeek under the supervision of Madame Albert (later Blum), the Home de la-Bas in Aische-en-Refail, Home Lindebeek, Les Moineux (in Uccle), and a crèche (Etterbeek). Some 682 children stayed at the orphanages, with 500 being found in the various homes at liberation.

Jonas Tiefenbrunner and his wife Ruth ran the only *frum* (strictly kosher and Jewish law abiding) orphanage. They made every effort to celebrate the Jewish Holy Days as best they could. For *Hanukkah*, each child made a present for another child. During *Sukkoth*, they built a

Sukkah (temporary shelter) in the back yard.[345] The children were taught about Judaism and Jewish customs, such as the meaning of *Pesach* (Passover), *Brochas* (blessings) before dinner, and *Benchen* (blessings) after dinner.[346] Jonas was 29 years old when he started running this orphanage. Both he and Ruth had papers that would have allowed them to escape Belgium, but both decided to remain with the children. Jonas and Ruth's daughter, Judit Schreiber (born in 1945), testified that her father lived for the children. He rarely talked about these years other than to say they were the hardest but nicest years of his life. While he was loved by the children, Ruth was the one who cooked, cleaned, and cared for the children's needs, but was regarded by them as the strict one. Only one child had parents who both returned after the war's end. For some, only one parent returned. Even though all lived in hope that their parents would return, they were often disappointed when they did: the parents were not recognizable, were often too destitute to care for them and took years to recover from their Holocaust experiences. Many of the children did not want to return to their parents but chose to stay with Jonas and Ruth. At the end of the war, when the orphanage was closed, the couple continued to care for the remaining children in their own home, together with others who had been hidden in Christian homes and institutions. Eventually the children grew up and married or left home to establish their own lives. The last of them left the home in 1960. Jonas died in 1962 of a heart attack. As his daughter Judit Schreiber reports, no longer caring for the children broke his heart both physically and emotionally. Many of the children emigrated to Israel and the Tiefenbrunner family held a reunion, in 2002, of about 50-60 children who had lived in the orphanage but were then living in Israel.

In contrast, Madame Marie Albert-Blum, a Belgian born Jewish woman who ran the orphanage at Wezembeek, did not impose a religious atmosphere or practices but enthused the children with Zionism.[347] Raizel Warman (now Roni Luck Wolf), was about two years old when her parents were rounded up and deported to the camps. She and her sister, who was a few years older, were taken to the Wezembeek orphanage where they remained until liberation. Twenty-six-year-old Madame Albert, who ran the home, tried to find foster homes for the children: she would photograph them with a teddy bear to make them appear more appealing and advertised them for adoption. Roni's older sister was taken home by a Catholic woman, but the child refused to eat or drink no matter what was tried to encourage her to do so. She was, luckily for Roni, returned to the orphanage where she and Roni remained together. Roni remembers the orphanage with pleasure: as the youngest child there, among about 150, she was fussed over, picked up and loved by all the caretakers and has few if any unpleasant memories of her years there, unlike her older sister who was more aware of the dangers and horrors of the times.

Towards the end of the war, the Germans decided to evacuate all the children and move them to the camps. Madame Albert attempted to save the children from deportation by lying to the Nazis. She claimed that some of the children had infectious diseases. The Germans discounted this and transported the remaining fifty-eight children, who had not yet been adopted, to the railway station. There, however, the train guards believed Madame Albert, and refused to allow the children to board, sending them to a nearby shed to await return to their orphanage. *En route* to the shed, Madame Albert came across seven other Jewish children: she persuaded the guards to allow her to take these children with her. All the children were saved.[348]

At the end of the war, Roni's uncle and aunt (her mother's brother and his wife), who had been living in England, found the girls and eventually arranged to take them back to the UK, despite Roni's objections. Leaving her orphanage home was traumatic for Roni, but both she and her sister were discouraged from ever talking about their Holocaust experiences. About five years later, at about eleven-years-old, Roni, and her older sister, were formally adopted by her uncle's family. Some years later, Roni moved to Israel and joined the army where she met her future husband Ivor Wolf. After some years living in South Africa with his family the couple made *Aliyah* to Israel. During all these years, Roni never talked about her childhood experiences in Belgium until one day, Yad Vashem published a one-page article including photographs of unknown children from the Shoah. Roni's daughter recognized the photograph of her mother as a child, taken with the teddy bear that was used to encourage potential adoptive parents to take in children from the Wezembeek orphanage. It was only at this stage that Roni began to talk about her early life and became an educator about Holocaust events. She and her husband have stayed in touch with many of the children who moved to Israel and especially with Madame Albert-Blum.[349]

Italy

Matilda Cassim

Matilda Cassim was based in Florence. At the age of seventeen, with the onset of World War II she helped refugees who arrived in Italy. She worked with the DELASEM Organization that helped Jewish refugees in Florence. She was required to locate refugees at the train station and direct them to the organization's offices from where they would be assisted to find hiding places. She and a Jewish-Christian underground kept in touch with the refugee children trying to make them happy by sending them sweets and books. She also moved between monasteries that housed refugees providing them with fake IDs, food, and clothing, and passing along information. She persuaded nuns to shelter refugees. Her group saved between 300 and 400 Jews. In November 1943, the SS raided one of the group's meetings and sent them all to Auschwitz. Matilda escaped arrest as she was late for the meeting. In July 1944 she and her brother fled to Switzerland. After the war, she helped set up an orphanage in Selvino, northern Italy, for children who had survived. There she helped prepare them for immigration to Israel.[350]

Bella Hazan

Bella Hazan was a resistance worker during the war who served as a courier because of her Aryan appearance. During her time with the resistance, she passed as an Aryan named Bronislawa Limanovska. After about a year of underground work, she was captured, imprisoned, and tortured but did not reveal any secrets. She survived four months in the notorious Gestapo-run Pawiak prison in Warsaw and was then sent to Auschwitz-Birkenau as a Polish prisoner, where she passed as a nurse, although not qualified in that profession.[351] After surviving a death march and multiple concentration camps (Ravensbrück, Malchow and Buchenwald), she arrived at a DP camp in southern Italy where she instructed a group of forty-three orphaned girls aged six to fourteen, known as the Frumka group, until they were all able to emigrate to British Mandatory Palestine in November 1945.[352] She came from a religious family and was a member of a socialist youth movement, Hechalutz-Dror, dedicated to helping others.

Sweden

Chava Unger was born in Germany and, from 1933-1938, managed a Jewish children's home for approximately 250 children in Hamburg, where she was known as "the woman with the big heart."[353] After her father's arrest on *Kristallnacht*, she obtained permission for 500 Jewish children to leave Germany and live with Swedish families. Chava cared for them in Sweden and by 1941 had arranged visas for many to emigrate to British Mandatory Palestine. In 1943 she funded a fishing boat to rescue more than 200 Jews from Denmark by sailing them to Sweden.[354]

British Mandatory Palestine

Haviva Reich was a fellow parachutist of Hannah Senesh, the highly honoured and courageous Israeli Jewish resistance fighter who, in March 1944, was dropped into Yugoslavia by parachute to help fight the Nazis. She moved to Hungary where she was captured and later killed. Haviva Reich requested that she be dropped into Slovakia where she organized food and shelter for thousands of refugees, rescued Allied servicemen, and helped children escape.[355] She was captured in October 1944 and executed.

Children Rescuing Children

Children were not only rescued, they were also, occasionally, the rescuers. Just as Jewish women found ways to rescue children, so too did Jewish girls. Stories of Jewish girls saving the lives of their peers have emerged from Belorussia, France, and Belgium.

Belorussia

In Belorussia, a group of young girls were responsible for rescuing children out of the Minsk ghetto. The girls were primarily young teenagers, with a few as young as ten-years-old. Bronya Gammer, Sima Fitterson, Fanya Gimpel' and Roza Rubenchik[356] were all between ten and twelve years old. Most of the girls did not look stereotypically Jewish, which made it less likely that they would be immediately identified as Jews. The girls had found a way to enter the ghetto, where they would stay for a few days to gather a group of a few dozen children. They would then lead the small group out of the ghetto and escort them to partisan groups in the nearby forests. Although we know that these rescue attempts occurred, we know little of the details of how the girls were able to enter and leave the ghettos, the obstacles the groups faced, or the risks they encountered.

France

Another remarkable story of children rescuing other children is that of Fanny Eyal (later Ben Ami). At the age of thirteen, Fanny led a group of children through forests and along roads until they passed from France to Switzerland. There were twenty-eight children in the group. An older boy of seventeen who had been leading them decided to leave the group when they encountered a large German presence close to the Swiss border. He decided to return home, leaving Fanny to rescue the children.[357] Fanny smuggled the children onto a postal train that took them to Annemasse, and then tried to get to the border in trucks. They were caught by French *gendarmes*, interrogated, and interned in prison. Fanny managed to get the children out through a bathroom window. They then marched, singing as though they were on holiday, so as not to arouse suspicion. The children made their way to the forest and from there crossed into Switzerland, with the older children carrying the younger ones on their shoulders.[358]

Belgium

Some Jewish children also helped their peers cope with the increasingly repressive conditions imposed on them by the Nazis. Jewish children were barred from attending public schools in Belgium in 1941, following the invasion of that country by the Nazis the previous year.[359] In response, Henri Zylberminc and a number of his friends set up a group called the Jewish Students Group, to help each other cope with the absence of their interactions with school friends. Two dozen boys and girls were the first to meet but the group rapidly expanded to nearly a hundred youngsters. It became more than just a social group but a secret network of students who helped others, sometimes risking their lives.[360]

Bella Blitz, a fourteen-year-old girl, was chosen to serve as a secretary and was responsible for introducing about seventy students to the group. She took notes of their meetings, made sure that everyone had the phone numbers of the group's leaders, and collected the phone numbers of all the members.[361] Later, Bella and many others in the group were arrested and sent to a work camp, Malines. Bella found a way to send a letter to warn Henri and the members of the Jewish Students Group about the camp. Henri's parents went into hiding, while he and his younger brother Jack escaped capture and survived by hiding on the streets. By the spring of 1944, it became too dangerous for Henri and Jack to remain as fugitives on the streets and they joined their parents in hiding. Six months later Belgium was liberated.

Mirjam (unknown surname), an outgoing girl in the group, managed to find a teaching job caring for Jewish children in an orphanage in Brussels, after her family had been captured and sent away. Some time later a story circulated indicating that the Nazis were going to deport people from old age homes and orphanages. Mirjam volunteered to escort twelve children from the orphanage to Switzerland with the help of the Belgian and French underground.[362] Sadly, Mirjam and the children she was escorting did not make it: they reached the border but either they were turned over to the Germans by a French collaborator or the Swiss border guards would not let them through, and the Germans caught them.[363]

After the war, Henri hoped to have a reunion of the Jewish Student's Group, but few had survived. Mirjam and her group never returned from the war. Bella perished in Auschwitz.[364] Out of the nearly 100 members of the group, only eleven survived: the majority were sent to Auschwitz and were murdered.[365]

Hiding

The complexity of hiding children is revealed by these brief reports of Jewish women rescuers. Every rescue was unique, with rescuers using whatever skills or resources they could summon to adapt to highly dangerous contexts. They took unbelievable risks, sometimes resulting in the loss of their own lives, and certainly exposing them to capture, imprisonment and torture.

There was no template for the type of person who became a rescuer, but there are some similarities worth noting. Many of the women whose stories have been included here had studied or worked as social workers, nurses, or psychologists. They all valued helping others. Most of these women were very young. In addition to the children who helped save other children, many Jewish women rescuers were under thirty years old. In 1940, Mila Racine, Marianne Cohn and Charlotte Sorkine were all under twenty years old. Vivette Hermann-Samuel was in her twenties, while Andrée Salomon was thirty-two.[366]

Most of the women discussed in this chapter worked in collaboration with larger organizations, which included both Jews and non-Jews. As beneficial as it could be to work with larger organizations, it also came with increased risks of exposure and betrayal, capture and death. Few of the rescuers of which we are aware worked alone, or in small groups, such as Odette and Moussa Abadi in France, or the Krauses in the USA. Hundreds of rescuers, both Jewish and non-Jewish, worked to bring the children to safety, either in hiding or across borders to safer countries. Uniquely, dozens of both Jewish and non-Jewish rescuers moved 5,000 Jews, including children, to the French village of Le Chambon-sur-Lignon and its surrounding region (population 24,000) whose largely Protestant residents hid them between December 1940 to September 1944, and saved them.[367]

The ways in which Jewish women rescued children were as varied as the rescuers themselves. Some hid children, others moved them from one place to another for safety, yet others provided food or practical assistance, and some worked as document forgers. Some offered housing to children, others provided educational activities, or even created or contributed to children's libraries or schools. All were dedicated to saving them in whatever way they could, for however long they could. All their rescue efforts involved secrecy, and reflected an urgent need to resist and oppose the Nazi effort to murder all Jews and Jewish children.

Chapter 6: Smuggling

In regions that shared borders with non-occupied nations, an alternative to hiding children to save them was to facilitate their immigration to neutral countries across borders or to smuggle them into safer nations when legal immigration was not possible. In Europe during the war, there were very few non-occupied nations, with Switzerland and Spain being the most likely destinations for children seeking safe havens.

The route to Spain, leading through the Pyrenees, was more difficult than the one to Switzerland, but Jews were frequently turned away at the Swiss border. The Spanish route was therefore preferred. Crossing the border into Switzerland became far more difficult after October, 1938, when the Swiss government asked Germany to stamp a "J" on all Jewish passports to make identification of Jews easier.[368] Even prior to this, the Swiss required all refugees from Germany to have permission to emigrate from a Swiss consulate entered into their passports. The Swiss argued that by not granting admission of Jews to their country they would prevent the development of an antisemitic movement. By October 1939, a few children under sixteen or eighteen, sometimes pregnant women, or families with small children were occasionally admitted.[369] By the end of the war, Switzerland had admitted approximately 300,000 refugees, but only about 25,000 were Jews.[370]

The Guides

Smuggling Jews across borders was both dangerous and difficult. Not only did Jews need to leave their existing places of residence, often undetected, but they would then need to make their way to a friendly border, which may be a significant distance away. Locals who helped guide Jews to the Swiss or Spanish borders, in France called *passeurs,* would only help them find their way to the border; they rarely helped them pass through, and charged high fees if they did.

Smuggling children across long stretches of land with, at times, difficult terrain, was always challenging. In many cases, the children in a group being escorted to the border spoke different languages and were always traumatized by being uprooted from the lives to which they were accustomed. *Passeurs* had to be innovative and patient to encourage the children to listen to them and to follow their requirements for safety. One notable example is the approach used by Marcel Marceau (born Mangel).[371] He, together with his father were both part of the Scouts network and rescued more than 100 Jewish children.[372] Georges Loinger, of the Scouts of France and Marceau's cousin, asked Marcel Marceau to help smuggle children across the border to safety when a wealthy Strasbourg landowner brought 123 Jewish, German-speaking children to the French resistance. (Georges Loinger himself moved hundreds of children across the Swiss border and was one of the most audacious child smugglers.)[373] Unable to speak German, Marcel used mime to communicate with the children he helped escape into Switzerland. His first simple hand gesture, a hand passed over his face changing expressions from happy to sad and back again, became a signature action of his later artistic performances. He developed the art of mime into a life-long, immensely successful, global career in its performance.[374] His career was further influenced by his Holocaust related experiences. He is famous for his mime character "Bip" (a sad clown with a white face, striped jumper, and battered hat sprouting a limp flower).[375] The name of this endearing persona is sometimes attributed to the character Pip from Charles Dickens' *David Copperfield* (because the name of Philip Pirrip in the book was apparently too difficult to pronounce and was shortened to Pip).[376] It is, however, more likely that the name came from the documents he produced to give forged papers to the children he helped rescue, which were known as "bifs."[377] Marceau was involved in three operations to save children.

Not every person offering "help" to Jews trying to cross the borders did so as honestly or altruistically as Marcel Marceau. They typically charged for their services. In many cases they blackmailed Jews for more money to ensure the guides would not denounce them. Sometimes, after being paid, guides would abscond, abandoning the refugees and forcing them to find their own way across the border.[378]

Guides who genuinely tried to help Jewish children find safety would typically take small groups of children to the border and provide them with forged documentation to cross into Switzerland or Spain. While some tried to pass through border patrols with these forged documents others simply tried to cross the borders undetected, but were frequently caught. Border guards often denied Jews entry and those caught trying to escape into Switzerland undetected were frequently sent back across the border. Many of the Jews sent back to France at the borders died in concentration camps: few if any survived.[379]

Most of the stories discussed in this chapter are those of Jewish women living in France and helping to guide children to the border and smuggle them across. They include Mila Racine, Marianne Cohn, Charlotte Sorkine, Jan Letcheber, Sarah Knot and Judith Marcus, Elizabeth Hirsch, Denise Siekierski, Nicole Salon and Huguette Wahl, and Margo Wolff. In addition, there were a few Swiss citizens that also assisted refugees who managed to cross the border including Aimée Stitelmann.

Mila Racine

On the eve of the occupation of Paris by the German army, Mila Racine's family fled to southern France. They were a Zionist, traditionally religious family. She joined the French underground with her brother, Emanual, while her sister, Sarah, joined the resistance. Simon Lévitte, the director of the EIF scouting movement, engaged

Mila to work in the documentation centre in Moissac near the youth movement's dormitory. In November 1942, Lévitte moved the documentation centre to Grenoble (Isère), in the Italian-occupied area. Racine moved with it.

The documentation centre was operated both by the Zionist movement MJS and the EIF, and was an intelligence gathering centre for information on the hidden children, including their identities, origins, and hiding places. After the Germans overran the Italian-occupied area in September 1943, the MJS assembled a group of volunteers to smuggle children and young people across the Swiss border. Racine was a major activist in the group, but on 21 October 1943, she was arrested by the German border police, together with children she was guiding. The mayor of Annemasse, where she was held, Jean Deffaugt, secured the release of some of the children and offered to rescue Mila as well, but she refused to leave the remaining children. She concealed her Jewish identity and was ultimately deported to Ravensbrück. The remaining children were rescued by members of the underground. In late March 1945, she was killed in an Allied aerial bombardment on Ravensbrück, although some reports claim she died near Mauthausen.[380]

Marianne Cohn

In 1943, Marianne Cohn, was sent by the MJS to replace Mila Racine in the documentation centre, after Mila was arrested. Cohn had previously been active forging passports for the underground. After taking over Racine's work, Cohn smuggled many groups of youth to Switzerland until she was arrested on 31 May 1944, together with a group of twenty-eight children aged between four and fifteen, just as they approached the Swiss border. All of them were imprisoned in Annemasse.[381] Two days later the mayor of Annemasse, Jean Deffaugt, who forged documents for Jews and helped many to escape to Switzerland, convinced the Nazi commandant to send the seventeen youngest children to a local orphanage. Every day for three days, Marianne and the remaining eleven children were marched through the town to the Nazi headquarters in the Hôtel de France to work in the kitchens. At night she was interrogated and beaten by the Gestapo. The Maquis (resistance group) sent word to her that they would rescue her. Like Racine, Cohn refused to be rescued by the underground for fear that if she were, the Nazis would murder the remaining children.[382] The members of the underground sent a message to the Gestapo commandant, threatening to kill him if the children were harmed. All the children were eventually rescued through the assistance of Jean Deffaugt, who had to sign an agreement to return the children to the security services if ordered to do so. The released children were placed in a summer camp and later led to safety across the Swiss border into Geneva. On 8 July 1944, however, several weeks before the children were released, Marianne and three other prisoners were murdered. She was brutally tortured before being killed.[383] On 18 August, the Germans in Annemasse surrendered to the Maquis.[384] Marianne Cohn's body was discovered after the war ended.

Charlotte Sorkine

After Marianne Cohn's capture and death, Charlotte Sorkine took over the role of escorting children to the Swiss border and later to Spain. At seventeen, she had joined the Armée Juive (AJ) which was a fighting unit rather than a rescue organization. She did so after opening the door to a synagogue where, unknown to her, a resistance group was meeting, and decided to join them.[385] She was involved in smuggling weapons, explosives, and forged documents, to members of the resistance who needed them, hidden in a false bottom in the basket of her bicycle. By March 1943, however, she began to escort groups of Jews to safety at the Swiss border. She also forged hundreds, if not thousands of papers for Jews.[386] In March 1944, at the initiative of Andrée Salomon of the OSE, the AJ established a branch called the SERE (the Evacuation and Relocation Service for Children or the Service d'évacuation se de regroupement des enfants). The SERE took small groups of children – usually fewer than twelve at a time – to Spain. Sorkine worked with them as a guide for these groups. From April to August 1944, eighty-eight children were rescued: some report this number to be higher, up to 134.

Jan Letcheber

Jan Letcheber was born in France and lived in the Grenoble area. She was active in the Zionist underground from 1942 until liberation in 1944. She was a widow, the mother of two boys aged eleven and eight, whose home offered a warm welcome to young members of the organization. As a French citizen she was able to rent houses and she used this ability to create safe houses for children seeking refuge. Dozens of children were able to find refuge in her houses on their way to Switzerland.[387] Both Marianne Cohn and Mila Racine brought children to her houses as they guided them out of Nazi occupied France. They would stay overnight in small groups and be taken to the train station the following morning, equipped with forged documents that would allow them to cross the Swiss border. By offering these children shelter, she risked her own life and the lives of her own children.

Sarah Knot and Judith Marcus

David and Sarah Knot (who was born Ariadna Scriabina, the daughter of Russian composer Alexander Scriabin, but who converted to Judaism after marrying David) were founders of the "Jewish Army" (Armée Juive). Their first branch was established in Toulouse and was under Sarah's command. Through this, Sarah and her daughter, Betty Knot (from a previous marriage to a French Jew, a pianist and composer, Daniel Lazarus), were able to save many Jews, including children, whom she helped smuggle to Switzerland or Spain after their parents had been sent to the camps. Sarah Knot was also active in hiding children in monasteries and farms, in addition to sabotaging Nazi activities.[388] A month before the liberation of Paris, Knot was killed by French militia gunfire after they ambushed underground operatives.

Judith Marcus joined the Communist underground in Paris and was part of the Armée Juive. She carried false documents to Jews and spread news, money and weapons to those in the underground. One method she used to carry out these activities was to pretend to be a social worker. Under that guise, she carried heavy luggage containing household accessories that would justify her movements. This baggage also carried children's toys, including a wooden duck whose stomach opened to reveal important documents and money. She helped dozens of orphaned children and families. When she was ultimately caught, she claimed she was a French woman working for the Red Cross and had nothing to do with Jews. She was tortured to the point of exhaustion but did not reveal any information about her resistance tasks. She survived and later emigrated to Israel.[389]

Elizabeth "Böszi" Hirsch

Elizabeth "Böszi" Hirsch was a qualified social worker. She was asked by Andrée Salomon of the OSE to join the team of voluntary resident social workers in Gurs camp. Through that work, she and her team rescued hundreds of children, both legally or otherwise. She also participated in rescuing 108 children from Vénissieux camp. With her sister Charlotte "Shatta" Simon, she organized children's convoys across the borders to Switzerland and Spain. She personally escorted twelve children aged between eight and fourteen safely through the High Pyrenees mountains into Spain. They eventually arrived in British Mandatory Palestine in October 1944.[390]

Denise Siekierski

Denise Siekierski *née* Caraco was an only child raised by her grandparents. She joined the Jewish Scouts youth movement (later the Sixth) at the age of eleven and became a scout leader. She was nicknamed *Colibri* (hummingbird) during her early Scout days. In 1942, when Vichy France was occupied by the Germans, she was active in the Sixth, finding homes for young Jewish fugitives, producing false documents, guiding people to the Swiss and Spanish borders, making monthly visits to those who were hidden, and traveling to places in the South of France carrying illegal documents. She maintained close ties with the thousands of Jews and Jewish children hidden in Le Chambon-sur-Lignon. In January 1943, Siekierski helped organize a hiding operation. She interviewed applicants and supplied them with false documents. As her own life was in danger, she moved around Marseille, sleeping in a different location every night. She finally had to leave town and went to Grenoble. Returning in June 1943, she met Joseph Bass and joined his resistance group. Denise was Bass' principal assistant, narrowly escaping arrest several times.[391]

Nicole Salon and Huguette Wahl

In November 1943, Nicole Weil (who married Jacques Salon, one of the leaders of the Scouts), was sent by the Scouts, together with Huguette Wahl, a social worker, to Nice to try to save as many children as possible. They collaborated with both the Garel Network and the Marcel Network in these activities. While preparing one convoy of children to be smuggled to Switzerland, they were arrested. Both were sent to Drancy where they looked after a small group of children. All were subsequently transported to Auschwitz, arriving on 23 November 1943. On arrival, Both Nicole and Huguette were approved as fit for entry into the camp but both refused to abandon the children, and instead, were sent to a gas chamber with them.[392]

Margo Wolff

Margo Wolff, a journalist, escaped Nazi Germany at the beginning of the Nazi regime but was arrested in France in 1939. She was sent to Gurs internment camp but escaped to Marseille where she obtained a Czech passport that enabled her to save Jewish children. She drew on her drama background to stage a play about the Maccabees that prepared the children for group transfers to the Swiss or Spanish border. Several groups were saved, although Margo was arrested twice by the Gestapo and held in a Swiss internment camp. After the war she continued her work in journalism, earning many honours.[393]

Swiss Helpers

Aimée Stitelmann, a Swiss citizen, was the daughter of a Russian-Polish-Swiss Jew living in Switzerland. She helped approximately seventeen children get into the country and assisted them in finding safety with Swiss families. She was, however, caught several times and imprisoned for short periods as a result.[394]

Chapter 7: Emotional Support

Most children and adults were murdered on arrival in extermination camps such as Treblinka, Sobibor, Majdanek, or Belzec. Children over thirteen – or younger if they could pass as older – were usually admitted to labour camps, including Auschwitz, as they were judged as potentially able workers. Some, especially those under thirteen, who found themselves in transit or labour camps, had a greater chance of survival, especially if they were helped by others. That said, few children under thirteen survived any of the camps. For example, on liberation, 180 children under eighteen years of age were found in Auschwitz, only fifty-two of them were under eight years old, all of whom were the subjects of medical experiments.[395] There were 149 children in Bergen-Belsen on liberation,[396] 700 in Buchenwald,[397] and 120 in Theresienstadt.[398]

Physical escape from extermination camps was virtually impossible. Escape from labour or transit camps was extremely rare, especially for children. Instead, alleviating the horrors of their experiences was the most optimistic goal that any rescuers could offer to the mostly teenage children who were admitted to labour camps.

Friedl Dicker-Brandeis

Conditions in Theresienstadt were atrocious. Children were separated from their families, siblings and friends and lived in overcrowded children's homes surrounded by cruelty and starvation. Friedl Dicker-Brandeis brought art into their worlds, helping over 600 children to cope with their feelings of loss, sorrow, fear, and uncertainty.[399]

Friedl-Dicker Brandeis was born in Vienna and studied art at the Weimar Bauhaus under Johannes Itten and Paul Klee. The Bauhaus taught not only art, but a philosophical approach based on empathy.[400] Friedl was a multifaceted artist working in a large variety of media including photography, textiles, printing presses, metal work, weaving, architectural themes, furniture, and interior design, as well as traditional art forms. Her work was creative and received multiple awards. The varied nature of her art stood her in good stead for the contributions she later made to the lives of children in Theresienstadt.[401]

Friedl was arrested for communist activities in 1934 and imprisoned. After her release she moved to Czechoslovakia where she married her cousin, Pavel Brandeis. She became active in the Czech underground. In 1938, her friends obtained a visa for her to go to British Mandatory Palestine, but she refused to leave, not wanting to separate from her husband or friends.[402] On 12 December 1942, both she and her husband were deported to Theresienstadt. She was instructed not to bring more than fifty kilograms of luggage.[403] Most Jews packed clothing, valuables, and photos when deported, but Friedl packed art supplies to ensure she would have materials with which to teach art to the hundreds of children she presumed would value this in the camp.[404]

Her goal in teaching art was to restore the shaken inner world of the children.[405] Lessons taught techniques such as watercolour, paper weaving, collage, and drawing but, drawing on her Bauhaus groundings, also encouraged the children to dig deeper into their true feelings and emotions and to create drawings of these sensations. She encouraged the children to explore and express their imaginations.[406] Her art resembled freedom, intending that this freedom could take the children out of the boundaries of their confinement and away from the horrors of their daily lives. One of her students, Eva Dorian, said her lessons were "emancipated meditation."[407] Another of her pupils, Helga Polláková-Kinsky painted pictures, reporting

> in her world there was no danger, no threat of
> transport, and while she was drawing, she felt safe

and good. From morning to night, in their free time, the children kept drawing. Friedl encouraged the children to talk about their artwork. Discussion helped calm them down and restore their hope.[408]

Helga added that "She wanted us to get away and go into a nice world."[409] Another student, Erna Furman said, "the times spent drawing with her, are among the fondest memories of my life."[410]

At the end of every lesson, she told the children to sign their names on their work. She returned their identities back to them in a world that referred to them only by number.[411]

Friedl's artistic activities in Theresienstadt drew on her multifaceted experiences. She and her colleagues helped the children to stage a production of *Fireflies*, a Czech fairy-tale, working with the children to design and make the costumes. They used dyed sheets that she had brought into the ghetto with her, and any scraps of material they could find including underwear, shirts, and even burial shrouds. She also contributed to the famed production of *Brundibar*, the children's opera composed in 1938 by Hans Krása, with lyrics by Adolf Hoffmeister, that was performed fifty-five times in Theresienstadt in 1943 and 1944.[412]

On 28 September 1944, Friedl's husband was sent to Auschwitz on a transport of men only. He survived. Eight days later, she volunteered to be sent on the next transport in the hope of finding him. On 6 October she was sent with thirty[413] (some say sixty[414]) of her students to Auschwitz-Birkenau. All were murdered.

After her departure, Raja Englanderová-Žákníková, one of her teenage students, found 5,000 of the children's drawings in two suitcases in the attic of L410, a room/space Friedl used in Theresienstadt. She gave the suitcases to Willi Groag, head tutor of L410. Willi took the suitcases with him to Prague after the war where they sat untouched for twenty years. Their contents were eventually discovered and are now exhibited around the world. They belong to the State Jewish Museum in Prague and Beit Theresienstadt in Israel where they have been carefully cataloged and preserved.[415] Over 130 of Friedl's paintings were discovered in the 1980's and are now in the Simon Wiesenthal Centre in Los Angeles.[416] One of Friedl's own paintings, of a girl's face, created while in Theresienstadt, appears on the cover of this book, in her honour.

Hadassah Rosensaft (*née* Bimko)

Hadassah Rosensaft was a dentist but was forced to work as a doctor in Auschwitz-Birkenau. In November 1944, after fifteen months, Mengele sent her, together with eight other Jewish women, to Bergen-Belsen in Germany.[417] Bergen-Belsen held Jews, prisoners of war, Roma and Sinti, political prisoners, and other targets of Nazi persecution. As Allied and Soviet forces advanced into Germany in late 1944 and early 1945, thousands of Jewish prisoners were sent there from camps closer to the front, including women and a few surviving children. In July 1944 there were 7,300 prisoners in Bergen-Belsen: by April 1945, there were 60,000.[418] Towards the end of 1944, the SS organized a *Kinderheim* (children's house) in the camp: before then, this had been a family home of Dutch Jews who had papers as American citizens.[419]

One month after Hadassah Rosensaft's arrival, forty-nine Dutch Jewish children were assigned to her care by the SS guards, followed by other children deported to Bergen-Belsen from Buchenwald and Theresienstadt. Hadassah walked from block to block seeking children. She took them to the *Kinderheim*, her "Children's home," loved them and looked after them.[420] Eventually she, with other women prisoners, kept 149 children (ranging in age from infants to teenagers) alive throughout the winter and spring of 1944-5. As Hela Jafe, one of her co-workers, reports:

> The children were small and sick, and we had to wash them, clothe them, calm them and feed them. [...] Ada was the one who could get injections, chocolates, pills and vitamins. I don't know how she did it. Although most of the children were sick, thanks to Ada nearly all of them survived.[421]

Hadassah reports that:

> We talked to them, played with them, tried to make them laugh, listened to them, comforted them when they cried and had nightmares. When they were sick with typhus, we sat beside them telling them fairy tales. I sang songs to them in Polish, Yiddish, and Hebrew – whatever I remembered – just to calm them until they fell asleep.[422]

All but one of the children survived. All the children from Hadassah's *Kinderheim* were sent to Israel.[423] On 9 April 1949, Dr. Bimko accompanied the first transport of 100 children and twenty expectant mothers (two of whom gave birth on the journey) to Israel.[424]

Luba Tryszynska

Like Hadassah Rosensaft, Luba Tryszynska, a Jewish nurse from White Russia (Belarus), was sent from Auschwitz to Bergen-Belsen in November 1944.[425] Like some of the other rescuers in this book, she too began caring for camp children, with the permission of the camp doctor and the SS officials, in December 1944. Luba and Hermina Krantz, a Jewish woman from Slovakia, also transferred from Auschwitz, were placed in charge of, and cared for, ninety orphaned children from less than one-year-old to twelve. Luba became the provider, scrounging food and other provisions like wood from the camp, while Hermina cared directly for the children, washing them, cooking for them, and feeding them. Together they kept the children within the barrack to which they had been assigned, and kept them sheltered from the worst of the horrors of the camp. After liberation Luba became the manager of a new children's home under British direction, and Hermina became its chief cook. Later Luba accompanied some children back to the Netherlands and others to Sweden. Luba was referred to as the Angel of Belsen.

Yehoshua and Hennie Birnbaum

Yehoshua (Otto) Birnbaum and Hennie Weiden Birnbaum were born in Poland to Orthodox families and emigrated to Germany as children. They married in 1927 and had six children between 1928 and 1938. In the summer of 1938, the German government rounded up Polish-born Jewish men, including Yehoshua, and deported them to Zbąszyń, Poland. Hennie, pregnant with her sixth child, maintained the household, their business, and their religious lifestyle, after her husband's deportation.[426]

Harassed by the Germans, Hennie sent her five children to the Netherlands to live with an aunt. They travelled on their own by train. Their uncle did not meet the children's train, however, and local community members looked after the children: four of them with one family and one with another. After a few weeks, the four children were transferred to an orphanage. Hennie could not obtain legal documents allowing her to go to the Netherlands. Instead, she boarded a train knowing that her sixth baby was due to be born. Once in the Netherlands she claimed to be in labour and was taken off the train and admitted to a Catholic hospital where she was cared for by a young doctor who was the son-in-law of a Dutch minister. The minister wrote to Hennie saying her husband could enter the Netherlands if he agreed to go to a refugee centre that was being built in Westerbork to house German refugees. Yehoshua Birnbaum was reunited with his wife, and ultimately with their children, and all moved to Westerbork. From there they made their way to Leeuwarden. In May 1940 the Germans invaded the Netherlands and the Birnbaums were again sent to Westerbork, which had been converted into a transit camp from where the Germans shipped Dutch Jews to extermination camps in Poland.[427]

Many of the transports of Jews to Westerbork arrived at night. Hennie and Yehoshua Birnbaum would meet the trains and rescue the children who were without their parents. They were taken to Barrack 35 and housed there in four dormitories. The Birnbaums took personal responsibility for this make-shift orphanage. Forged documents were produced for the children claiming imaginary baptism or that the children were illegitimate offspring of German soldiers.[428]

On 15 March 1945, as the war was nearing its end, the Birnbaums were sent to Bergen-Belsen together with about 200 orphans still under their care.[429] Soon after, three of their own children contracted polio with one of them experiencing temporary paralysis of the legs. Despite this, the Birnbaums continued to care for the orphans, who survived.

On 10 April 1945, the family was sent on an evacuation train to Theresienstadt during which journey Hennie and their oldest child contracted typhus. Soviet soldiers liberated the train on 23 April 1945. The Birnbaums together with their children as well as many of the orphans moved from place to place, seeking refuge, ultimately arriving in the Netherlands. In the meantime, two of their own children were sent to a sanitarium in Switzerland to recover from tuberculosis. The Birnbaums continued to care for about forty remaining orphans, who had survived and not found alternative homes, and in 1950 they moved to Israel with all of them, and were reunited with their own children who had, by then, recovered from the polio, typhus, and tuberculosis that some of them had contracted. Over the years, the Birnbaum's cared for a total of approximately 350 children, with the youngest being only six months old.[430] Despite their own family hardships and illnesses, the Birnbaums remained loyal to their commitment to care for the Dutch orphans that came their way through Westerbork and Bergen-Belsen.

Ellen Loeb

Ellen Loeb also assisted with the rescue of children in Westerbork. She and her family were deported to Westerbork where she worked as a nurse, although she was not qualified to do so. She accomplished this by watching others and learning from their examples. She describes a transport of twenty children to Westerbork:

> We were frightened of what we were seeing because the lines of carts just didn't stop. There were more and more, sometimes three children on one stretcher. Many were babies under one year old. [...] there were also children of two and three years of age up to fourteen, all of them very, very ill. They were half naked or wrapped only in a thin blanket. Most of them cried miserably and were totally exhausted and hungry. [...] eventually we had a

total of forty-five children with all kinds of diseases. [...] Many had pneumonia after having had measles. Others had otitis media, chicken pox, whooping cough and many other children's diseases. Almost all the children had terrible diarrhea. You were actually fighting for each child.[431]

All except five of the children recovered. Ellen and her coworkers tried to keep the children from being sent on to camps in the east. For example, one child who was well and likely to be deported was given an injection of milk to give him a fever. That allowed him to stay safe with his family for a little longer. Ellen cared for the children between June 1943 and February 1944 when she was sent to Auschwitz and later to Mauthausen. She survived, as did her mother.[432]

Fella Cajtak Meiboom and Esther Maestro Sadikario

Fella Cajtak, a nurse, was deported from Poland to Auschwitz-Birkenau in 1942. She was forced to work in a dental clinic where she had access to drugs, clothing, and food. She distributed these items to prisoners. She became the *Blockälteste* (Block leader) of Block 8, a part of the punishment lager, where she was in charge of more than 1,000 Jewish girls aged twelve to sixteen. She was able to bribe the SS men with items given to her by the Jewish inmates in exchange for hiding the weak and sick among them, thus evading death.[433] She personally did her best to care for and give medical assistance and hope to about sixty girls.[434]

Esther Maestro Sadikario was a Greek Jewish woman deported to Auschwitz. She saved 181 girls from Block 25 in Birkenau who were supposed to be sent to the gas chambers. She helped them sneak out of the window of the barrack to get to a nearby barrack.[435] This happened not once but over a series of three selections.

These stories are unique examples of heroism in the camps. Although the women were themselves exposed to all the horrors of the camps, they found the emotional energy and the will to help the children they encountered. There are tens of thousands of testimonies and memoirs relating women's stories of their lives in camps. None were easy. All reflect the physical, mental, and emotional horrors of those experiences. Many of these women helped a friend or even a few others, but it was rare for anyone to provide assistance to dozens or even hundreds of others. The women described in this chapter did, not only by saving the lives of numerous children in many instances, but especially by providing them with emotional support, care and love.

Chapter 8: Retrieving Children

At the end of the war there were thousands of Jews known as the "remnants" (*She'erit Hapletah*),[436] including Jewish children that had been separated from their parents, siblings, or other family members, and from their Jewish roots. Six million Jews had been murdered, two-thirds of the pre-war Jewish population of Europe, among them as many as one and a half million children. Children who had been hidden had the greatest chance of survival, although only about 10% of the Jewish children of Europe survived.[437] Most had been orphaned, many were placed in Christian homes, some baptised into Catholicism, while others survived in labour or concentration camps, among partisans, hidden in forests, or escaped Europe through rescue efforts as described in this book. Some found themselves alone on the streets, having been thrown out of the homes in which they had been hidden. Given the continuing prevalence of antisemitism in Europe after the war, families feared exposure for having hidden Jewish children, resulting in the children's eviction. Many wandered the countryside or cities living independently as what we would now call, "street children." The same antisemitism that led families who had hidden children to evict them out of fear also threatened Jewish orphans.

Major efforts were instituted by Rabbis, Jewish organizations, family members, parents, siblings, and family friends or relatives to find the children and to return them to their families whenever possible, or at least, to their pre-war Jewish way of life. At the time, the predominant feeling in the Jewish community was that, after the decimation of the Jewish population in Europe, Jewish children who had survived – usually in hiding and by converting or identifying as

Christians – should be returned to their family or relatives, or if this was not possible, at least to Judaism. They believed that not returning them to Judaism would have supported Hitler's goal of eradicating the Jews from Europe. Additionally, as so many Jews had been killed, every remaining Jewish child was precious.

Multiple obstacles stood in the way of these retrieval efforts, ranging from resistance from Church institutions, or families who had cared for the children for years and had become attached to them, and from the children themselves who, in many cases, could not remember their original family and knew no other loved ones other than the homes in which they now lived. Returning to their surviving family members was difficult: the children often felt abandoned by their families rather than saved by them through their actions. Some children perceived having been sent away from their families as rejection. For example, Vera Schaufeld was nine years old when she was sent from Prague on a *Kindertransport*. She last heard from her parents in November 1940.

> I imagined that my parents must have forgotten me
> or that I must have done something really terrible to
> deserve to be in England. [...] I used to go through
> all the things that I had ever done wrong as a child,
> and said that it was because I had done these things
> that I didn't deserve to be with my parents.[438]

Not all children who were sent to Aryan families were taken there by their parents or by rescuers. Some had been left along highways, or on doorsteps, or by the wall of a convent, in the hope that someone would help them. Such children developed strong feelings of abandonment, particularly if they remembered such actions.[439]

Those that survived in camps, or on the streets, had been deprived of any sense of love and support from adults, and were distrustful of adults, resistant to authority, and independently mature far beyond their young years. Returning to any form of Judaism, which they perceived in many cases to have been the cause of their horrific experiences under the Nazis, was not always a welcome prospect.

Nevertheless, despite these obstacles, and with many misgivings about the further disruption they would cause in these children's lives, many rescuers undertook the task of reuniting these children with a semblance of normal Jewish life. This chapter explores the perspectives and experiences of the children, the families that had cared for them, the Church, and the Jewish organizations that implemented efforts to retrieve these children and to return them to their families or to Judaism.

How Children Survived

The exact number of Jewish children who survived the war is unknown.[440] Early postwar estimates from the Joint Distribution Committee are that 150,000 survived, out of a prewar population of about 1.5 million. Children under seventeen or eighteen were usually included in these figures.[441]

After the war, children were found in homes, camps, forests, with partisan groups, and in both neutral and allied countries, making an accurate tally of how many children survived, and how they survived, challenging.[442] One estimate of the contexts in which children survived emerged from post-war Lodz, and is based on 1,246 surviving children under the age of fourteen who had registered with different Jewish committees. This indicates that 59% of children survived on the Aryan side, presumably hidden by Christians, 22% survived in camps, 10% in forests, 5% in the Lodz ghetto and 3% with partisan groups.[443] In the chaos that was post-war Europe and the world, there were few means to assess child survivor rates accurately. As the majority of child survivors appeared to be those who had been hidden with Christian families and institutions, retrieving them from these places of shelter became a priority at the end of the war.

Children's Experiences

For many children the post-war years became some of the worst they experienced.[444] This applied especially to those who had formed deep bonds with the families that had sheltered and who had loved them during the war years. For some children, and especially the younger ones who had been placed in Christian homes, these were the only parents they knew or remembered. Some continued to stay with these families but others were removed to return to their parents, relatives, or temporarily to Jewish care homes or orphanages where they could be found more easily by their relatives or parents, or until they could emigrate to Israel.[445] The younger ones in particular no longer spoke their parents' language, and few of them had any memories of Jewish traditions or customs. In addition, children had learned for years that being Jewish was dangerous and they had been forced or encouraged to forget their Jewish roots, traditions, and languages. The youngest ones never even knew about their Jewish origins.[446] Many, like Leah Nebenzahl (*née* Hirschman), had been sheltered in homes that were antisemitic, as was common at the time, and grew up believing and expressing antisemitic tropes learned from their foster homes.[447]

Superficially, it may appear that holding antisemitic views while rescuing Jewish children is paradoxical. It is, however, likely that many families that offered to hide Jewish children did not know they were Jewish, so raising the children with antisemitic views is not, necessarily, antithetical. Others, however, that did know of their rescued child's Jewish origins, may have been influenced by the prevailing antisemitism of the time and shared these views with the children. Also, children expressing such antisemitic views may have been better protected from discovery than if they had held, or expressed, more tolerant views towards Jews and Judaism.

Surviving parents too were often in no condition to care for children, physically, financially, emotionally, or mentally.[448] In addition, prejudice against camp survivors was strong: they were seen as morally compromised and emotionally and behaviourally damaged.[449] Notwithstanding these difficulties, most western countries believed that children should return to their parents if they had survived, except in the Netherlands. The Netherlands regarded Jewish children as wards of the state and did not automatically return them to their parents, despite Jewish organizations' opposition to this approach. Host families in this country were able to keep the children they had sheltered more often than in any other country.[450] In the Netherlands, parents were denied access to their children on the grounds that the parents were so traumatised by their experiences that the children would be better off staying with their adoptive families. As Polak writes:

> If a Jewish child had been separated from its parents during the war, and these parents had survived, it was not given in Dutch law that parent and child would be reconciled. On matters of family reconciliation, Dutch law seemed to have been written to protect the children from their parents, especially if the parents were Jewish, and Dutch courts soon became clogged with hysterical mothers and fathers who just wanted their kids back.
>
> [...] You came back from Bergen-Belsen, and Theresienstadt, physically and emotionally devastated, having no certainty that anyone in your family is alive – not even your children. You then engage in what must be history's most desperate, harrowing manhunt for your missing child, and when in some moment of divine grace, you locate your child, the authorities tell you your child is no longer yours – that the child's adoptive parents, who have hidden them all these months and years, are more competent than you are in your laughingly humiliated, compromised and shaken condition, and that these adoptive parents now get to keep your son, your daughter. Such a parent is left feeling that where the Nazis did not ultimately succeed in separating parent and child, the Dutch did.
>
> Even in those cases where the adoptive family is more competent than the hapless returning concentration camp survivors, the cruelty involved in refusing these parents their children, to me, overrides any consideration of "what's best for the children."[451]

In other countries, children removed from their hosting families were often moved from place to place until such time as they could emigrate to Israel or could join family or relatives in other countries. They could be moved first to a Jewish care home or orphanage or to a United Nations Relief and Rehabilitation Administration (UNRRA) reception centre, and then to a ship leaving Europe, to a new country, a new family, and a new language.[452]

A constant source of concern for Jewish agencies was how to enable the children to reconnect with Judaism. Their past years of secrecy regarding their Jewish origins and their minimal memory of Jewish traditions often made it difficult for them to understand the value of these practices. While some care homes/orphanages followed strict Orthodox customs, others did not force these on the children who did not find this desirable. These homes gradually introduced Jewish customs, without making it compulsory for children who were reluctant to participate.[453] Some children held on to the symbols of Christianity that they had, such as crucifixes or rosaries, for a long time. These reflected their beliefs and allegiance at the time or were a means of rebelling against their parting from their host families.[454] As Leah Hirschman experienced, she was allowed to follow Christian religious practices that her foster family had instilled in her while Jewish customs, such as lighting candles on Friday night, were slowly introduced, until a gradual replacement of Judaism for Christianity occurred.[455] Others, and particularly those strictly Orthodox organizations involved in retrieving children, rejected any practices other than strict Judaic customs, often with less acceptance by the children, at least at first.

At the end of the war, surviving children faced a number of possible life paths. For a very few, the nuclear family survived and remained or was reunited intact. For some, one parent survived and was reunited with their child. In both these situations being reunited with family, even though desperately wanted by most children, was often a difficult and distressing experience.[456] Surviving parents if alone, often remarried creating even more difficult family interactions.[457] Step-parents sometimes favoured their own biological offspring over their step-child. Sometimes, children returned to distant family members faced particular difficulties when the aunt or uncle who adopted them also had their own children. The adopted child often felt they were not treated in the same way, or as well as, the family's own natural children.[458]

After the war, these new families, no matter what their structure, faced health, income, lifestyle, career, and migration challenges, making optimal care for the children, especially when the parents themselves were in need of considerable support, extremely hard. These children faced the initial loss of their families, adjustment to their hiding families, and then readjustment back to their now, often largely forgotten, or even largely unknown, original families. This final change involved not only changes in caregivers, but further changes in language, religion, and identity. These children were not only survivors themselves, but now often became the children of survivors with all the challenging connotations that second generation children experienced added to their own. There were also situations in which they experienced abuse. For example, in 1945, Max, aged nine, was returned to his father, who had a new wife. It was not until four years later, at the age of thirteen, that he learned that the woman he regarded as his mother was his stepmother and also, that he was Jewish – facts that his father had decided to keep from him after the war. His stepmother was emotionally and physically abusive, behaviours that culminated, when he was fourteen, in sexual abuse. After four years of forced sexual activity with her, usually following beatings, he left home at the age of eighteen.[459]

In addition, surviving parents often thought their own suffering had been so great that their children's experiences could not compare. Nor did they want to talk about their children's hiding family or about a parent or siblings who had died. Alternatively, parents talked incessantly about their own experiences.[460] A considerable number of children who were reunited with one or both parents were eventually placed in *kibbutzim* or in care homes as their parents realized these could offer their children a better life than they could provide. The longer the children stayed in such institutions, the more difficult it became for them to return to their families.[461] In Poland, for example, about three-quarters of the 866 children in care homes had at least one surviving parent.[462] In France, about 49% of children in post-war children's homes had two living parents and an additional 34% had one surviving parent. True orphans in care homes were, surprisingly, relatively rare.[463] The difficulties faced by children who were reintegrated into their surviving or newly created family environments after the war raise questions about the decisions made by the Dutch to leave rescued children with their foster families rather than to return them to their biological parents. Were the Dutch right in their decision? Or was it best to give the original family unit a chance to try to reunite happily before choosing to place their children in *kibbutzim* or shared child care homes if family life proved to be non-optimal?

Life in Care Homes or in Families

Some hidden children were placed in orphanages where they could more easily be traced by Jewish families seeking their remaining family members, and from where they were occasionally claimed by distant relatives, again requiring multiple adjustments to differing family environments and interpersonal relationships. Some relatives tried to claim children because of genuine affection for the children of relatives, others out of a sense of duty to their murdered loved ones, and others because they were the only relatives still alive.[464]

An alternative option to family life faced other surviving children: life in care homes/orphanages, or rapid attainment of independence. Many aid agencies favoured placing children in foster homes, believing that family life was the best place for a young child or adolescent.

Life in care homes or orphanages, as compared to family settings, was often happier for children as they could share their memories with others who understood them.[465] Children housed with relatives often fared worse than those placed in collective homes or with foster parents. By 1948, up to half of placements with relatives had failed.[466] Unrealistic expectations were often the cause of these failures. Those placed in foster homes hoped that the family would be able to get their parents or siblings back from Europe to join them. Also, some foster parents took in children because they wanted servants to help them in addition to believing they were doing a good deed. Neither set of expectations would lead to a happy experience.[467] In contrast, and for example, Hélène Ekhajser became a counsellor at a care home in Taverny in France. She had been deported to Auschwitz in February 1944 at the age of sixteen. She forged a bond with the children in the care home through story-telling. Felice, one of the children, remembered that Hélène told them horrific stories, which the children loved. One of these was the story Hélène had witnessed on the death march from Auschwitz to Ravensbrück in January 1945:

> [In the story] everybody was walking in the snow, and this little girl wanted to…she couldn't walk anymore, so they asked the Germans if she could ride in the truck. And they said sure. So [the Germans] took her up in the truck, and they killed her. And we thought – wow! That's a wonderful story![468]

Felice remembered this story as one of warmth and affection and excitement because they all had such memories in common. Such stories were shared histories that the care home supervisors could understand, unlike foster families who had no or little understanding or interest in the children's experiences.

The Canadian program that brought 1,115 or more (estimates vary) youngsters to Canada by 1952, initially tried to place them with foster families but this was not often successful and the children chose to return to life in a centre for these immigrant youth.[469] Canadian demands when bringing these children to the country were that they would be under eighteen years of age, orphans, physically and mentally fit, and would be supported financially by the Canadian Jewish Committee organizing this program. Most families wished to adopt small children, and especially girls, preferably from higher socio-economic family backgrounds, but few were available: most were boys between fifteen and seventeen years old. The children were also adept at concealing their past and the existence of living parents in order to emigrate, leading to further complications when this was revealed.[470] Foster homes proved to be unsuccessful placements and the youth were often moved back into reception centres arranged for them.

Not all foster homes were good for the children. Helga Weisz, who emigrated to the USA, reported:

> Whenever I tried to tell them what had happened to my family in Europe, they told me that I was making up stories and that I should just forget about those times. They also said that if my parents were punished it's probably because they did something bad against the government. They told me that I shouldn't talk about it anymore and that I should concentrate on becoming an American.[471]

Many were concerned about the children's psychological state after their harsh war experiences. Surviving children, not surprisingly, proved to be resilient and resourceful, adept at presenting a side of themselves that they thought might be beneficial for them.[472] Those that had been hidden had been forced to adopt such an "optimal" persona to remain undiscovered as Jews: those that had lived on farms, among partisans, or on the streets, were independent, precocious and "street wise." Returning to a traditional family life of subservience to adult authority was problematic.

Another reason to seek out orphaned Jewish children was to provide children for adoption for those who wanted to adopt a child.[473] Most adoptive parents wanted young children, girls, and those from higher social class families of origin.[474] Fewer of these survived than older children. On the other hand, the children were resourceful, having had to live by their wits for years. They were often able to play the roles that they thought adoptive parents or immigration agencies wanted them to play.[475] To survive, many children lied about their age during the war. Afterwards they might change their age to meet age limitations for emigration to British Mandatory Palestine or other countries.[476]

An example of the multiple roles played by children who progressed through the disruptions of family life due to the Nazi attacks on Jews is illustrated by the story of Pavel Friedländer, a German speaking Jewish child from Prague who became a French

Catholic named Paul-Henri Ferland when he worked underground in a Catholic boarding school near Vichy in France. After liberation he changed his name again and ultimately became an Israeli citizen, and later the historian Saul Friedländer. He later admitted that it was difficult to know which name belonged to him, even forty years later.[477]

Foster Families' Experiences

The experiences of foster families were as varied as those of the children, ranging from genuine love and care for the children through to using the children for financial benefit or outright abuse. At the end of World War II, families who protected Jewish children through the war were often reluctant to relinquish them, for a wide variety of reasons.[478] Some refused to part with the children because they loved them, or because they had baptised the children and wished to save their souls for Catholicism. Others took advantage of the children for their personal financial gain. In November 1945, between two and three thousand Jewish children were living in Christian homes in Poland, not out of compassion, but as a source of income for the family.[479] Those with an inclination towards profiteering from orphaned Jewish children used the opportunity to ransom the children back to their families or communities for large monetary rewards.[480]

There were foster families who considered it in the best interests of the children for them to return to their Jewish heritage and willingly relinquished them to the Jewish orphanages, asking for no compensation.[481] Other families that had hidden children handed them over but asked for compensation for the costs of their care. When communities granted those requests, the information spread and commerce in rescued children grew.[482] Many children were then "ransomed" back to Jewish rescue organizations, who offered to compensate the family for some of the expenses they had incurred by caring for the children over the years, in exchange for handing them over to the care homes established for Jewish child survivors.

For example, ten-year-old Marietta Klaphola had survived the war and eventually emigrated to British Mandatory Palestine but her Polish foster mother refused to disclose where Marietta was until she was paid $1,000.[483] While the original amount of compensation offered was low – in Poland, 14,000 złotys per child (approximately US $200) in April 1946 – the amount escalated rapidly as families realised that they could bargain to exchange the child. It rose to 140,000 złotys per child in April 1947[484] and continued to rise to between 200,000 and 400,000 złotys (approximately US $5,500) that year.[485] Viewed at today's rates, these amounts increased from approximately US $3,500 to over US $100,000 in the one-year period. There were even families that ransomed their children then returned a few days later and took them back by fraudulent means, albeit with the child's cooperation.[486]

Other foster families declared that the children had been left in their care by the parents with the understanding that if the parents did not return, the family would have the right to adopt the child and to inherit the families' assets. If distant relatives claimed a child, negotiations were sometimes entered into in the hope of receiving remuneration as well as the assets of the child's parents.[487] Alternatively, some foster families only agreed to relinquish the child to distant relatives if they could accompany the child.[488]

In other cases, there were children who were not identified by their foster families as Jews. Many of the hidden children were very young and knew nothing of their Jewish origins. They could not have returned to their Jewish roots on their own. Leah Hirschman, for example, tells of both her foster family and herself being unwilling for her to be taken back by an aunt: one of her deceased mother's sisters. In her case, Leah's aunt sought the judgement of the Polish courts. The testimony of the policeman to whom her mother had entrusted Leah as a baby confirmed her family identity and her Jewishness, leading to the courts awarding custody of Leah to her aunt. Despite this, it was only after a significant sum of money (US $1,500 in 1946, equivalent to approximately US $23,100 today), and Leah's family's possessions were promised to the foster family, that they agreed to relinquish Leah.[489]

The Church's Approach

Jewish families and organizations attempting to retrieve hidden children faced an additional set of complications regarding children who had been hidden in Catholic institutions. In many convents, hidden Jewish children had been baptised – often to hide them so they blended in with other non-Jewish children by their full participation in Catholic rituals and sacraments. For some nuns, this was a question of belief, and the conviction that all children living in a convent had to be baptised. For all children, however, the question of baptism became increasingly serious as children grew to an age when other sacraments would be administered, such as first communion and confirmation. In those cases, Jewish children would have had to participate in the sacraments or would have been identified by their peers as Jewish. Only children who have been baptised can take communion, and preparation for it and other sacraments are often extensive and part of community life. Jewish children living in secret in convents often had to be baptised in secret before participating in other sacraments, as public baptism, as older children, would have raised dangerous questions.[490] As a result of both baptism and participation in other Catholic sacraments, the nuns and priests no longer considered the children to be Jewish, and, consequently, had no intention of returning the children to the Jewish community.[491]

While Catholic belief identifies someone who has been baptised as Catholic, according to *Halakhah* (Jewish law), a Jew remains a Jew even if baptised.[492] Furthermore, according to Jewish law, death is preferable to conversion although clearly, those families that chose to save their child's life by hiding them with Christian families, did not abide by this ruling.[493] Some convents, if not most, viewed the children as Christian and did not encourage them, no matter how young, to leave and rejoin their families. In cases when they did relinquish the child, they informed the parents and the child that the child had been baptised and that they expected the child to continue practicing their Christian faith.[494]

In other situations, Jewish children, particularly toddlers and infants, hidden with the church, were placed with adoptive Christian families. One that is known about was even adopted by a German officer.[495] According to the Franciscan Sisters, who rescued many children but who were also ardent missionaries with proselytizing intentions, eighty such children survived in this way, although their fate is not known.[496] Records were haphazardly kept regarding these infants, and the nuns did not check to see if the children had parents or other relatives; all traces of the children were deliberately obscured.[497] The nuns kept the names of adoptive parents secret. At the war's end, when the children's parents or relatives came to collect them, the nuns refused to reveal the adoptive parents' identities,[498] a similar scenario to that played out in numerous Catholic orphanages and women's homes in Ireland with regard to children born out of wedlock, at about the same time.[499]

The Catholic Church had an established history of using baptism to remove Jewish children from their homes and communities. Almost a century before the Holocaust, in 1858, a Jewish child named Edgardo Mortara had been baptised by his nanny in his home. He was subsequently kidnapped from his parents to be raised as a Catholic with the blessing of Pope Pius IX. Although Jewish activists in Europe protested vociferously, he was never returned to his family and at the age of twenty-one, became a monk with the support of a trust fund from the Pope.[500] The merits and demerits of this incident are still debated today.

Some families went to extreme lengths to avoid returning children to their Jewish relatives or lifestyle. A similar story to that of Edgardo Mortara emerged in France after World War II, this time regarding the two sons of Fritz and Annie Finaly. Robert was born in 1940 and Gerard in 1941. Both boys had been circumcised by their parents before the couple was arrested and deported through Drancy to Auschwitz, where they died. In 1942, before they were deported, Robert and Gerard's parents gave the boys to a neighbour to look after them. The neighbour subsequently asked the sisters of the Order of Notre Dame de Sion to hide them. The sisters placed them in the municipal crèche in Grenoble under the care of Antoinette Brun. In 1945, the children's aunt, Grete Fischer, inquired after the fate of her brother's children. She met with Brun, who assured her that the boys were not baptised. But Brun avoided returning them to their aunt, saying they were too poorly to travel. Brun later revealed that she wanted to care for them until their own parents returned. Grete Fischer, as well as her sister and brother-in-law Yehudit and Moshe Rossner, wanted to adopt the children but Brun evaded all attempts to return them. In 1948 Brun had the two boys baptised. The Rossners took legal action which made its way to the Supreme Court of France which, in 1951, ordered Brun to return the children to their relatives. Brun defied the court and shortly afterwards the boys disappeared. With the help of clergy, the boys had been taken to Spain and hidden there by monks. Eventually the Grand Rabbi of Paris and members of the French government arranged for the return of the boys, now aged ten and eleven, to the Rossners. Shortly after their return, they moved to Israel where they learned Hebrew and transitioned back to their cultural heritage.[501]

The convents have never disclosed how many Jewish children were placed in their institutions and nor were records always kept by rescuers (for fear of discovery and endangering the children's lives). If records were kept, they were not found after the war.[502] Nor is the number of Jewish children who were saved by convents and who did not return to Judaism known.[503] The difficulties with removing Jewish children from convents occurred across Europe. Some estimate that dozens, if not hundreds of Jewish children remained in convents in Poland alone and could not be restored to their Jewish heritage.[504] There is only one known instance in which nuns handed over the children they had hidden to a Jewish children's home. The Convent of the Sacred Hearts in Przemyśl, Poland, handed over thirteen children they had rescued. This convent was also unusual in that it did not baptise the children, objecting to the practice on principle. One older child from this convent refused to move to a Jewish children's home and later converted to Christianity.[505] Some of the children rescued by convents (a handful) decided as a gesture of gratitude, and in identification with the sisters, to take their religious vows.[506] Many who were relinquished from the convents emerged with feelings of alienation and inferiority compounded by their frequent exposure in the convents to abusive epithets in Christian antisemitic tradition. Convent education included negative imagery of Jews related to their supposed act of deicide and torture of the Son of God. These children felt torn between the devoted care given to them by the nuns and their remarks about Jews, contributing to guilt on account of their alleged sins.[507]

Rabbi Yitzchak Halevi Herzog, the Chief Rabbi of British Mandatory Palestine, repeatedly visited Pope Pius XII (towards the end of the war, in April 1945, in September 1945, in March 1946),[508] with appeals to issue an unequivocal statement that Catholic Clergy were to refrain from pressuring those Jews whom they saved to convert. His requests were ignored.

In the UK, a significant number of *Kindertransport* children who had been hosted by Christian families abandoned their Jewish faith in adulthood. There are claims that although many Jewish families had offered to take the children in, the British government mandated that the children be dispersed widely across Britain to avoid antisemitic backlash against the program if a large contingent of Jewish children were placed in any one community. The lack of emphasis on maintaining the children's Jewish affiliation led to complications in later years.[509]

Jewish families and communities feared that allowing their children to live in convents to save their lives would lead to their conversion. They were correct: the children were not necessarily "forced" to convert as their total immersion in Christian life made their conversion virtually inevitable.[510] Some of those who were raised as Catholic even became priests or nuns, and one became a Cardinal, Cardinal Lustiger.[511] Additionally, while Christian religious institutions did not necessarily accept Jewish children in order to convert them, many Christian educators and members of religious orders saw it as their vocation to encourage those under their care to become pious Christians. Assessments indicate that most of the Jewish children hidden in Christian institutions in Poland and Ukraine converted to Christianity. At times, such conversion was a condition for offering shelter.[512] The Catholic Church in France, at least, forbade Jewish children who had been baptised from being told they were born Jewish or from being handed over to non-Catholic rescuers.[513] Claiming their souls for Christianity became as, if not more, important than saving their lives.

Jewish Agency Experiences

Retrieving children and helping them return to Judaism was one goal of Jewish agencies such as the Zionist Coordinating Committee in Poland, especially if children had been hidden with Christian families.[514] Jewish agencies, however, overestimated the number of children hidden in Christian homes.[515] Despite the numerous obstacles to this objective discussed in this chapter, the vast majority of children who were hidden with Christian families were retrieved without difficulty, either by their own Jewish family members or relatives, or handed over to Jewish organizations seeking these children. For example, in Belgium, only 87 of the 1,816 children sheltered by Christian families had not been retrieved by Jewish agencies by the end of 1946.[516] In France, where about 10,000 children had been hidden with Christian, mostly Catholic families, only 59 Jewish children remained with their host families in 1948. Nevertheless, Jewish agencies still feared that not returning hidden children was being used as yet another way of eliminating the Jewish nation, justifying their aggressive search for these children.

The question of whether to retrieve these children from their foster families raises numerous concerns. When the foster parents and the children all agreed to be moved to Jewish care homes or to their families, there was no difficulty. But when the children were happy where they were and did not want to leave their foster family, or when the foster parents did not want to relinquish the child that they had cared for, matters became much more challenging. At issue was whether it was important to respect the children's own Jewish parents' wishes for their child to be both saved and to live life as a Jewish child, or whether saving the children's lives was the priority concern.

Jewish organizations and Jews in general wished to save whatever remnants of the Jewish people they could after Hitler's efforts to exterminate them had been halted. While they might have been concerned about the unhappiness caused to the children in removing them from their foster families, child care beliefs at that time were far more controlling than they are now. It was commonly believed (even if erroneously in hindsight) that children would probably not even remember the trauma this separation might incur: that children would simply move on and forget this unhappy phase of life. Such thinking led to those retrieving the children to resort to persuasion, coercion, or even kidnapping/abduction on occasion, to retrieve the child from their foster home.

The varied approaches to this have led to controversy about the appropriate terminology to use to describe these actions: "rescue" is not an ideal descriptor as these children were usually not in danger, unhappy, or requiring "rescue." "Redeem" is another word often used, and carries religious overtones: were the children redeemed to Judaism? Was this enough to justify their detachment from loving homes? We have used the word "retrieved" as this more clearly describes the actions of removing the children from their homes whether willingly, by coercion or manipulation, or even by force.

Young Jewish women searched the countryside for these children.[517] When, occasionally, foster families resisted parting with the children for which they had cared, families or agencies applied to the courts to retrieve the children, as in the case of Leah Hirschman.[518] In other instances, they resorted to deception, or even kidnapping or abduction to retrieve the child.[519] In Leah's case, she was manipulated into willingly going for a sightseeing ride with an "uncle" who had befriended her – with her foster family's collaboration – and moved to her Jewish relative's home. Some time later, Leah encountered her foster mother again, but the woman denied knowing Leah, perhaps concerned that if the child were to return to her, she might have to forfeit the payments that had been made to her. Leah Hirschman's experience resulted in anguish for some time, and later acceptance, and gratitude for this "rescue" years later.[520]

Finding Hidden Children

Many Jewish women helped to retrieve or care for Jewish child survivors in the aftermath of the war. For several of these women, their post-war activities were a natural evolution of their wartime resistance activities. For example, Recha Sternbuch, a Swiss, war time, rescue activist who worked alongside her husband, Isaac, to assist refugees to find safe havens outside of Nazi Europe, devoted her efforts after the war to finding Jewish children hidden with non-Jews.[521] Some of the women who dedicated themselves to finding hidden Jewish children after the war included Devora Fleischer, Chasia/Hasya Bornstein-Bielicka and Hela Leneman, Franciska Schechter (Tzipora Agmon), Hélène Cazes-Benatar, Ruth Eliav-Kliger and Sarah (Shner) Nishmit, whose stories are told here.

Devora Fleischer

One of the Jewish women who helped find hidden children after the war was Devora Fleischer. When the Germans invaded the Soviet Union, Devora fled to the forests: her entire family had been murdered. She was hidden by a Polish noblewoman and helped the woman with her boarding house during the war. After the war, Devora searched, unsuccessfully, for members of her family, eventually losing her will to live. At that point she met a courier from Israel, Arye Sarid (Leibl Goldberg), who persuaded her to help him find Jewish children who had been hidden with Poles. She searched for children in the Lublin area. She learned from local peasants that a Jewish girl was hidden in a monastery in Turkowice. When she reached the monastery, the nuns denied there were any Jewish children in the area. But when an eight-year-old girl entered the room, Devora hugged her and called her Feigle, her Jewish name. The girl hugged her and agreed to go with her. Devora found twenty-four children in six months before she emigrated to British Mandatory Palestine in November 1946.[522]

Chasia/Hasya Bornstein-Bielicka and Hela Leneman

Chasia/Hasya Bornstein-Bielicka and Hela Leneman were both teachers in children's homes run by the Koordynacja (The Zionist Co-ordination for the redemption of children in Poland) for rescued children.[523] Hela Leneman ran one of these homes. Chasia's/Hasya's post-war activities retrieving Jewish child survivors was, in some ways, a continuation of her work as a member of the resistance during the war. During the war, Chasia/Hasya joined Hashomer Hatza'ir (a Zionist youth movement) as a twelve-year-old and was active in this group, becoming an underground courier who created weapons, obtained firearms, and forged documents. After the war, she collected orphaned Jewish children in Poland and lived with them in the Zionist children's home. In March 1946, she boarded an illegal immigrant ship with the children heading for British Mandatory Palestine but they were diverted to Cyprus. She stayed with the children in a detention camp and continued to educate them until they were permitted to enter Israel. The children were then housed in Kibbutz Gan Shmuel.[524]

Franciska Schechter (Tzipora Agmon)

Franciska Schechter in Hungary, like Hela Leneman in Poland, volunteered to work at children's homes established by the Zionist underground after the war.[525] Like Chasia Bornstein, during the war, Franciska joined Hashomer Hatza'ir as a sixteen-year-old and became active in the Hungarian underground, working as a courier. She delivered forged certificates, documents, money and clothing. She joined a double agent who worked for the Gestapo and pretended to be his family member. The two of them freed detainees who had been caught while trying to escape to Romania. Later Franciska volunteered to work at the children's homes providing assistance to orphaned children, giving them hope and some peace.

Hélène Cazes-Benatar

Hélène Cazes-Benatar was a successful lawyer who served in the Moroccan branch of WIZO, which she co-founded and where she served as its President. She became increasingly concerned about Jews as news of Nazi atrocities reached her. In the aftermath of the war, Hélène helped bring children from Paris to Morocco using fake visas, as legal visas to emigrate to countries outside of Europe such as British Mandatory Palestine/Israel were difficult to obtain. After the war she established a children's hospital in Tripoli and, in the early 1950's, helped bring tens of thousands of Jews to Israel.[526]

Ruth Eliav-Kliger

In 1944, Ben Gurion, the Head of the Jewish Agency in British Mandatory Palestine, sent Ruth Eliav-Kliger as the first Jewish Agency representative to France. She visited Bergen-Belsen a week after its liberation, helped look for children who had been hidden in monasteries in France, and organized a Passover seder for 4,000 surviving children, including surviving Buchenwald children, and 217 children that she found in hiding places in Berlin. In 1945, after meeting with General Dwight Eisenhower, she received permission from Colonel Ernest White to use the ship *Askanai* to take 2,500 Jewish refugees to Israel. She adopted and raised two children who were Holocaust survivors.[527]

Sarah (Shner) Nishmit

Sarah (Shner) Nishmit was born in a Polish *shtetl* (village) but educated in Lithuania and became interested in Zionism after hearing antisemitic comments. She joined a partisan group during the war and, at the war's end, helped retrieve Jewish children from their Christian hiding families in Poland. In Poland, around 600 of the 2,000 to 3,000 Jewish children that were living in Christian homes were retrieved by the Zionist organization, the Koordynacja, with the support of Rabbi David Kahane and Yeshayahu Drucker who worked on behalf of the Committee of Jewish Communities.[528] The Koordynacja (The Zionist Coordination for the Redemption of Children in Poland) was established in 1946.[529] Multiple Zionist organizations collaborated with them to retrieve Jewish children who were hidden in monasteries or with non-Jewish families. Its institutions took care of about 1,000 children until its operation was discontinued in 1949. Its mission was to return Jewish children to their people and to prevent Jewish children growing up in a world that disliked Jews. Their initial goal was to retrieve the children at any costs. They established children's *kibbutzim* for those aged three to thirteen to provide a Zionist education.[530]

Sara Dushnitski (later Sarah (Shner) Nishmit) was persuaded to assist Leibl Goldberg (Arye Sarid), an emissary from British Mandatory Palestine who was engaged in this work on behalf of the Koordynacja in Poland. Sarah and Leibl found dozens of hidden children who had been adopted by Christian families, whom they helped return to their Jewish heritage. Sarah was however, plagued by doubts about her work and often asked herself whether she had the right to remove children from homes where they were happy and adjusted and had no knowledge of their Jewish heritage.

Ethical Questions

Arye Sarid (later Arie Sarid and also known as Leibl Goldberg), the founder of the Polish, Zionist Koordynacja, along with others involved in retrieving children who had been hidden with Christian families or in institutions, agonized about the heartache caused by taking children from their Christian foster homes,[531] and wrote:

> There are those who ask me if it would not have been better to leave the children with their adoptive families and not shatter their tranquility, particularly if coercion was used. [...] And there are some who ask whether I have no pangs of conscience for thrusting these children into a fate of suffering, calamities, and new experiences. The truth is, that such thoughts did cross my mind [...] especially in the complex case of redeeming children who were lovingly cared for by a Christian family. But at that very moment I lacerated myself for such bursts of weakness. In the final analysis we are fulfilling the last request of their parents: to leave them descendants. We are ensuring that their child will remain Jewish and not become one of those who attack and murder Jews.[532]

Sarah (Shner) Neshmit expressed similar feelings:

> Sometimes we had serious qualms about whether we had the right to remove a child from the home of his adoptive parents and thrust him into a psychological crisis. It was hard to be a witness to the tears shed by children when they parted from their Christian adopters, in whose home they had been so warmly treated. It was also hard to be a witness to the tears in the eyes of the adoptive mother when she handed over the child she had nurtured. Frequently we were apprehensive about the wrong that we were doing to both the children and to their "parent."[533]

Not all the foster families from which Jewish children were retrieved were safe havens. In a number of cases, Sarah (Shner) Neshmit reported finding the children had been physically and/or sexually abused by their adoptive families. She decided that these examples justified the removal of Jewish children from such danger.[534]

At that time, children's experiences in the Holocaust were discounted and it was believed they would forget their experiences and not remember any trauma. Those who retrieved children, like Sarah, likely believed that they would not do any lasting harm to the children psychologically by removing them from their hiding families.[535] With the benefit of hindsight, we now know that these tumultuous experiences might have had lasting effects. The children suddenly found themselves back in a Jewish world from which they had barely managed to escape and because of which they had suffered so cruelly. They were again traumatized.[536] Even children who had been taken to the UK on the *Kindertransport* and who have been, until recently, regarded as the lucky ones who escaped from the horrors of the Holocaust by being rescued by apparently loving foster parents, experienced considerable traumas including loss of their families, changes in language, culture, religion, lifestyle, and social status. Like hidden children in Europe, many were unhappy and were abused emotionally, physically and

131

occasionally sexually in their foster families, and were generally helpless to avoid such misuse.[537] Few were reunited with their families and most had to make their own way in life with little educational training to support them.[538] Loss of family remained a severe source of trauma for these children from which many, if not most, hardly ever recovered.[539] Mental illness and subjects such as sexual abuse among the children have often been ignored, glossed over, or minimized, making their exposure, though uncomfortable, an important corrective to commonly held redemptive images of this program.[540] Nevertheless, these traumas were faced by virtually all children who survived the Holocaust, whether they were sent away from Europe, or were hidden with families or in institutions to escape the Nazi net.

Despite the qualms expressed by agencies that sought to retrieve Jewish children raised as Christians and to return them to Judaism, some, today, would assert that removing an orphaned child from a loving adoptive family and re-traumatizing a child through this separation from virtually the only family they have known, simply to ensure they followed their religious heritage, is unconscionable. These view the wishes of the (deceased) parents to save their child as of paramount importance and not their wish to ensure the child's adherence to Judaism. Even one of the organizers of these Polish rescue measures testified to having second thoughts about these actions:

> It is hard to say that the abductions of children were
> appropriate, because, after all, the people who had
> rescued them had taken care of them and risked their
> lives. But we did not delve into the moral problem:
> the shock of the Holocaust was so powerful that we
> thought saving one soul for the Jewish people was a
> tremendous achievement. Looking back at this from
> the perspective of time, I don't know if it was really
> so essential, if such drastic measures were necessary.
> I don't know if there was sufficient justification to
> entitle us to act.[541]

As with many issues raised by the Holocaust, this ethical dilemma is a most challenging one. After the decimation of Jews by the Nazis, the importance of saving Jewish lives was undeniable. In addition, post war relations between Jews and Christians in Europe were acrimonious; the antisemitic climate of the times was not a safe society for the children to return to if they were to live as Jews.[542] On the other hand, causing even further distress to the children is horrifying given the traumas they had already endured. Also, removing a child from a loving family would have been heartbreaking for the foster parents, despite their probable prior knowledge that the child was only temporarily entrusted to them. While some hid the knowledge that their fostered child was Jewish from both the child and/or authorities, which would have made the realization of their Jewishness shocking for the child, others planned for this eventual relinquishment and gave up the child, lovingly, along with a narrative account of his/her life, to the rescuing parents or agencies.[543] Parting from nuns was, however, for many, not as traumatic as parting from families, as relationships were less intimate in convents.[544]

Of somewhat greater concern is the approach taken to children who were retrieved. As was in keeping with child rearing attitudes of the times, few took the time to explain to children what was happening, or to seek their involvement in the decision about returning to family members or to Judaism. Nor did they always develop friendships with the children prior to their extraction from their foster family, a move requiring time and sensitivity. Leah Hirschman repeatedly reiterated how nothing was explained to her, making her resistance to removal from her foster family understandable.[545] In contrast, Eric Rosen, also a very young child, who was retrieved by Rabbi Schonberg, reports being involved in the decision to leave his happy foster family to move to the UK under the auspices of Rabbi Schonberg. He willingly, and independently, chose to leave after numerous visits to his foster family and to him by those seeking to return him to Judaism, explaining to him what would be involved and what his father had wanted when entrusting him as a baby to his foster family.[546] Neither Leah who was forcibly removed, nor Eric who had responsibility for his decision to leave, regretted those moves as their lives unfolded.

Chapter 9: Moving Abroad

Against this complex background of psychological, physical, economic, and social trauma among the children, and the conflicting values, methods, and retrieval efforts to return children to their families, or at least to Judaism, some Jewish women stand out as being remarkable rescuers, helping large numbers of Jews and particularly children to escape from Europe, or at least to reunite them with any remaining relatives.

Ruth Gruber

Towards the end of the war, in June 1944, Franklin Delano Roosevelt finally agreed to allow 1,000 refugees to be brought to the USA from Italy, where the war had ended with Italy's surrender to the Allies on 8 September 1943.[547] The history of the USA's unwillingness to allow refugees, let alone Jewish refugees, to reach American shores during the pre-war years is well known and discussed in Chapter 4.[548] This attitude of rejection of refugees, and especially Jewish refugees, continued during the war years despite increasing awareness of the plight of Jewish people in Europe. Antisemitism remained widespread among the American population and government.[549] Knowledge of the Nazi's extermination of Jews was sent to the USA repeatedly, from as early as 1942, but was frequently suppressed or ignored.[550] The suppressed cables were discovered in late 1943. A report on this issue, dated 13 January 1944, named Breckinridge Long as the archvillain in the government's "Acquiescence to the murder of Jews."[551] He falsely claimed that the USA had admitted 580,000 refugees into the USA within the quota limits and implied that the USA had gone out of its way to assist Jewish refugees. The USA was permitted to allow 150,000 immigrants per year according to the quota, but only 23,725 had been admitted the previous year and of these only 4,750 were Jews fleeing the Nazis.[552] Notably, however, over 100,000 prisoners of war had been brought to the USA to work on farms and in factories. Most of these were captured Nazi soldiers. They had been transported in two ships that formed part of a flotilla of twenty-nine vessels crossing the Atlantic: thirteen warships escorted sixteen troop carriers and cargo ships. Only 1,000 refugees were allowed into the USA in that time.[553]

Roosevelt was advised that if this information became known to the public it would reveal the antisemitism of the State Department and would reflect on the White House. A few days later, Roosevelt created a War Refugee Board with the responsibility for rescuing Jews. As a result of this action, ships were leased to Sweden to assist in rescuing Jews from the Balkans. In addition, in July 1944, Raoul Wallenberg was sent to Hungary where he saved at least 70,000-80,000 Jews singlehandedly.[554] The lack of cooperation from the State and War departments of the USA government meant that the War Refugee Board could not act as quickly or as effectively as they would have wished.[555]

The special assistant to the Secretary of the Interior, Harold L. Ickes, asked Ruth Gruber to go to Italy in 1944, after Italy had surrendered to the Allies, and accompany 1,000 Jewish and Christian refugees to America to be settled in a former internment camp in Oswego, New York State. Ruth did so, travelling with them across the Atlantic. They turned to her with their stories, wishes and hopes, regarding her as their guardian angel. She organized English lessons and entertainment for them on board. Once in Oswego she continued to act as their advocate, helping them to overcome obstacles that arose for them. She arranged for them to be allowed into the town of Oswego instead of being confined behind the barbed wire surrounding their internment camp – like a concentration camp. She helped the children access schools in the town and to reach college and university education as these became needed goals for some. She organized furnishings, bassinets, clothing, and essentials that helped people regain some of their dignity. She negotiated permission for some to marry and when babies were born, she helped them gain permission for the newborn to obtain American citizenship. Antisemitism was still rife in the USA and there were some who insisted that the refugees be only temporarily allowed in the USA and be forced to return to their countries of origin at the cessation of hostilities. Each of these goals was a source of conflict and debate. Gruber was, however supported by the Secretary of the Interior, Harold Ickes, throughout, even when she finally advocated successfully for all the refugees to be allowed to remain in the USA after about a year living in Oswego.[556]

Lena Küchler-Silberman

Lena Küchler-Silberman was born in Poland in Wieliczka but moved to Warsaw where she helped smuggle children out of the ghetto. One story tells how she found a baby lying on the corpse of its mother. She hid the baby under her coat and smuggled it out of the ghetto taking it to a monastery for refuge. During the war years, she passed for Aryan, serving as a nanny for two Polish children in a small, rural village.

After the war Lena returned to Kraków where she came across dozens of children huddled in a room at the Jewish Committee in Długa Street.[557] She began to care for them, scrubbing them clean, finding clothes for them, caring for their sores, boils, scabs, frozen fingers and toes, and broken bones.[558] Some of the children had hidden in underground bunkers, some had jumped off trains on the way to camps, and one had deep wounds on her scalp after being beaten by Ukrainians. One twelve-year-old boy saved his own life when an old woman allowed him to live in an unused kennel in exchange for teaching her to read Ukrainian.[559] Another child at the centre was listless and expressionless. She was around four years old, with a shorn head covered with scars. Lena was told:

> Her name is Zosia Fener. [...] her parents managed
> to get a Gentile woman janitor to hide her in the city
> [Warsaw]. This woman hid Zosia in a closet in her
> apartment in a basement, warning her never to
> speak and never to come out. For two years she

137

never left the closet except at night, when she slept
in the apartment itself. In the morning she would go
back to the closet. […] The janitor left the apartment
one day and never returned. Apparently, she died in
the fighting [in Warsaw].[560]

A member of the Underground knew about the child and checked
on her, found her, and brought her to the Committee. The child did not
speak or move. She was emaciated and covered with lice, unable to
walk or talk when she emerged. When they found her, she had been
without food for two days.

After the war, David Boder, using innovative (for the time) tape-
recording equipment, interviewed and recorded Lena and three of the
children she rescued. In her interview, translated into English from the
original Polish, Lena described some of the children she rescued.

I have children who sat in hiding places for a year
or two with the legs doubled up, so that when they
left these hiding places they had complete atrophy
of the leg muscles. A part of the children were
hidden in Polish cloisters. But in the cloisters the
children were converted, and later on the priests did
not want to return these children. Only from a few
orphanages where there reigned a terrible hunger,
where they could not feed the children, even the
Polish children, there they first of all tried to get rid
of the Jewish children, and they would bring them
to the Committee.[561]

Lena experienced the impact of local gossip among Gentiles who
had hidden children that the Jews would pay good money to get them
back. One day a peasant woman arrived with a four or five-year-old
little girl. Without embarrassment she demanded:

I've brought you a Jewish girl. […] A Jewish girl,
not a Catholic! I have her real name and where she
was born – everything is on a piece of paper […].

Now I took care of her for two years you understand?
And I didn't do it for nothing. I came here to collect
my payment, what her mother promised me before
the Germans took her away. One hundred thousand
złotys and a house in town! It's nearly four months
already since the war ended and the mother has not
come back, and now I want to settle this account.[562]

Lena and the committee protested that they did not have that kind
of money. Lena called for the doorman to get the police and the woman
retracted her demands. Eventually they gave the woman some sugar,
promising her more in a month's time. The child's name was Miriam
Mozner, born 30 August 1940 in Lwów. Lena's own little girl's birthday
was the same date and her own child, who had died earlier in Lena's
life, had also been named Miriam.[563]

In collaboration with the Jewish Committee she founded a care
home that could house 100 orphaned Jewish children in a large,
unoccupied rest home in Zakopane, an environmentally healthy
section of Poland.[564] A second home was also set up nearby in
Rabka.[565] She originally started a school for the children in the home
but later enrolled the children in the local school.[566] Unfortunately,
antisemitism was rife in Poland and, one day, the children were
attacked with rocks and sticks by the remaining Gentile students.[567]
Lena herself was attacked one evening as she was walking home from
the town. She was hit with a heavy metal bar, was robbed, and kicked
until she lost consciousness. Some hours later she awoke and managed
to drag herself home.[568]

The second school in Rabka was also attacked. The children in
Rabka then joined those in the Zakopane home.[569] As a consequence of
these attacks, Lena decided that the children could not stay safely in
Poland.[570] She also learned that five Jewish children were hidden in a
convent high in the mountains nearby, where all the children were
living in abject poverty. All the children had been baptised and the
sister in charge insisted that they all be allowed to follow Christianity.
With some difficulty, Lena managed to obtain the papers required by
the convent and eventually succeeded in rescuing the five children.[571]

139

At the start of the war, Lena's husband left her for a German woman who he believed would hide him during the war. At the end of the war, he changed his mind, and returned to Lena in Zakopane, hoping to restart their life together. Lena refused and formally divorced him,[572] after which she escaped with her 100 children. Although they encountered some difficulties at the border crossing, the guard's wife took pity on them and persuaded her husband to let them cross into France, where Lena and the children stayed for two years. In 1948, Lena and the children made their way to Haifa on a battered vessel.[573] She remarried some time later and, when already in her forties, gave birth to a son. She called him her 101st child. Many of "her" children stayed in touch with her, as in particular did Miriam, and visited her throughout the remainder of their lives.[574]

The Marcel Network: Moussa Abadi and Odette Rosenstock

Moussa Abadi and Odette Rosenstock (typically referred to as "the Abadis") hid over 500 children in France during the war years but also spent a great deal of time attempting to reunite these children with any surviving family members after the war. Their stories reflect some of the negative experiences they encountered with some frequency. They report that many of the parents whose children they had saved never thanked them and a number were decidedly unpleasant about their efforts. For example, the Buras, whose children had been hidden by the Marcel Network for eighteen months, did not come to Moussa's office to collect their children but arranged for them to be put on a bus and sent to them. They never acknowledged the Abadis' help with a letter of thanks or even acknowledged that the children had arrived in good health and were safe.[575]

Another parent complained to the Abadis about the family selected to care for his son. He had been a sickly baby that no one wanted to look after. Odette found him a home with a peasant woman, Madame Belliol, who was willing to take on his care. She fed him, loved him, and nursed him back to health so he grew into a strong little boy. His biological mother died in Auschwitz, but his father, Monsieur Lazarovich, survived and was horrified that his son had been given to a Christian family. "How is it possible that you put my son with these *goyem* [non-Jews]?" He complained to Moussa and Odette, "What you did was unthinkable. I demand that you give him back to me immediately."[576]

There were also some who tried to make money out of the situation. For example, one man who was reunited with his children through Moussa and Odette submitted a bill to the OSE office in June for school supplies he said he had bought for them. The next month, July, he submitted a similar bill even though the schools were closed for the summer. Moussa and Odette doubted he even needed the money as he received enough money from two other charities to support his family. His case was apparently not unique.[577]

A further case involved the headmistress of an elite girl's school in Nice. She hid a Jewish girl, Sarah Krechman, in the school from 1942. Sarah's parents paid the school fees but were arrested and sent to Auschwitz a year later. The headmistress kept Sarah in the school without receiving any payments for her schooling. She told Moussa and Odette that she had kept her promise to Sarah's parents. At the war's end Moussa asked the headmistress if he should place Sarah in an OSE children's home but she declined saying she would keep Sarah in the school, without asking for any payment for this. After Sarah had spent three years in the school, Moussa and Odette learned what had really happened. A cousin of Sarah's from Paris said he would take over Sarah's care but asked what had happened to the valuable piece of jewelry that Sarah's parents had entrusted to the headmistress. The headmistress confirmed that Sarah's parents had done so. When Moussa asked that she return the jewelry to Sarah's cousin, the headmistress said she had sold it to cover Sarah's expenses and that in fact, Sarah's account was now in debt. Moussa and Odette realised that the headmistress had agreed to keep Sarah in the school to cover the value of the jewelry and to build up a bill for the family. The cousin agreed to pay the bill in order to get Sarah back. In Moussa and Odette's eyes this was "black-market charity."[578]

Ethically questionable actions for financial gain after the war were common given the total disruption that the war had brought to all in

Europe, the desperate situation facing most, and the continuing antisemitism that prevailed. Such demands, while unconscionable, were not surprising, or uncommon.

Like many Jewish rescuers, Moussa and Odette were never honoured for their efforts and even refrained from talking about their rescue efforts after the war. Their lives were severely affected by the events they experienced, possibly contributing to their silence about their activities. In 1948 Moussa resigned from the French rescue organization that he assisted, the OSE (the Oeuvre de Secours aux Enfants). He was exhausted and emotionally drained from searching for lost parents, the pain of telling children they were orphans, and the shortages and hardships engendered by the war.[579] Odette had been so traumatized from caring for patients in Nazi death camps that she struggled to face patients again.[580] Moussa became severely depressed and descended into a gambling addiction from which it took ten years for him to recover. He then became an internationally known theatre critic with a globally broadcast, weekly radio program.[581]

Many of the people who had helped Moussa and Odette hide children were honoured by Yad Vashem as Righteous Among Nations, including Paul Rémond, Alban and Germaine Fort who hid Jewish children at their children's home in Cannes, Father Vincent Simeoni and Father Michel Blain who saved Jewish children at the Dom Boscoe vocational school in Nice, and Pasters Edmond Evrard and Pierre-Gagnier who helped Odette place Jewish children with Protestant families. Moussa and Odette, however, were Jewish and consequently Yad Vashem would not honour them, possibly leading to little if any perceived need to highlight the role they played. Their story remained hidden as each of their collaborators did not reveal it.[582]

In 1989 they married in a religious ceremony. Moussa was seventy-nine and Odette seventy-five. They had lived together for eighteen years and had married earlier in a civil ceremony.[583] Neither of them talked about their wartime activities or sought any recognition for their actions, simply saying they were there at the right time and in the right place.[584] Only when Holocaust denial became a more pressing, public issue did they agree to talk about their rescue activities. When Moussa was eighty-three, he agreed to tell his story as long as he could preview the text before it was published to check for accuracy. In 1993, one of the children he had hidden created an association: The Children and Friends of the Abadis. They arranged to have a square in Paris, near where the Abadis lived, named after them.[585] Moussa died in 1997 at the age of eighty-seven. Odette never wanted to live after his death. She spent two years sorting out Moussa's papers and then took her own life, at the age of eighty-four.[586]

It is impossible to know whether earlier recognition of this courageous couple would have bettered their lives, but it would have acknowledged the remarkable role played by these Jewish rescuers, even if only by historians and Holocaust scholars.

Other Rescue Efforts

In Poland, the Central Committee for Jews assisted thousands of children. They operated eleven children's homes for 1,224 children in July 1946, as well as forty-five boarding houses with over 4,067 residents, a psychology clinic, and a child-tracing service to help reclaim children from Gentile families. Their school department operated twenty-eight schools for 2,236 children in 1946.[587]

There were many people and organizations that sought to return Jewish children to their origins. Notable among these were Rabbi Yitzhak Halevi Herzog who, with the help of Yeshayahu Drucker, reclaimed about 500 children across Europe and moved them to Israel/ British Mandatory Palestine. Rabbi Herzog was, at that time (1946), the Chief Ashkenazi Rabbi for Mandatory Palestine and in 1948, the first Ashkenazi Chief Rabbi of Israel.

Rabbi Solomon Schonfeld was an extremely religious Charedi British Rabbi[588] who also rescued many thousands of Jews from Nazi forces between 1938 and 1948. His rescue efforts were under the auspices of the Chief Rabbi of England's Religious Emergency Council, which he created with the approval of Chief Rabbi Joseph Hertz, his father-in-law.[589] Among these rescue efforts was the organization of a *Kindertransport* of about 300 Orthodox Jewish children.[590] After the war, he continued to assist several hundred children, who had survived in concentration camps or in hiding, to move to England and receive a Jewish education and life there.[591] He arrived in Poland in November 1945 with a truck, food, medicine, and clothing for religious congregations, returning twice more in 1946 with further aid and taking 250 children and youth back to the UK.[592]

A further pioneering effort to reclaim Jewish children involved bringing a group of 300 boys who had survived in Theresienstadt to the Lake District in England. They became known as the Windermere Children.[593] Uniquely, the children received no counselling but were encouraged to swim in the nearby lake, play football, and learn English. The goal was to bring them together with other children with similar experiences and to let them help each other adjust to the past and their present situation. The initiative was supported by the Committee for the Care of Children from Concentration Camps established by British philanthropist Leonard Montefiore. Altogether about 650 boys and 80 girls between the ages of eight and sixteen were brought to England with his help.[594]

Another major group rescue effort was directed to the rescue of 430 of the Buchenwald boys, who were invited by the French government to recuperate in France, in Écouis, including Elie Wiesel.[595] They were mostly between twelve and twenty-one. Only thirty were between eight and twelve. Collective life for these boys was particularly difficult as they rejected any authority and any routines that reminded them of camp life.[596] Although they were eager to talk about the camps, no one was willing to listen to them and they were told to forget about the past.[597]

Rescuing Jewish children in large numbers was a difficult challenge in the disorder and chaos of the post-war period. It was fraught with challenges including caring for traumatized children, who if they survived at all, had to adopt false identities, become independent beyond their years, were skilled at adapting to or manipulating adverse environments to facilitate their survival, and who had little or no formal schooling to prepare them for independent life. Rescuers also had to face the ethical challenges that confronted them when retrieving children from their places of hiding and returning them to lives they were unlikely to immediately welcome. The sometimes-conflicting question of whether to save their lives or to save their religious identity remained a dilemma facing many. For some it was a choice between rebuilding the Jewish people, or allowing Hitler's policies, directed towards exterminating the Jews, to succeed.

Chapter 10: Memory and Ethics

While rescuers underwent horrors, hardships, imprisonment, torture, abandonment of their personal lives, and danger, they also experienced fulfillment. André Trocmé and his wife Magda recalled that they were never happier than during the years of rescue in Le Chambon-sur-Lignon. Madeleine Dreyfus was left with profound joy resulting from her ability to transcend herself during her years of rescue.[598] These and other rescuers were ordinary people from all backgrounds. Some were religious, like Recha Freier, others secular like Magda Trocmé. Some were upper class, as were Wilfred Israel and Raoul Wallenberg, and others altruistic peasants, like Madame Belliol, who saved Monsieur Lazarovich's sickly baby son. But all valued decency, hospitality, shelter for the young and defenceless, and kindness. Some were hailed as heroes or heroines, such as Irena Sendler and Nicholas Winton, while others went mostly unrecognized for much of their lives, such as the Krauses[599] and the Abadis.[600] The Krauses sought no recognition for their actions and lived in anonymity after the war. The Abadis kept quiet about their activities and saw relatively few of the children they rescued ever again.[601]

Women Rescuers in Film

In addition to being granted some national honours and awards, some Holocaust heroes and heroines have been commemorated in film, and their stories should be told through this medium more often. Women took a major role in the rescue of children, and in rescue organizations women were central contributors. Jewish parents were also more inclined to trust women to hide their children.[602] Despite this, women are seldom commemorated in film as rescuers. On the rare occasions that they are portrayed as heroic rescuers, there is almost always a romantic element to their role that forces the female characters into traditional stereotyped roles of beautiful women who are the object of men's desire. In most European films depicting women rescuers, the female lead is played by famous film stars such as Hellen Mirren in *The Door* (2012), Catherine Deneuve in *The Last Metro* (2009), and Romy Schneider in *The Passerby* (1982). While such famous stars will increase the box-office appeal of the movie, they do not always reflect the reality that ordinary women were rescuers. These films almost never reflect true stories but are fictionalized and romanticized accounts of what were horrific and dangerous experiences for the real women who rescued children. *The Search*, starring Montgomery Clift and Aline MacMahon, portraying the remarkable reunification of a Gentile child from Auschwitz with his mother after a year or more of her seemingly futile search for him, won two academy awards in 1948, including Best Picture. While sentimentally entertaining, this imagined tale is typical of the trend that followed when producing films commemorating women in Holocaust child rescue films. The preference for romanticized, fictional scripts and a lack of factual accuracy underlying the screen characters and real people or events, as well as the choice of beautiful and famous actresses for the leading roles, reflects the ongoing tendency to dissociate historical and memorial sources, and to downplay the real virtue of women, and particularly, Jewish women rescuers.[603]

The representation of women as rescuers is further influenced by the country of origin of the films. Many of the films that portray women as rescuers emerge from perpetrator or collaborator countries such as Germany and France. Many of these distort reality by presenting resistance efforts and, in so doing, soften the historic record to present these countries in a more positive light. In contrast, male rescuers are portrayed more often in films from occupied countries such as Poland, the former Czechoslovakia, the Netherlands, and neutral Sweden.[604] Despite recent acknowledgement of female resistance activities in

Holocaust literature, few films reflect this reality, with male rescuers predominating.[605] This approach is likely due to a combination of the long history of relegating women to peripheral positions in films with a dominant male focus, and the similar history of neglecting to recognize female rescuers in Holocaust historiography. They also reflect how countries would like to present their past role in the war.[606] One example is the film made about Irena Sendler in Poland, who rescued a few hundred children from the Warsaw ghetto, although this figure is usually reported or portrayed as up to 2,500 children.[607] This exaggerated figure emerged from a student project written by four girls in a Kansas school who wrote a ten-minute play claiming that Irena saved 2,500 children. The story persisted and the figure of 2,500 children saved by Irena became a popular portrayal of her activities as in the film.[608] The film (*The Courageous Heart of Irena Sendler*) honours a Gentile woman whose bravery goes far towards creating a more positive image of Polish activities while ignoring the more negative aspects of this country's war-time involvement. Irena Sendler has been extensively honoured both in Israel (as Righteous Among Nations in 1965, and as an honorary citizen of Israel in 1991) and by Poland, where she received the country's highest order of honour, The Order of the White Eagle, and in 2007, an award from the Polish Government for her bravery.[609]

The absence of Jewish women rescuers from most films about Holocaust rescue is striking. One notable exception is the film made about Lena Küchler-Silberman (*Lena: My 100 Children*) that does tell her heroic story.[610] Although she has been honoured in Israel, Küchler's story is not well known beyond its borders.

Superheroes and the Holocaust

One of the most famous superheroes of the film world is Superman. Few are aware of the origins of this story in European Jewish history from the late 19th and early 20th centuries. In 1938, Action Comics published a story that included a hero named Superman. By June of the following year, Superman had become popular and was presented in comics titled in his name. Superman's story relates how he was born on a distant planet that was on the verge of destruction. His parents saved their son by sending the child, unaccompanied, to a safer world. There he was adopted by loving foster parents who treasured their new son's emerging superpowers and encouraged him to reach his potential as America's greatest defender. Superman's story was created by American born Jerry Siegal and Canadian born Joel Schuster, who were both Jews. They were the children of immigrants from Lithuania, the Netherlands, and Ukraine who had fled from antisemitism in Europe.

The parallels between Superman's story and those of Jewish children fleeing Nazism and antisemitism in Europe are abundant. Superman is born on Krypton, a world about to be destroyed. His given name was Kal-El and his father's name was Jor-El. "El" in Hebrew is one of the names of God. In Hebrew the name "Jor," Superman's father's name, is similar to the word "*Jareh*," meaning fear, while Superman's name "Kal" is similar to the Hebrew word "*Kol*," meaning voice. Superman's name, Kal-El, could translate to "Voice of God," a fitting name for the defender of America.[611] To save his life, Kal-El is sent far away, unaccompanied, much like the children of Jews in Europe who were sent away to save their lives, or were entrusted to strangers who promised to hide them. Kal-El is rescued by his foster/adoptive parents, Jonathan and Martha Kent, (variously named in differing versions of the Superman series) who hid him (and especially his superpowers) to enable him to become a super defender of the world. The parallel with hidden Jewish children in the Nazi era continues with this aspect of Superman's life. Jewish children who were rescued by or hidden with non-Jewish parents were forced to create and live with an entirely false persona that concealed all aspects of their Jewish roots. Superman too created the character of Clark Kent to hide his superpowers and alien origins. The Kents, his foster family and later adoptive parents, assisted Kal-El to create this alias to allow him to survive and use his abilities for the betterment of the world. Although never as popular a character as Superman, Supergirl's origins, although less clearly defined, also stem from Krypton, and she is also assisted by Kal-El's adoptive parents, the Kents. Her life likewise encompasses a hidden persona until exposed as a superheroine.

Jerry Siegel and Joel Schuster were influenced by their Jewish refugee families' experiences of escaping antisemitism in Europe and by global events occurring in Germany at the time of the creation of the Superman character in 1938/1939 and the years following.[612] The popularity of Superman's, and to an extent Supergirl's, characters, in combination with increasing feminist movements and social awareness of women's limited roles in society that emerged from both World Wars during which women had taken on positions traditionally occupied only by men, likely contributed to the creation of multiple superheroes, including a slew of female super-heroines such as Wonder Woman (1941), Batwoman (1956), Supergirl, (1959), Black Widow (1964), Captain Marvel (1967), and Storm (1975), among others, that continues to this day.

Women during the Holocaust, and among them, many Jewish women, were indeed, heroines, despite many, if not most, going unrecognized. Unlike their fictionalized representations, Holocaust heroes and heroines faced more difficult ethical challenges than their comic strip and film counterparts.

Ethics

Conflict, war, and genocide provide almost endless scope for difficult, even impossible ethical choices: Parents forced to choose which child to save, or to die with their children; families forced to choose between their lives and their religion or identity; and entire communities facing decisions over survival of the community balanced with that of the individual. The Jewish women rescuers discussed in this book contended with these and other ethical challenges, often resulting in significant personal turmoil and deep struggles with the actions they had to take. Analysing ethical decision making with the luxury of eighty years of hindsight and historical study, however, is a problematic activity at best. Any discussion of ethics must be placed in context, with the full situational and emotional implications that entails. We undertake this analysis because it is essential to understanding the work that Jewish women who rescued Jewish children did, with the full understanding that no analysis will be complete, free of bias, or fully representative of the experiences of the rescuers, organizations, or children.

The underlying premise of this book is that saving children's lives, almost always by removing them from their homes and families, was, in many, if not most, circumstances, an act of heroism. Within this broad premise, however, are a range of circumstances that can change this determination. This brief discussion will focus on five broad ethical concepts that repeatedly emerge in the experiences of Jewish women who rescued Jewish children: the moral ambiguity known as The Grey Zone, in which people faced choiceless choices, forced on them by the context of the Holocaust and Nazi actions; the impact of intent and consent on determining ethical actions; the influence of religion and ideology; the ethics of recognition and representation; and the morally unambiguous situations, where right and wrong can be determined, even within this complex and highly tumultuous context.

The Grey Zone

When writing about the Holocaust, it can be temptingly easy to withdraw from ethical analysis by relying on Levi's concept of a Grey Zone[613] in which we cannot judge the "choiceless choices"[614] that were forced on those in the Holocaust. In many contexts, this is a fair and entirely necessary ethical construct, where it is impossible and even reprehensible for us, with the privilege of eighty years of hindsight, to judge those embroiled in the horrors of the Holocaust. This is not, however, true of every situation and every context, nor does it obviate our responsibility to consider and learn from these difficult moral and ethical dilemmas.

We need ask whether rescuing/saving/retrieving children by removing them from their parents – which was a prerequisite for their survival in most cases – was a morally appropriate choice. Almost all who took children from their parents, including the Krauses, Irena Sendler, and others who smuggled children out of ghettos, the women who persuaded mothers in French detention camps to agree that their children be taken to care homes for safety, those that parted with their children who were sent on the *Kindertransport,* and the Christian foster families and religious institutions who looked after hidden children and then had to part with them later, expressed and experienced anguish about these separations. The children themselves were traumatized at each parting. Was saving their lives by clutching them from the Nazi's hands and in so doing causing immeasurable emotional pain to parents and children alike, the right thing to do? Some Rabbis at the time thought not.[615] Clearly, those who rescued or saved such children, often at risk to their own lives, did their utmost to save the children and believed such separations were worth it. We cannot ask the parents, as few survived the war and none are left alive today. The children themselves were often traumatized and many remained so for years, although such emotional pain is the aftermath of the multiple horrors they experienced as a result of the Nazis, including the deaths of their parent/s and the hardships of their lives after the war, and not only from the acts surrounding their rescue. Many of the foster parents who cared for and loved the children they had hidden for years were also traumatized by relinquishing the children back to the parents/relatives or Jewish agencies in the years after the war. Others sought and received financial rewards for doing so, while yet more recognized their temporary role in rescuing children and relinquished them readily.

The dilemma regarding retrieving these children from happy foster homes, is further compounded when the question of retrieving them to Judaism, rather than to a family member, is added. Given the disastrous effects of Hitler's antisemitic policies on the extermination of the Jewish people of Europe, the importance of retrieving as many Jewish children back to Judaism as possible, is understandable.

Choiceless choices also arose when children or babies, in particular, were hidden together with groups of adults. Was it best to smother a crying child who was in hiding with a group to avoid the potential disclosure of the entire group's hiding place? Rabbinic responses contradict each other, depending on the experiences of the Rabbis asked to resolve this dilemma. Some, such as Rabbi Shimon Efrati, was asked whether a Jew in hiding in a ghetto must pay respect for having inadvertently smothered a crying infant to avoid detection.

His *responsum*, published in 1961, concluded that *Halakhah* (Jewish law) does not require that the infant be killed: rather it is optional. If one chooses to die rather than the infant be killed, one shall be called holy. However, the individual who unintentionally suffocated the child should not have a bad conscience because he acted to save Jewish lives. Rabbi Efrati was probably influenced by the fact that his own brother had been hiding in a bunker during such a search when a baby burst out crying. The Rabbi in the bunker ordered that no one should risk harming the child and, as a result, all twenty people, including Rabbi Efrati's brother, were discovered and murdered by the Nazis.[616]

Intent

In some instances, we can question the intent behind the actions taken to save some children. Today, we can ask whether it was correct for families to prevent their Jewish children being rescued by Christians for fear that they might be converted to Catholicism or Christianity. Was preserving their Judaic heritage more important than saving their lives? Were the Rabbis who advised them not to give their children to rescuers to prevent such *shmad* (conversion) giving valuable guidance?

In retrospect we know that some children who were raised by Christians survived as non-Jews. Not only did some convert to Christianity but a few even became members of the clergy. Would their parents have still wished for their survival knowing this might happen, or would they have preferred their child's death rather than conversion? For some, such as Bieta Koppe, whose grandfather smuggled a Christening dress and crucifix to the baby in hiding, the choice was clear: Survival was more important than religious affiliation. For others, such as Manya who chose to die with her son Artek, rather than give him to others to rescue, there was no wish to be separated.

In contrast, were the actions of Jan Dobraczyński and his colleague Jaga Piotrowsak, who insisted that children rescued from the Warsaw ghetto be baptised as a condition of their being saved. Such intent throws doubt on the honesty of their actions regarding rescuing Jewish children. Was their intention an ardent desire to save children or a means of killing the Jew in the child – a furtherance of Hitler's exterminationist objectives? In the ghettos, was it acceptable to give children "mercy deaths" to prevent them from falling into Nazi hands and being exterminated on arrival in camps? Might some of those children have survived if they had not been killed to prevent their suffering? The actions of Dr. Adina Blady Szwajger[617] who chose to murder the children under her medical care to prevent them from falling into Nazi hands, is debated. From one perspective, she was driven by an altruistic motive of saving them from the cruelty of deportation and likely death in the camps. The less noble alternative, however, is that she knew she was exempt from deportation but had promised the children she would not be parted from them. In this interpretation, she killed them rather than let them know she had abandoned them despite her promise; that she was willing to leave them to go to their deaths rather than face that fate with them. Either choice is difficult to judge in retrospect, however the intent behind her actions is essential to understanding them and their ethical implications.

A further example of questionable intent arises from consideration of the *Kindertransport* children. Was it acceptable for Britain to enforce a wide distribution of Jewish *Kindertransport* children across the UK so as not to cluster a large number of Jewish children in any one centre to avoid antisemitic repercussions? Was it ethical that the British government forced children to be housed in non-Jewish homes, even when many Jewish households in Britain were willing to take them? The possible antisemitic undertones of this decision remain a blight on the otherwise honourable actions taken to save 10,000 children, especially when few if any other countries offered such relief. The clearly antisemitic intentions behind the decisions of countries such as the USA and Canada, which refused to admit many Jewish child refugees, remains a shadow or, rather, a dark cloud, over their honour.

Religion and Ideology

There are many dubious aspects to the role played by religion and ideology in the rescue of Jewish children. Was it morally acceptable for religious institutions that sheltered children to baptise Jewish children?

Should their Jewish identity have been respected both before the performance of these rituals and afterwards? There is no question that such actions were often, if not always, essential to hide their Jewishness. Children unable to participate in the rituals required by religious observance would have been immediately exposed as Jewish, and their lives endangered. Given that context, however, was the performance of such ceremonies as baptism and first holy communion "under duress" (as was the case to save their lives) a valid practice? According to Catholicism, baptism and such sacraments are understood to be an outward sign of inner grace. Would those who are sincere in their beliefs truly accept that such "conversions" were spiritually sincere? Apparently, however, at the time of the Holocaust, even at the highest level, such conversions were sanctioned by the Church. Pope Pius XII, despite being repeatedly requested to do so by Rabbi Herzog, refused to order the return of Jewish children to those who wished to retrieve them, suggesting that the performance of rituals such as baptism, communion, and confirmation, even when those were performed simply on pragmatic grounds, to provide a safe appearance for the children, was regarded as spiritually significant. This position is not surprising given the history of the Church recognizing and endorsing forced and coerced conversions in other related contexts, despite claims to oppose such acts. Notable examples of the history of forcing Jews to convert to Christianity are the forced conversions in the Iberian Peninsula that took place repeatedly as early as the 7th century and peaking through the 14th to 16th centuries.[618] Even these centuries old examples continue to fuel the debate regarding whether coercion and faith can coexist.[619]

Questions regarding the Church's role in the Holocaust remain widely debated today with the Church's objective to present their actions in a positive light remaining of paramount importance. Controversy still reigns regarding the potential beatification of Pope Pius XII. Surprisingly, Pope Francis, in 2023, chose to beatify a single Polish family of nine who were murdered for helping Jews. One can only ask whether this was a symbolic apology for papal omissions in the Nazi era, or an endorsement of attempts to rewrite aspects of Holocaust history, particularly in Poland?

Perhaps, however, we need look further to the role of ideology in determining our lives, and our answers to these challenging questions. Nazism was based on an ideology: that the Aryan/German race was superior to all others. This, indeed, is one contributing cause of World War II and the Holocaust. But so too is religious ideology a contributor to our dilemmas. Both Jewish religious extremism as well as Catholic/ Christian fanaticism add to our quandaries. While many Jews asked where God was in the Holocaust, some saying he was present and others believing he had deserted the Jews,[620] belief in God, either a Jewish or a Christian God, certainly drove many of the choices and decisions we note, often to the detriment of the children. Father Patrick Desbois, after examining Holocaust atrocity crimes for decades, also questions the value of ideology saying that he believes he belongs to a race that kills two-year-old children.[621] I have agreed with him, adding that we may also abuse them physically, emotionally and sexually first.[622] Examining the stories of child rescuers in the Holocaust suggests that, sometimes driven by ideologies, and even when we have the best intentions, we may also discount children's needs, views, wishes, hopes, and feelings in the process of helping them. While the Nazis must rightly be condemned for implementing the Holocaust and creating the conditions under which such horrific choices were forced upon Jews, and while we must honour and respect the frequently unsung Jewish heroines who rescued children whenever they could, we need to remain alert to the ambivalent insights and nuances of understanding that these rescues raise.

Recognition and Representation

Even within the film world, it has been common practice, and presumably, therefore, acceptable to create heroic stories of rescuers that either intentionally, or perhaps unintentionally, whitewash the antisemitic or Nazi-allied actions of the country they now depict as heroic in rescuing Jewish children. The Czech filmmaker Matej Mináč's, and that government's lauding of Nicholas Winton's rescue of Czech children through the *Kindertransport*, serves not only to honour his activities inappropriately but also to present Czechoslovakia as a victim of the Nazis and not as allied to them, and to present the

Czech people as heroic rescuers of children rather than as their murderers. In addition, within the film world, is it acceptable to portray Jewish Holocaust heroines in films that, while honouring them, also romanticize their roles or sexualize them, presumably to titillate audiences? Male rescuers are reflected in film as heroes: women rescuers, if portrayed at all, are more likely to be presented as sexual objects.

Is it acceptable for Yad Vashem to only offer national recognition for Gentile rescuers or should they actively embrace and incorporate current developments by B'nai B'rith and others that are now seeking to honour Jewish rescuers as well? Should these endeavours be incorporated into the Yad Vashem Act as we recognize this disparity in honours more clearly today? To date, this formal recognition has been denied. It is likely clear that we believe recognition should be offered to all those who rescued others, regardless of their sex or religious affiliation. Likewise, representation in film and other popular culture should embrace the reality and complexity of the rescuers and the contexts in which their heroism took place. While it is beyond the scope of this book, it is also essential that the stories of other victims of the Nazis (and their rescuers) be recorded, recognized, and shared, with as much attention paid towards, for example, the Roma and Sinti, Homosexuals, or Disabled people murdered by the Nazis as has been paid to the Jewish victims of the Shoah.

Morally Unambiguous: Right and Wrong

Although we have questioned the ethics behind many challenges encountered in the Holocaust, particularly regarding the rescue or saving of Jewish children, there are some morally unambiguous questions. On balance, the act of rescuing and protecting children is unambiguously right. On the other hand, removing children from loving foster homes to put them into Jewish run institutions becomes unequivocally unethical when implemented through extremely dishonest, deceptive, and dangerous methods that prioritized the preservation of Judaism over the needs of the child.[623] There is also little moral ambiguity regarding the refusal of countries like the USA and Canada to admit Jewish child refugees when they could easily have done so.

We cannot, however, doubt, for a moment, that blame for all these actions lies on Nazi hands rather than on the rescuers or retrievers of the children. The Nazis established the circumstances and world in which such actions and horrific choices were necessary. Within that context however, there were, on occasion, moments when individuals and nations had options in how to respond; some were choiceless choices, others heavily influenced by ideology and religion, and still others were simply and unequivocally right or wrong. The Nazis imposed a world of horror and brutality, but within that world, there were individuals and groups, including the extraordinary Jewish women discussed in this text, who stood against this Nazi imposed terror and rescued children, against all odds, and endured immense personal trauma in the process. They should be remembered; and they should be honoured.

Appendix: 108 Women

Pre-war Rescuers

Anna Braude-Heller[624] (Poland). Helped children in Warsaw ghetto

Marysia Bronka Feinmesser[625] (Poland). Rescued children from Warsaw ghetto

Ella Golomb-Grynberg[626] (Poland). Rescued children in Warsaw ghetto

Helena Jockel[627] (Hungary). Chose to stay with children in ghetto

Vladka Meed[628] (Poland). Rescued children from Warsaw ghetto

Tola Mintz[629] (Poland). Physician in an orphanage in the ghetto

Fela Perlman[630] (Poland). Created a school for children

Ewa Rechtman[631] (Poland). Assisted Irena Sendler in Warsaw ghetto

Maria Rotblatt[632] (Poland). Ran an orphanage in Warsaw ghetto

(Inka) Adina Blady Szwajger[633] (Poland). Rescued children from Warsaw ghetto

Stefania Wilczynska[634] (Poland). Janusz Korczak's assistant

Rescue from Europe

Beate Berger[635] (Germany). Brought 300 children to Palestine

Recha Freier[636] (Germany). Started Youth Aliyah: saved 1,000 children

Hela Jafe[637] (Bergen-Belsen). Cared for children in camp

161

Eleanor Kraus (Gilbert Kraus)[638] (USA). Took fifty children from Vienna to USA

Henrietta Szold[639] (Israel). Collaborated on Youth Aliyah

Cecilia Razovsky[640] (USA). Brought 1,000 children to USA

Kate Rosenheim[641] (Germany). Collaborated with Cecelia Razovsky

Marie Schmolka[642] (Czechoslovakia). Facilitated *Kindertransport*

Rebecca Sieff[643] (UK). Organized 2,000 permits for Jewish youth

Hiding Children

Hansi (and Joel) Brand[644] (Hungary). Supported children's homes

Basia Temkin-Berman (and Adolf)[645] (Poland). Helped hidden children and mothers

Marie Albert-Blum[646] (Belgium). Ran Jewish orphanage

Rebecca Boas[647] (the Netherlands). Rescued children from Jewish daycare centre

Matilda Cassim[648] (Italy). Established child refugee organization

Alice Cohn[649] (the Netherlands). Forged documents for children

Margot Cohn[650] (France). Helped hide children

Innese Cohen[651] (the Netherlands). Rescued children from Jewish daycare centre

Viri (and Harry) Cohen[652] (the Netherlands). Rescued children from Jewish daycare centre

Madeleine Dreyfus[653] (France). Helped hide children

Sabine Elzon[654] (France). Helped hide children

Denise Gamzon[655] (France). Rescued children from internment camps/passeur

Chava Richer Halevi[656] (Hungary). Rescued orphans

(Maurice and) Ester Heiber[657] (Belgium). Administration and planning of rescues

Aviva (Ingeborg) Simon (Igael)[658] (France). Rescued from internment camps/passeur

Fela Botek Izbutsky[659] (France). Helped hide and rescue children after the war

Hilde Jacobsthal[660] (the Netherlands). Rescued children from Jewish daycare centre

Hava (and Hertz) Jospa[661] (Belgium). Hid over 3,000 children

Zivia Kapit[662] (Lithuania). Rescued children from Kaunas ghetto

Pesia Karnovsky[663] (Lithuania). Rescued children from Kaunas ghetto

Sieny Kattenberg[664] (the Netherlands). Rescued children from Jewish daycare centre

Rachela Katz[665] (Lithuania). Rescued children from Kaunas ghetto

Paula Kaufman[666] (the Netherlands). Hid children/smuggled across borders

Pesia Kissen[667] (Lithuania). Rescued children from Kaunas ghetto

Leah Kozel[668] (Lithuania). Rescued children from Kaunas ghetto

Shulamit Lerman[669] (Lithuania). Rescued children from Kaunas ghetto

Rachel Ida Lifchitz[670] (France). Helped hide children

Sonia Lifshitz-Goldschnidt[671] (Lithuania). Rescued children from Kaunas ghetto

Liza Magon[672] (Lithuania). Encouraged children to flee Ashmiani ghetto

Betty Odkerk[673] (the Netherlands). Rescued children from Jewish daycare centre

Henrietta Pimentel[674] (the Netherlands). Rescued children from Jewish daycare centre

Malka Pogetsky-Shamali[675] (Lithuania). Rescued children from Kaunas ghetto

Haviva Reich[676] (Israel). Helped Slovak children escape

Odette Rosenstock (Moussa Abadi)[677] (France). Hid children in safe homes/institutions

Rona Rosenthal[678] (Lithuania). Rescued children from Kaunas ghetto

Letty Rudelsheim[679] (the Netherlands). Helped hide children

Vivette Hermann-Samuel[680] (France). Rescued children from internment camps/passeurs

Adeline Finkelstein-Salomé[681] (the Netherlands). Rescued children from Jewish daycare centre

Andrée Salomon[682] (France). Rescued children from internment camps/passeurs

Lyuba Schwartz[683] (Lithuania). Rescued children from Kaunas ghetto

Juliette Stern[684] (France). Helped hide children

Ida Sterno[685] (Belgium). Helped hide children

Ruth (and Jonas) Tiefenbrunner[686] (Belgium). Ran Jewish orphanage

Chava Unger[687] (Sweden). Ran children's homes in Hamburg, Sewden

Huguette Wahl[688] (France). Assisted the Abadis

Mirjam Waterman[689] (the Netherlands). Hid children/smuggled across borders

Nicole Weil[690] (France). Assisted the Abadis

Sophia Werber[691] (Belgium). Assisted Hava Jospa

Bella Hazan[692] (Italy). Cared for children from Frumka group

Child Rescuers

Fanny Eyal (Ben Ami)[693] (France). Escorted children across borders

Bella Blitz[694] (Belgium). Jewish Student Group member

Sima Fitterson[695] (Belorussia). Escorted Jews to forest partisans

Bronya Gammer[696] (Belorussia). Escorted Jews to forest partisans

Fanya Gimpel[697] (Belorussia). Escorted Jews to forest partisans

Roza Rubenchik[698] (Belorussia). Escorted Jews to forest partisans

Mirjam (?)[699] (Belgium). Jewish Student Group and escort for children

Smuggling Across Borders

Marianne Cohn[700] (France). Smuggled children across borders

Elizabeth "Böszi" Hirsch[701] (France). Rescued children from internment camps/passeur

Charlotte "Shatta" Simon[702] (France). Smuggled children

Sarah (and David) Knot[703] (France). Established *Armée Juive*/ smuggled children

Betty Knot[704] (France). Smuggled children

Jan Letcheber[705] (France). Provided safe houses for children

Judith Marcus[706] (France). Helped hidden Jewish children

Mila Racine[707] (France). Rescued children from internment camps/ passeur

Nicole Salon[708] (France). Rescued children in Nice and Drancy

Denise Siekierski *née* Caraco[709] (France). Helped hide children

Charlotte Sorkine[710] (France). Smuggled children across borders

Aimée Stitelmann[711] (Switzerland). Helped seventeen children enter Switzerland

Margo Wolff[712] (France). Helped hide childern

Rescuers in Camps

Hennie (and Yehoshua) Birnbaum[713] (Westerbork/Bergen-Belsen). Cared for children

Friedl Dicker-Brandeis[714] (Theresienstadt). Taught art to children

Hermina Krantz[715] (Bergen-Belsen). Cared for children in camp

Ellen Loeb[716] (Westerbork). Cared for children

Fella Cajtak Meiboom[717] (Birkenau). *Blokalteste*: helped 1,000 girls

Hadassah Rosensaft[718] (Bergen-Belsen). Cared for children in camp

Esther Maestro Sadikario[719] (Birkenau). Saved 181 girls from Block 25

Luba Tryszynska[720] (Bergen-Belsen). Cared for children in camp

Retrieving Children

Franciska Schechter[721] (Hungary). Worked in care home for children

Hélène Cazes-Benatar[722] (Morocco). Set up children's hospital in Tripoli

Chasia/Hasya Bornstein-Bielicka[723] (Poland). Retrieved children

Hélène Ekhajser[724] (France). Counseller in care home for children

Devora Fleischer[725] (Poland). Retrieved children from Christians

Ruth Gruber[726] (USA). Took 1,000 from Italy to Oswego, USA

Ruth Eliav-Kliger[727] (Israel). Rescued children hidden in Berlin

Hela Leneman[728] (Poland). Teacher in post-war children's home

Sarah Shner Nishmit[729] (Poland). Retrieved children from Christians

Recha Sternbuch[730] (Poland). Retrieved children

Lena Küchler-Silberman[731] (Poland). Took 100 children from Kraków to Israel

Notes

1 Elena Makarova, "Friedl Dicker-Brandies 1898-1944," Jewish Women's Archive, 1999, accessed 21 October, 2021, https://jwa.org/encyclopedia/article/dicker-brandeis-friedl.
2 Terezin Files, Friedl Dicker-Brandeis, 1995, 30.7.1898.
3 Yad Vashem, "Names of Righteous by Country," Yad Vashem, 2022, accessed 29 April, 2022, https://www.yadvashem.org/righteous/statistics.html, Simmy Allen, "Family of Holocaust Survivor and Righteous among the Nations from Poland Visited Yad Vashem," *Yad Vashem*, 2 June, 2022.
4 Yad Vashem, "The Righteous among Nations Database," Yad Vashem, 2022, https://righteous.yadvashem.org/?search=Female&searchType=righteous_only&language=en.
5 B'nai B'rith, "B'nai B'rith World Center and Keren Kayemeth Leisrael Hold Unique Holocaust Day Ceremony Marking the Heroism of Jewish Rescuers," Centre Stage, 2016, accessed 22 June, 2021.
6 Patrick Henry, *We Only Know Men* (Washington, DC: The Catholic University of America Press, 2007), 142.
7 Henry, 142.
8 Moshe Gromb, *Jews Who Rescued Jews during the Holocaust, Research and Documentation of Jewish Rescue XIII: Women Who Paid with Their Lives* (Israel: Nadav Books, 2021), 33-9, Moshe Gromb, *Jews Who Rescued Jews during the Holocaust, Research and Documentation of Jewish Rescue XV: Jewish Women* (Israel: Nadav Books, 2021), 35-41.
9 Mordecai Paldiel, *Saving One's Own: Jewish Rescuers during the Holocaust* (Lincoln: University of Nebraska Press, 2017), 85-7, Chana Arnon, "Jews Rescued Jews during the Holocaust," Committee on Jews Rescued Jews, 2004, accessed 5 May, 2021, https://www.holocaustchild.org/jews-rescued-jews/presentation-given-at-yad-vashem-conference-june-2004/.
10 Etien G Klug et al., "Child Abuse and Neglect by Parents and Other Caregivers," in *World Report on Violence and Health* (Geneva: World Health Organization, 2002).
11 Deborah Dwork, *Children with a Star: Jewish Youth in Nazi Europe* (New Haven: Yale University Press, 1991), xlii.

12 Beverley Chalmers, *Betrayed: Child Sex Abuse in the Holocaust* (UK: Grosvenor House Publishers, 2020), 9, Julie Heifetz, *Too Young to Remember* (Detroit: Wayne State University Press, 1989), 19.

13 USHMM, "Plight of Jewish Children," USHMM, accessed 16 November, 2015, www.ushmm.org/wic/en/article.php?ModuleId=10006124.

14 Nahum Bogner, *At the Mercy of Strangers: The Rescue of Jewish Children with Assumed Identities in Poland* (Jerusalem: Yad Vashem, 2009), 12.

15 Bradley E Smith, and Agnes F Peterson, *Heinrich Himmler: Geheimreden 1933 Bis 1945* (Frankfort 1974).

16 Paldiel.

17 Arnon, Chana Arnon, "Jewish Rescuers Who Lived in Israel after the Shoah," World Federation of Jewish Child Survivors of the Holocaust & Descendants, 2021, accessed 7 May, 2021, https://www.holocaustchild. org/jews-rescued-jews/jewish-rescuers-living-in-israel/, Paldiel, Mordecai Paldiel, "Jewish Women Rescuers of Jews," in *Women Defying Hitler*, ed. Nathan Stoltzfus, Mordecai Paldiel, and Judy Baumel-Schwartz (London: Bloomsbury, 2021), Judith Baumel Schwartz, "Saving Jewish Children after the Holocaust," Research Gate, 2-13, accessed 12 January, 2021, https://www.researchgate.net/publication/293439961_Saving_Jewish_ Children_After_the_Holocaust, Nathan Stoltzfus, Mordecai Paldiel, and Judy Baumel-Schwartz, *Women Defying Hitler: Rescue and Resistance under the Nazis* (London: Bloomsbury Academic, 2021).

18 Gromb, *Jews Who Rescued Jews during the Holocaust, Research and Documentation of Jewish Rescue XV: Jewish Women*, Gromb, *Jews Who Rescued Jews during the Holocaust, Research and Documentation of Jewish Rescue XIII: Women Who Paid with Their Lives*.

19 Mikhal Dekel, *Tehran Children: A Holocaust Refugee Odyssey* (New York: WW Noton and Co., 2019).

20 Judith Hemmendinger, and Robert Krell, *The Children of Buchenwald: Child Survivors of the Holocaust and Their Post-War Lives* (Jerusalem: Geffen, 2000), Martin Gilbert, *The Boys: The Story of 732 Young Concentration Camp Survivors* (New York: Henry Holt and Company, 1996).

21 *The Windermere Children*, (Wall to Wall and Warner Bros, Germany 2020).

22 Steven Pressman, *50 Children: One Ordinary American Couple's Extraordinary Rescue Mission into the Heart of Nazi Germany* (New York: HarperCollins Publishers, 2014).

23 Fred Coleman, *The Marcel Network: How One French Couple Saved 527 Children from the Holocaust* (Washington: Potomac Books, 2013).

24 Mark Jonathan Harris, and Deborah Oppenheimer, *Into the Arms of Strangers: Stories of the Kindertransport* (London: Bloomsbury Publishing, 2000), Ernest Goodman, and Melissa Hacker, "Kindertransport,"

Encyclopaedia Britannica, 2020, accessed 19 June, 2021, https://www.britannica.com/print/article/1983860, National Holocaust Centre and Museum, "Kindertransport," Unknown, accessed 11 May 2022, https://www.holocaust.org.uk/kindertransport-overview, USHMM, "Kindertransport, 1938-40," USHMM, 2021, accessed 12 January, 2021, https://encyclopedia.ushmm.org/content/en/article/kindertransport-1938-40?series=137, Jennifer Craig- Norton, *The Kindertransport: Contesting Memory* (Bloomington, Indiana: Indiana University Press, 2019), Yavneh Memorial and Education Centre, "Kindertransports from North Rhine-Westphalia: The Yavneh Kindertransports," Yavneh Memorial and Education Centre, 2021, accessed 19 June, 2021, http://www.kindertransporte-nrw.eu/kindertransporte_jawne_e.html.

25 Ruth Gruber, *Haven: The Dramatic Story of 1,000 World War II Refugees and How They Came to America* (New York: Three Rivers Press, 2000).

26 Bogner, Susanne Vromen, *Hidden Children of the Holocaust: Belgian Nuns and Their Daring Rescue of Young Jews from the Nazis* (New York: Oxford University Press, 2008), Andre Stein, *Hidden Children: Forgotten Survivors of the Holocaust* (Canada: Penguin Books, 1993), Jane Marks, *The Hidden Children: The Secret Survivors of the Holocaust* (Great Britain: Bantam Books, 1995), Maxine B Rosenberg, *Hiding to Survive: Stories of Jewish Children Rescued from the Holocaust* (New York: Clarion Books, 1994), Dan Michman, ed., *Hiding, Sheltering, and Borrowing Identities: Avenues of Rescue during the Holocaust* (Jerusalem: Yad Vashem, 2017), Tara Zahra, *The Lost Children: Reconstructing Europe's Families after World War II* (Cambridge Massachusetts: Harvard University Press, 2011), Rebecca Clifford, *Survivors: Children's Lives after the Holocaust* (New Haven, USA: Yale University Press, 2020).

27 Alan Rosen, *The Wonder of Their Voices: The 1946 Holocaust Interviews of David Boder* (Oxford, UK: Oxford University Press, 2010).

28 Henry, 137.

29 Henry, 137.

30 Doreen Rappaport, *Beyond Courage: The Untold Story of Jewish Resistance during the Holocaust* (Massachusetts, USA: Candlewick Press, 2012), 31.

31 Paldiel, *Saving One's Own: Jewish Rescuers during the Holocaust*, xix, Tsila Herscho et al., "All Our Brothers and Sisters: Jews Saving Jews in the Holocaust" (Israel2022).

32 *Resistance*, (Shout Factory, 2019).

33 Paldiel, *Saving One's Own: Jewish Rescuers during the Holocaust*, xix, Herscho et al.

34 David Hogan, and David Aretha, eds., *The Holocaust Chronicle* (Illinois: Publications International, 2001), 405-7.

35 Henry, 138.

36 Thomas Keneally, *Schindler's List* (New York: Simon and Schuster, 1982), *Schindler's List*, (1993).

37 Henry, 144-5, Eva Fogelman, *Conscience and Courage: The Rescuers of Jews during the Holocaust* (New York: Doubleday, 1994), 303-4.

38 Paldiel, *Saving One's Own: Jewish Rescuers during the Holocaust*, xiv.

39 Gromb, *Jews Who Rescued Jews during the Holocaust, Research and Documentation of Jewish Rescue XIII: Women Who Paid with Their Lives*, 20.

40 Gromb, *Jews Who Rescued Jews during the Holocaust, Research and Documentation of Jewish Rescue XV: Jewish Women*, 16.

41 Miriam Gillis-Carlebach, *Each Child Is My Only One: Lotte Carlebach-Preuss, the Portrait of a Mother and Rabbi's Wife* (New York: Peter Lang, 2014), 159-60.

42 Henry, 141.

43 Henry, 160-1.

44 Henry, 99.

45 Paldiel, "Jewish Women Rescuers of Jews," in *Women Defying Hitler*, 151.

46 Yad Vashem, "Rescue by Jews during the Holocaust," *Yad Vashem Newsletter* 94, no. Winter 2021 (2021), https://view.publitas.com/yad-vashem/yad-vashem-magazine-94/page/32-33.

47 Yad Vashem, "Rescue by Jews during the Holocaust," 1.

48 Yad Vashem, "Rescue by Jews during the Holocaust," 1.

49 Gromb, *Jews Who Rescued Jews during the Holocaust, Research and Documentation of Jewish Rescue XIII: Women Who Paid with Their Lives*, 21-2.

50 Yad Vashem, "Rescue by Jews during the Holocaust Solidarity in a Disintegrating World: Unto Every Person There Is a Name," Yad Vashem, 2020, accessed 3 April, 2024, embassies.gov.il/zagreb/NewsAndEvents/Documents/every-person.pdf.

51 Avraham Burg, "The Righteous yet Unrecognized: The Muslims Who Saved Jewish Children during WWII," Haaretz, 2022, accessed 28 March, 2022.

52 Burg

53 Henry, 10.

54 Arnon, "Jews Rescued Jews during the Holocaust."

55 Arnon, "Jews Rescued Jews during the Holocaust."

56 Arnon, "Jews Rescued Jews during the Holocaust."

57 Stoltzfus, Paldiel, and Baumel-Schwartz, 73.

58 Paldiel, "Jewish Women Rescuers of Jews," in *Women Defying Hitler*, 163.

59 Laura E. Brade, and Rose Holmes, "Troublesome Sainthood: Nicholas Winton and the Contested History of Child Rescue in Prague,

1938–1940," *History & Memory* 29, no. 1 (2017): 11-22, https://marieschmolka.files.wordpress.com/2019/03/brade-holmes.pdf.

60 Brade, and Holmes 27.

61 Brade, and Holmes 24.

62 Brade, and Holmes 24.

63 Brade, and Holmes 25.

64 Brade, and Holmes 26-7.

65 Brade, and Holmes 26-7.

66 Brade, and Holmes 27.

67 Henry, 167, Berel Lang, *The Future of the Holocaust: Between History and Memory* (Ithaca, New York: Cornell University Press, 1999), 120.

68 Henry, 167, Lang, 120.

69 Henry, 168.

70 Henry, 141.

71 Henry, 103.

72 Hogan, and Aretha, 211-3, 38, 93-5.

73 Hogan, and Aretha, 211-3, 38, 93-5.

74 Beverley Chalmers, *Birth, Sex and Abuse: Women's Voices under Nazi Rule* (UK: Grosvenor House Publishers, 2015), 270-1.

75 Vladka Meed, *On Both Sides of the Wall* (Washington: Holocaust Library, 1993), 111.

76 Meed, 111-2.

77 Meed, 111-2.

78 Meed, 114.

79 Meed, 116.

80 Meed, 201, Joseph Ziemian, *The Cigarette Sellers of Three Crosses Square: Searing Testament to Human Courage* (New York: Avon Publishers, 1975).

81 Miriam Offer, *White Coats in the Ghetto: Jewish Medicine in Poland during the Holocaust* (Israel: Yad Vashem, 2020), 87.

82 Rochelle Saidel, "Remembering a Hero of the Holocaust," Remember the Women Institute, 2022, accessed 5 August, 2022, https://myemail.constantcontact.com/Remembering-a-Hero-of-the-Holocaust.html?sod=1111778380172&aid=v-iuIWkXC8I.

83 Maria Ciesielska, "To Care for Children on Their Way and Beyond... History of Female Doctors from the Warsaw Ghetto Who Stood by Their Patients until the Very End." (paper presented at the Heroines of the Holocaust: Nurses and Doctors as Resistors in Genocide Conference, New York 2023).

84 Helena Jockel, *We Sang in Hushed Voices* (Canada: The Azrieli Foundation, 2014), 14-7.

85 Jockel, 16.

86 Adina Blady Szwajger, *I Remember Nothing More: The Warsaw Children's Hospital and Jewish Resistance* (New York: Simon and Schuster, 1988).

87 Offer, 268-9.

88 Offer, 273.

89 Offer, 256.

90 Offer, 255-6.

91 Gromb, *Jews Who Rescued Jews during the Holocaust, Research and Documentation of Jewish Rescue XIII: Women Who Paid with Their Lives*, 61.

92 Offer, 582.

93 Wikipedia, "Lejb Rotblat," Wikipedia, 2022, accessed 7 June 2022, https://en.wikipedia.org/wiki/Lejb_Rotblat, Anna Bikont, *Sendlerowa. W Ukryciu ('Sendler: In Hiding')17,* (Wołowiec Wydawnictwo Czarne, 2017).

94 Offer, 282.

95 Raul Hilberg, *Perpetrators Victims Bystanders: The Jewish Catastrophe 1933-1945* (New York: Harper Collins Publishers, 1992), 165.

96 Chalmers, *Birth, Sex and Abuse: Women's Voices under Nazi Rule*, 255.

97 Offer, 518.

98 Offer, 516.

99 Chalmers, *Birth, Sex and Abuse: Women's Voices under Nazi Rule*, 90.

100 Lynn H. Nicholas, *Cruel World: The Children of Europe in the Nazi Web* (New York: Vintage Books, 2006), 373.

101 Henry Friedman, *I'm No Hero: Journeys of a Holocaust Survivor* (Seattle, USA: University of Washington Press, 1999), 26-7.

102 Mark Klempner, *The Heart Has Reasons: Dutch Rescuers of Jewish Children during the Holocaust* (Amsterdam: Night Stand Books, 2012), 3.

103 Larry Loftis, *The Watchmaker's Daughter* (New York: Harper Collins, 2023), 64.

104 Pressman, 37.

105 Pressman, 126.

106 Anne Nelson, *Suzanne's Children: A Daring Rescue in Nazi Paris* (New York: Simon and Schuster, 2017), 89.

107 Tilar Mazzeo, *Irena's Children: A True Story of Courage* (New York: Gallery Books, 2016), 200.

108 Emunah Nachamy Gafny, *Dividing Hearts: The Removal of Jewish Children from Gentile Families in Poland in the Immediate Post Holocaust Years* (Jerusalem: Yad Vashem, 2009), 44-5.

109 Friedman, 43.

110 Gafny, 44-5, Offer, 477-9.

111 Gafny, 43.

112   Bikont, Anna Bikont, "Knowledge under Siege: Irena Sendler in Hiding," 2023, https://www.youtube.com/watch?v=yyqFiuWQLHQ.

113   Mazzeo, 139.

114   Bikont, *Sendlerowa. W Ukryciu ('Sendler: In Hiding')17,*.

115   Meed, 111.

116   Gafny, 45-6.

117   Gafny, 35.

118   Gafny, 36.

119   Abraham Werner, *Ordeal and Deliverance*, trans. Shula Werner (Raanana, Israel: Docostory Publishing House Ltd., 2003), 72-5.

120   Ziemian.

121   Ziemian, 9-10.

122   Mazzeo, 140.

123   Gafny, 35.

124   Nelson, 117.

125   Mazzeo, 140.

126   Mazzeo, 140.

127   Mazzeo, 140.

128   Mazzeo, 139.

129   Gafny, 43.

130   Mazzeo, 142-3.

131   Wiktoria Sliwowska, ed., *The Last Eyewitnesses: Children of the Holocaust Speak* (Evanston, illionois: Northwestern University Press, 1998), 274.

132   Mazzeo, 142-3.

133   Sliwowska, 274.

134   Gafny, 55.

135   Leah Nebenzahl, "The Miraculous Story Hidden Child in a Monastary and with a Polish Family, Leah Nebenzahl," interview by Les Glassman, *Youtube*, February 14, 2023, Israel, https:/youtu.be/cMOKLZ4cHjk.

136   Samuel Oliner, and Pearl Oliner, *The Altruistic Personality: Rescuers of Jews in Nazi Europe* (New York: The Free Press, 1988), 155, Fogelman, 163, Henry, 151.

137   David Gushee, *The Righteous Gentiles of the Holocaust: A Christian Interpretation* (Minneapolis, Minnesota: Fortress Press, 1994), 112, Henry.

138   Nechama Tec, *When Light Pierced the Darkness: Christian Rescue of Jews in Nazi Occupied Poland* (New York: Oxford University Press, 1986), 189.

139   Henry, 164.

140   Herscho et al.

141   Henry, 151.

142 Barbie Latza Nadeau, "Catholic Church to Beatify Polish Family, Including Newborn Baby, Killed by Nazis for Hiding Jews," CNN, 2023, accessed 8 September, 2023, https://www.cnn.com/2023/09/06/world/ulma-family-beatify-nazis-intl-scli.

143 Mazzeo, 140.

144 Gafny, 11.

145 Mazzeo, 141.

146 *Convention on the Prevention and Punishment of the Crime of Genocide*, by United Nations (Geneva: United Nations, 1948).

147 Gafny, 32.

148 March of the Living, "Uncovering Holocaust Perpetrators Where Few Have Looked," March of the Living, 2016, https://www.motl.org/uncovering-holocaust-perpetrators-where-few-have-looked/.

149 Rosemary Sullivan, *The Betrayal of Anne Frank: A Cold Case Investigation* (USA: Harper, 2022), 88.

150 Gafny, 46.

151 Gafny, 46.

152 Gafny, 47.

153 Gafny, 32-3.

154 Gafny, 44-5.

155 Gafny, 52.

156 Gafny, 53.

157 Mazzeo, 1.

158 Gafny, 49.

159 Gafny, 51.

160 Chalmers, *Betrayed: Child Sex Abuse in the Holocaust*, 116-46, Clifford, 20.

161 Chalmers, *Betrayed: Child Sex Abuse in the Holocaust*.

162 Gafny, 55.

163 Klempner, 133.

164 Chalmers, *Betrayed: Child Sex Abuse in the Holocaust*.

165 Paldiel, *Saving One's Own: Jewish Rescuers during the Holocaust*, 274.

166 Gromb, *Jews Who Rescued Jews during the Holocaust, Research and Documentation of Jewish Rescue XV: Jewish Women*, 110.

167 Ahavah, "Pleasure to Meet You," Ahavah, 2023, accessed April 26, 2023, https://ahava-v.org.il/en/nice-to-meet-you/.

168 Gromb, *Jews Who Rescued Jews during the Holocaust, Research and Documentation of Jewish Rescue XV: Jewish Women*, 57.

169 Bikont, *Sendlerowa. W Ukryciu ('Sendler: In Hiding')17,*.

170 *The Courageous Heart of Irena Sendler*, (Hallmark Hall of Fame Productions, 2009), Yad Vashem, "Irene Sendler," Yad Vashem, 2021, accessed 12 January, 2021, https://www.yadvashem.org/yv/en/exhibitions/righteous-women/sendler.asp.

171 Clodagh Finn, *A Time to Risk All* (Dublin, Ireland: Gill Books, 2017).

172 *Marion Pritchard: Courage and Valor*, (Vimeo, 2021), C:\Users\Bev\ AppData\Local\Microsoft\Windows\INetCache\Content.Outlook\70K2 E5L6\email.mht.

173 Nelson, Yad Vashem, "Suzanne Spaak," Yad Vashem, 2021, accessed 12 January, 2021, https://www.yadvashem.org/yv/en/exhibitions/righteous-women/spaak.asp.

174 Joe Miller, "Rescuing Jewish Children: The Story of Lois Gunden," MCC, 2020, accessed 12 January, 2021, https://mcccanada.ca/ centennial/100-stories/rescuing-jewish-children-story-lois-gunden, Yad Vashem, "Lois Gunden," Yad Vashem, 2021, accessed 12 Janaury, 2021, https://www.yadvashem.org/yv/en/exhibitions/righteous-women/ gunden.asp, Yad Vashem, "Women of Valor: Stories of Women Who Rescued Jews during the Holocaust," Yad Vashem, 2021, accessed 12 Janaury, 2021, https://www.yadvashem.org/yv/en/exhibitions/righteous-women/index.asp.

175 Yad Vashem, "Women of Valor: Stories of Women Who Rescued Jews during the Holocaust."

176 Paldiel, *Saving One's Own: Jewish Rescuers during the Holocaust*, 254-8.

177 Rafael Medoff, *America and the Holocaust: A Documentary History* (Lincoln, Nebraska: University of Nebraska Press, 2022), 154.

178 Pressman, 55.

179 Medoff, 98-112.

180 Medoff, 90.

181 Pressman, 66-7.

182 Pressman, 69.

183 Pressman, 73, Medoff, 103-4.

184 Medoff, 112.

185 Bat-Ami Zucker, "Cecilia Razovsky, the American Activist Who Rescued German Jewish Children (1933-1945)," *Women in Judaism: A Multidisciplinary e-Journal* 17, no. 2 (2020).

186 Pressman, 76-8.

187 Michael Danty, "Cecelia Razovsky," One Thousand Children, YIVO Institute for Jewish Research, 2021, accessed 28 October, 2021, https:// onethousandchildren.yivo.org/Cecilia-Razovsky.

188 Medoff, 117-20.

189 Pressman, 61.

190 Medoff, 118.

191 Pressman, 85.

192 Pressman, 119, USHMM, "Eleanor and Gilbert Kraus," USHMM, 2021, accessed 17 May, 2021, https://exhibitions.ushmm.org/americans-and-the-holocaust/personal-story/eleanor-gilbert-kraus?utm_source=

mkto&utm_medium=email&utm_campaign=E20210509MKT
EMB&utm_term=read&utm_content=historical&mkt_tok=MTY1LUtZ
Ty02MTYAAAF88GhWAtLWSeGARTpBZ5Lq5i8KIXB1UpHPxa6l7
V3UKAvgYd00QPdlIJrskBUqFT4xaIvLkYzvcwOG8RS0I3mfaWjd6R
YUw-7JB99rhe4AyQ.

193 Pressman, 136.
194 USHMM, "The Rescue Mission of Gilbert and Eleanor Kraus,"
    USHMM, 2021, accessed 23 May 2022, https://encyclopedia.ushmm.
    org/content/en/article/the-rescue-mission-of-gilbert-and-eleanor-kraus.
195 Pressman, 148.
196 USHMM, "The Rescue Mission of Gilbert and Eleanor Kraus."
197 Pressman, 148.
198 USHMM, "Eleanor and Gilbert Kraus."
199 Pressman, 160-1.
200 Pressman, 232.
201 Arnon, "Jews Rescued Jews during the Holocaust."
202 Paldiel, *Saving One's Own: Jewish Rescuers during the Holocaust*, 3-11.
203 Arnon, "Jews Rescued Jews during the Holocaust."
204 Paldiel, *Saving One's Own: Jewish Rescuers during the Holocaust*, 3-11.
205 Paldiel, *Saving One's Own: Jewish Rescuers during the Holocaust*, 3-11.
206 Arnon, "Jews Rescued Jews during the Holocaust."
207 Arnon, "Jews Rescued Jews during the Holocaust."
208 Paldiel, *Saving One's Own: Jewish Rescuers during the Holocaust*, 3-11.
209 USHMM, "Beate Berger, Director of the Beith Ahawah Children's
    Home.," USHMM, 2009, accessed 13 June, 2022, https://collections.
    ushmm.org/search/catalog/pa1167888.
210 USHMM, "Beate Berger, Director of the Beith Ahawah Children's
    Home."
211 USHMM, "Beate Berger, Director of the Beith Ahawah Children's
    Home."
212 Harris, and Oppenheimer, 8-9.
213 USHMM, "Kindertransport, 1938-40."
214 Lauren Young, *Hitler's Girl* (Canada: Harper, 2022), 60.
215 Harris, and Oppenheimer.
216 Harris, and Oppenheimer, 15.
217 Norton, 246.
218 Harris, and Oppenheimer, 13.
219 Anna Hájková, *Marie Schmolka, Who Inspired the Kindertransport*
    (UK: Jewish Voice for Labour, 2017). https://www.jewishvoiceforlabour.
    org.uk/article/marie-schmolka-inspired-kindertransport/.
220 Brade, and Holmes 21.
221 Brade, and Holmes 23.
222 Hájková.

223 Hájková.

224 Anna Hájková, "Marie Schmolka Society," 2022, accessed June 10, 2022, https://marieschmolka.org/.

225 Paul Bartop, and Samantha Lakin, *Heroines of Vichy France: Rescuing French Jews during the Holocaust* (California, USA: Praeger, 2019), xx.

226 Arnon, "Jews Rescued Jews during the Holocaust."

227 Paldiel, *Saving One's Own: Jewish Rescuers during the Holocaust*, 346.

228 Werner.

229 Kathryn Berman, "Hidden Children in France during the Holocaust," Yad Vashem, 2023, accessed 27 October, 2023, https://www.yadvashem. org/articles/general/hidden-children.html.

230 Berman

231 Berman

232 USHMM, "Jewish Aid and Rescue: Rescue of Children," USHMM, 2021, accessed 12 January, 2021, https://encyclopedia.ushmm.org/ content/en/article/jewish-aid-and-rescue.

233 Coleman, 33.

234 Shoah Resource Centre, "Jewish Army, France," Yad Vashem,, accessed 8 February, 2024, https://www.yadvashem.org/odot_pdf/Microsoft%20 Word%20-%206363.pdf.

235 Yad Vashem, "Rescue of Children," Yad Vashem, 2018, accessed 9 July 2018, 2018, www.yadvashem.org/odot_pdf/Microsoft%20Word%20 -%205820.pdf

236 Dekel, 300-1.

237 USHMM, "Jewish Aid and Rescue: Rescue of Children."

238 Yad Vashem, "Rescue of Children."

239 Yad Vashem, "Rescue of Children."

240 Yad Vashem, "Rescue of Children."

241 Holocaust Education and Archive Research Team, "The Story of Walter Suskind," Holocaust Education and Archive Research Team, 2012, accessed 9 February, 2021, http://www.holocaustresearchproject.org/ survivor/suskind.html.

242 Rappaport, 28.

243 Charlotte Decoster, "Jewish Hidden Children in Belgium during the Holocaust: A Comparative Study of Their Hiding Places at Christian Establishments, Private Families and Jewish Orphanages." (University of North Texas, 2006), 62, Roni Wolf, "Saved in a Jewish Orphanage during the Holocaust My Story with Roni and Igor Wolf," interview by Les Glassman, Israel, 2023, Les Glassman, Youtube, https://www. youtube.com/watch?v=87mVNDQwq_8.

244 Decoster, 64.

245 Paldiel, *Saving One's Own: Jewish Rescuers during the Holocaust*, 33, 209, Henry, 14.

246 Paldiel, *Saving One's Own: Jewish Rescuers during the Holocaust*, 33, 209, Henry, 14.

247 Arnon, "Jews Rescued Jews during the Holocaust."

248 Arnon, "Jews Rescued Jews during the Holocaust."

249 Arnon, "Jews Rescued Jews during the Holocaust."

250 Arnon, "Jews Rescued Jews during the Holocaust."

251 Arnon, "Jews Rescued Jews during the Holocaust."

252 Paldiel, *Saving One's Own: Jewish Rescuers during the Holocaust*, 230.

253 Lucien Lazare, "Resistance, Jewish Organizations in France: 1940-1944," Shalvi/Hyman Encyclopedia of Jewish Women, 2021, accessed 26 April, 2022, https://jwa.org/encyclopedia/article/resistance-jewish-organizations-in-france-1940-1944.

254 Lazare

255 Paldiel, *Saving One's Own: Jewish Rescuers during the Holocaust*, 242-4.

256 Lazare

257 Arnon, "Jews Rescued Jews during the Holocaust."

258 Gromb, *Jews Who Rescued Jews during the Holocaust, Research and Documentation of Jewish Rescue XV: Jewish Women*, 88-9.

259 B'nai B'rith International, "B'nai B'rith World Center and the Committee to Recognize Heroism of Jewish Rescuers during the Holocaust to Fete 20 Jewish Rescuers on Holocaust Martyrs' and Heroes' Remembrance Day," B'nai B'rith International, 2020, accessed 13 June, 2022, https://www.bnaibrith.org/press-releases/april-20th-2020.

260 Paldiel, *Saving One's Own: Jewish Rescuers during the Holocaust*, 239-42.

261 Berman

262 Pressman, 76-8.

263 Paldiel, *Saving One's Own: Jewish Rescuers during the Holocaust*, 239-42.

264 Paldiel, *Saving One's Own: Jewish Rescuers during the Holocaust*, 239-43.

265 Yad Vashem, "Names of Righteous by Country.", Allen,

266 Vivette Samuel, *Rescuing the Children: A Holocaust Memoir* (Madison, Wisconsin: The University of Wisconsin Press, 2002), 38, Paldiel, *Saving One's Own: Jewish Rescuers during the Holocaust*, 242-4.

267 Samuel, 44.

268 Samuel, 55-6.

269 Samuel, 55-6.

270 Samuel, 75.

271 Samuel, 85.

272 Paldiel, *Saving One's Own: Jewish Rescuers during the Holocaust*, 242-4.

273 Paldiel, *Saving One's Own: Jewish Rescuers during the Holocaust*, 244-6.
274 Henry, 69.
275 Paldiel, *Saving One's Own: Jewish Rescuers during the Holocaust*, 244-6.
276 Henry, 68.
277 Lazare
278 Henry, 73.
279 Henry, 73.
280 Henry, 94.
281 Lazare
282 Gromb, *Jews Who Rescued Jews during the Holocaust, Research and Documentation of Jewish Rescue XV: Jewish Women*, 71-2.
283 Lazare
284 B'nai B'rith International
285 Gromb, *Jews Who Rescued Jews during the Holocaust, Research and Documentation of Jewish Rescue XV: Jewish Women*, 122.
286 Gromb, *Jews Who Rescued Jews during the Holocaust, Research and Documentation of Jewish Rescue XV: Jewish Women*, 88-9.
287 Gromb, *Jews Who Rescued Jews during the Holocaust, Research and Documentation of Jewish Rescue XV: Jewish Women*, 88-9.
288 Arnon, "Jews Rescued Jews during the Holocaust."
289 AJPN, "Rachel Lifchitz," AJPN.org, 2022, accessed 26 July, 2022, https://www-ajpn-org.translate.goog/personne-Rachel-Lifchitz-9274.html?_x_tr_sch=http&_x_tr_sl=fr&_x_tr_tl=en&_x_tr_hl=en&_x_tr_pto=sc.
290 Coleman, 11.
291 Paldiel, *Saving One's Own: Jewish Rescuers during the Holocaust*, 232.
292 Coleman, 31.
293 Paldiel, *Saving One's Own: Jewish Rescuers during the Holocaust*, 232.
294 Arnon, "Jews Rescued Jews during the Holocaust."
295 Coleman, 33.
296 Paldiel, *Saving One's Own: Jewish Rescuers during the Holocaust*, 232.
297 Paldiel, *Saving One's Own: Jewish Rescuers during the Holocaust*, 232.
298 Coleman, 51.
299 Paldiel, *Saving One's Own: Jewish Rescuers during the Holocaust*, 232.
300 Coleman, 40.
301 Coleman, 75-6.
302 Coleman, 74.
303 Coleman, 99.
304 Coleman, 38.
305 Coleman, 39.
306 Paldiel, *Saving One's Own: Jewish Rescuers during the Holocaust*, 232.

307 Coleman, 85, 89.

308 Coleman, 142-3.

309 Gromb, *Jews Who Rescued Jews during the Holocaust, Research and Documentation of Jewish Rescue XIII: Women Who Paid with Their Lives*, 82-3.

310 Gromb, *Jews Who Rescued Jews during the Holocaust, Research and Documentation of Jewish Rescue XIII: Women Who Paid with Their Lives*, 83.C

311 USHMM, *Holocaust Encyclopedia, Kovno* (Washington, USA: United States Holocaust Memorial Museum, 2012), accessed 29 October 2023, https://encyclopedia.ushmm.org/content/en/article/kovno.

312 Gromb, *Jews Who Rescued Jews during the Holocaust, Research and Documentation of Jewish Rescue XIII: Women Who Paid with Their Lives*, 83.

313 Gromb, *Jews Who Rescued Jews during the Holocaust, Research and Documentation of Jewish Rescue XV: Jewish Women*, 92.

314 Gromb, *Jews Who Rescued Jews during the Holocaust, Research and Documentation of Jewish Rescue XIII: Women Who Paid with Their Lives*, 69-70.

315 Holocaust Education and Archive Research Team

316 Klempner, 152.

317 Gromb, *Jews Who Rescued Jews during the Holocaust, Research and Documentation of Jewish Rescue XIII: Women Who Paid with Their Lives*.

318 Holocaust Education and Archive Research Team

319 Holocaust Education and Archive Research Team

320 Cnaan Liphshiz, "Dutch-Jewish WWII Hero Betty Goudsmit-Oudkerk, Who Saved Hundreds of Children, Dies at 96," Global, 2020, accessed April 24, 2023.

321 Oorlogs Bronnen, "Rebecca Boas," Oorlogs Bronnen, 2023, accessed April 24, 2023, https://www.oorlogsbronnen.nl/tijdlijn/Rebecca-Boas/27/43140.

322 Holocaust Education and Archive Research Team

323 Gromb, *Jews Who Rescued Jews during the Holocaust, Research and Documentation of Jewish Rescue XV: Jewish Women*, 119.

324 Allan Zullo, and Mara Bovsun, *Heroes of the Holocaust: The Stories of the Rescues of Teens* (New York: Scholastic, 2005), 74-6, Zullo, and Bovsun.

325 Klempner, 15.

326 Klempner, 16.

327 Klempner, 141.

328 Rappaport, 28.

329 Gromb, *Jews Who Rescued Jews during the Holocaust, Research and Documentation of Jewish Rescue XV: Jewish Women*, 115.

330 Rappaport, 28.
331 Arnon, "Jews Rescued Jews during the Holocaust."
332 Gromb, *Jews Who Rescued Jews during the Holocaust, Research and Documentation of Jewish Rescue XV: Jewish Women*, 90.
333 Gromb, *Jews Who Rescued Jews during the Holocaust, Research and Documentation of Jewish Rescue XV: Jewish Women*, 70.
334 Gromb, *Jews Who Rescued Jews during the Holocaust, Research and Documentation of Jewish Rescue XV: Jewish Women*, 65-7.
335 Gromb, *Jews Who Rescued Jews during the Holocaust, Research and Documentation of Jewish Rescue XV: Jewish Women*, 85.
336 Paldiel, *Saving One's Own: Jewish Rescuers during the Holocaust*, 32-42.
337 Paldiel, *Saving One's Own: Jewish Rescuers during the Holocaust*, 36.
338 Paldiel, *Saving One's Own: Jewish Rescuers during the Holocaust*, 40.
339 Emanuel Ringelblum, *Ringelblumyoman Ve-Reshimot Mitkufat, Ha-Milhama [Diary and Notes from the Warsaw Ghetto: Sept 1939-December 1942]* (Jerusalem: Yad Vashem, September 1939-December 1942).
340 Rappaport, 30.
341 Gromb, *Jews Who Rescued Jews during the Holocaust, Research and Documentation of Jewish Rescue XV: Jewish Women*, 127-8.
342 Rappaport, 32.
343 Paldiel, *Saving One's Own: Jewish Rescuers during the Holocaust*, 276.
344 Decoster, 56-7.
345 Decoster, 64.
346 Decoster, 62.
347 Decoster, 62, Wolf, interview.
348 Marie Blum-Albert, *Le Recif De L'espoir: Souvenirs De Guerre Un Home D'ensfants Juifs* (Brussels: Presses interniversitaires, 1997).
349 Wolf, interview.
350 Gromb, *Jews Who Rescued Jews during the Holocaust, Research and Documentation of Jewish Rescue XV: Jewish Women*, 68.
351 Gromb, *Jews Who Rescued Jews during the Holocaust, Research and Documentation of Jewish Rescue XV: Jewish Women*, 132-3, Judy Batalion, *The Light of Days: The Untold Story of Women's Resistance Fighters in Hitler's Ghettos* (USA: William Morrow, 2020), 428.
352 Gromb, *Jews Who Rescued Jews during the Holocaust, Research and Documentation of Jewish Rescue XV: Jewish Women*, 132-3, Batalion, 428.
353 Gromb, *Jews Who Rescued Jews during the Holocaust, Research and Documentation of Jewish Rescue XV: Jewish Women*, 130.
354 Gromb, *Jews Who Rescued Jews during the Holocaust, Research and Documentation of Jewish Rescue XV: Jewish Women*, 130.

355 Batalion, 407.

356 Judith Springer, "The Quest for Rescue in Occupied Territory," in *Holocaust in Belorussia, 1941-1944*, ed. Leonid Smilovitsky, vol. 2023 F (Tel Aviv: Yiskor Book, 2000).

357 Yad Vashem, "Rescue by Jews during the Holocaust Solidarity in a Disintegrating World: Unto Every Person There Is a Name."

358 Gromb, *Jews Who Rescued Jews during the Holocaust, Research and Documentation of Jewish Rescue XV: Jewish Women*, 53.

359 Zullo, and Bovsun, 38-9.

360 Zullo, and Bovsun, 41.

361 Zullo, and Bovsun, 43.

362 Zullo, and Bovsun, 59.

363 Zullo, and Bovsun, 63.

364 Zullo, and Bovsun, 69.

365 Zullo, and Bovsun, 77.

366 Bartop, and Lakin, 120.

367 USHMM, "Holocaust Encyclopedia:Le Chambon-Sur-Lignon," United States Holocaust Memorial Museum, accessed 30 October, 2023, https://encyclopedia.ushmm.org/content/en/article/le-chambon-sur-lignon.

368 Bartop, and Lakin, 73.

369 Bartop, and Lakin, 74.

370 Bartop, and Lakin, 74.

371 Alun Palmer, "Renowned Mime Artist Marcel Marceau Saved Jewish Children from the Holocaust," The Mirror, 2020, accessed 12 January, 2021, https://www.mirror.co.uk/news/uk-news/renowned-mime-artist-marcel-marceau-22286631.

372 Palmer, Jakubowics, , Palmer

373 Paldiel, *Saving One's Own: Jewish Rescuers during the Holocaust*, 252-4.

374 Palmer

375 Palmer, Jakubowics, , Palmer

376 Palmer

377 Paldiel, *Saving One's Own: Jewish Rescuers during the Holocaust*, 218.

378 Bartop, and Lakin, 71.

379 Bartop, and Lakin, 98.

380 Lazare, Paldiel, *Saving One's Own: Jewish Rescuers during the Holocaust*, 261.

381 Bartop, and Lakin, 84-90, Lazare, Paldiel, *Saving One's Own: Jewish Rescuers during the Holocaust*, 247-51.

382 Rappaport, 44.

383 Lazare, Paldiel, *Saving One's Own: Jewish Rescuers during the Holocaust*, 247-51.

384 Rappaport, 44.

385 Myra Sklarew, "True History of an Unknown Hero of the French Jewish Resistance," Forward, 2013, accessed 19 April, 2023, https://forward.com/culture/178027/true-history-of-an-unknown-hero-of-the-french-jewi/.

386 Bartop, and Lakin, 26-8.

387 Gromb, *Jews Who Rescued Jews during the Holocaust, Research and Documentation of Jewish Rescue XV: Jewish Women*, 95.

388 Gromb, *Jews Who Rescued Jews during the Holocaust, Research and Documentation of Jewish Rescue XIII: Women Who Paid with Their Lives*, 64-5.

389 Gromb, *Jews Who Rescued Jews during the Holocaust, Research and Documentation of Jewish Rescue XV: Jewish Women*, 97-8.

390 Paldiel, *Saving One's Own: Jewish Rescuers during the Holocaust*, 246-7.

391 Arnon, "Jews Rescued Jews during the Holocaust."

392 Gromb, *Jews Who Rescued Jews during the Holocaust, Research and Documentation of Jewish Rescue XIII: Women Who Paid with Their Lives*, 84-5.

393 Margo Wolff, *The Boys of Mon Respos: Rescue Operation "Sesame" from Vichy France* (New York: Townhouse Press, 1986).

394 Bartop, and Lakin, 82.

395 *Liberation of Auschwitz: Child Survivors*, (1945), https://encyclopedia.ushmm.org/content/en/film/liberation-of-auschwitz-child-survivors.

396 Menachem Rosensaft, "My Mother Was a Jewish Heroine of the Shoah," New York Jewish Weekly, 2022, accessed 14 April, 2022, http://www.donate.jta.org/2016/12/20/default/my-mother-was-a-jewish-heroine-of-the-shoah-2.

397 Jack Werber, *Saving Children: Diary of a Buchenwald Survivor and Rescuer* (New Brunswick, USA: Transaction Publishers, 2014), 110.

398 USHMM, "Alphabetical List of Children Found at Terezin's Children's Home, Hauptstrasse 14 in April 1945. (Id: 30781)," USHMM, 1945, accessed 10 June, 2022, https://www.ushmm.org/online/hsv/source_view.php?SourceId=30781.

399 Liz Elsby, "Coping through Art - Friedl Dicker-Brandeis and the Children of Theresienstadt," Yad Vashem, 2021, accessed 21 October, 2021, https://www.yadvashem.org/articles/general/coping-through-art-brandeis-theresienstadt.html.

400 Elsby

401 Makarova

402 Makarova

403 Elsby

404 Susan Goldman Rubin, *Fireflies in the Dark: The Story of Friedl Dicker-Brandeis and the Children of Terezin* (New York: Holiday House, 2000), 41.

405 Makarova
406 Elsby
407 Linney Wix, "Aesthetic Empathy in Teaching Art to Children: The Work of Friedl Dicker-Brandeis in Terezin," *Art Therapy: Journal of the American Art Therapy Association* 26, no. 4 (2009).
408 Rubin, 25.
409 Rubin, 15.
410 Elsby
411 Rubin, 15.
412 Rubin, 29.
413 Rubin, 39.
414 Elsby
415 Rubin, 39.
416 Makarova
417 Paldiel, *Saving One's Own: Jewish Rescuers during the Holocaust,* 391-5.
418 USHMM, "Holocaust Encyclopedia: Bergen-Belsen," United States Holocaust Memorial Museum, 2023, accessed 5 November, 2023, https://encyclopedia.ushmm.org/content/en/article/bergen-belsen.
419 Roger A. Ritvo, and Diane M Plotkin, *Sisters in Sorrow: Voices of Care in the Holocaust* (College Station: Texas A & M University Press, 1998), 181.
420 Rosensaft
421 Ritvo, and Plotkin, 181-2.
422 Paldiel, "Jewish Women Rescuers of Jews," in *Women Defying Hitler*, 162.
423 Rosensaft
424 Gromb, *Jews Who Rescued Jews during the Holocaust, Research and Documentation of Jewish Rescue XV: Jewish Women*, 135.
425 Belsen Online Archive, "Luba Tryszynska - the Angel of Belsen," Belsen Online Archive, 1995, accessed 5 November, 2023, https://www.belsen.co.uk/luba-tryszynska/.
426 USHMM, "Studio Portrait of Hennie and Yehoshua Birnbaum and Their Baby Daughter Sonni," USHMM, 2014, accessed 13 June, 2022.
427 USHMM, "Studio Portrait of Hennie and Yehoshua Birnbaum and Their Baby Daughter Sonni."
428 USHMM, "Studio Portrait of Hennie and Yehoshua Birnbaum and Their Baby Daughter Sonni."
429 USHMM, "Studio Portrait of Hennie and Yehoshua Birnbaum and Their Baby Daughter Sonni."
430 USHMM, "Studio Portrait of Hennie and Yehoshua Birnbaum and Their Baby Daughter Sonni."
431 Ellen Loeb, "Liebe Trude, Liebe Rudy [Dear Trudy, Dear Rudy]," in *Sisters in Sorrow: Voices of Care in the Holocaust*, ed. Roger A Ritvo

and Diane M Plotkin (College Station, USA: Texas A&M University Press, 1998), 110.

432 Loeb, in *Sisters in Sorrow: Voices of Care in the Holocaust.* 110-1

433 Arnon, "Jews Rescued Jews during the Holocaust."

434 Gromb, *Jews Who Rescued Jews during the Holocaust, Research and Documentation of Jewish Rescue XV: Jewish Women*, 102-3.

435 Yitzchak Kerem, "Greek Women as Resistors and Rescuers in the Holocaust" (paper presented at the Heroines of the Holocaust Symposium, New York, 16 June, 2022).

436 Hemmendinger, and Krell, 169.

437 USHMM, "Plight of Jewish Children."

438 Zahra, 69.

439 Bogner, 50.

440 Mazzeo, 251.

441 Clifford, 5-6.

442 Clifford, 71.

443 Patricia Heberer, *Children during the Holocaust* (Lanham, USA: Rowman and Littlefield, 2011), xxvi.

444 Clifford, 21.

445 Clifford, 21.

446 Clifford, 63.

447 Nebenzahl, interview.

448 Clifford, 21.

449 Clifford, 96.

450 Michael Marrus, "The Vatican and the Custody of Jewish Child Survivors after the Holocaust," *Holocaust and Genocide Studies* 21, no. 3 (2007): 378-403, Chalmers, *Betrayed: Child Sex Abuse in the Holocaust*, 176-7.

451 Joseph Polak, *After the Holocaust the Bells Still Ring* (Jerusalem: Urim Publications, 2015), 102.

452 Clifford, 63-4.

453 Samuel, 139.

454 Clifford, 70.

455 Nebenzahl, interview.

456 Clifford, 92.

457 Clifford, 21.

458 Samuel, 133.

459 Diane Wolf, *Beyond Anne Frank: Hidden Children and Postwar Families in Holland* (Berkeley, California: University of California Press, 2007), 4.

460 Clifford, 101-9.

461 Clifford, 97.

462 Clifford, 98.

463 Clifford, 119.

464 Clifford, 62.

465 Samuel, 133.
466 Zahra, 74-5.
467 Zahra.
468 Clifford, 111.
469 Clifford, 81-88.
470 Clifford, 81-88.
471 Pressman, 227.
472 Clifford, 65.
473 Clifford, 62.
474 Clifford, 63-4.
475 Clifford, 65.
476 Zahra, 8.
477 Zahra, 21-2.
478 Clifford, 62.
479 Bogner, 223.
480 Clifford, 68-9.
481 Bogner, 199, 261.
482 Bogner, 199.
483 Zahra.
484 Bogner, 262.
485 Bogner, 289.
486 Bogner, 268.
487 Bogner, 257-8.
488 Bogner, 262.
489 Nebenzahl, interview.
490 Bogner, 166-9.
491 Bogner, 258.
492 Bogner, 279.
493 Bogner, 148.
494 Bogner, 285.
495 Bogner, 180.
496 Bogner, 180.
497 Bogner, 180.
498 Bogner, 180.
499 Beverley Chalmers, *Child Sex Abuse: Power, Profit, Perversion* (UK: Grosvenor House Publishers 2022), *Philomena*, (20th Century Fox 2013), Martin Sixsmith, *Philomena: A Mother, Her Son and a Fifty-Year Search* (London: Pan Books, 2010).
500 David I Kertzer, *The Kidnapping of Edgardo Mortara* (New York: Vintage Books, 1998), Zahra, 24-5.
501 Zahra, 138-43.
502 Bogner, 178.
503 Bogner, 178-9.

504 Bogner, 286.

505 Bogner, 278.

506 Bogner, 287.

507 Bogner, 163.

508 Bogner, 210-8.

509 Norton, 64,83.

510 Bogner, 174.

511 R D Rosen, *Such Good Girls: The Journey of the Holocaust's Hidden Child Survivors* (New York: Harper Perenial, 2014), 204-5.

512 Yaakov Ariel, "Turning to Christianity: Hiding Jews and Conversions during the Holocaust," in *Hiding, Sheltering, and Borrowing Identities: Avenues of Rescue during the Holocaust*, ed. Dan Michman (Jerusalem: Yad Vashem, 2017), 331.

513 Rebecca Benhamon, "Jewish Children Hidden Twice over by the Church," Times of Israel, 2013, accessed 15 May, 2019, www.timesofisrael.com/jewish-children-hidden-twice-over-by-the-church.

514 Clifford, 63.

515 Clifford, 63.

516 Clifford, 66.

517 Clifford, 67-8.

518 Nebenzahl, interview.

519 Clifford, 68-9.

520 Nebenzahl, interview.

521 Momentum, "Recha Sternbuch: A Wartime Story of Selflessness and Courage," Momentum, 2021, accessed 29 October, 2021, https://momentumunlimited.org/wov/recha-sternbuch-a-wartime-story-of-selflessness-and-courage/.

522 Bogner, 260.

523 Bogner, 309-10.

524 Gromb, *Jews Who Rescued Jews during the Holocaust, Research and Documentation of Jewish Rescue XV: Jewish Women*, 62-3.

525 Gromb, *Jews Who Rescued Jews during the Holocaust, Research and Documentation of Jewish Rescue XV: Jewish Women*, 48.

526 Gromb, *Jews Who Rescued Jews during the Holocaust, Research and Documentation of Jewish Rescue XV: Jewish Women*, 55.

527 Gromb, *Jews Who Rescued Jews during the Holocaust, Research and Documentation of Jewish Rescue XV: Jewish Women*, 74-5.

528 Bogner, 223, 92.

529 Beit Lohamei Haghetaot, ""The Koordynacja": The Zionist Koordinatsia for the Redemption of Children in Poland," Beit Lohamei Haghetaot / Ghetto Fighters' House, 2002, accessed 9 February, 2024, https://portal.ehri-project.eu/units/il-002806-kor_col.

530 Beit Lohamei Haghetaot

531 Bogner, 293.
532 Sandra Rosenfeld, "The Difficulties Involved in the Rescue of Children by Non-Jews - before and after Liberation," The International School for Holocaust Studies, Yad Vashem, 2018, accessed 9 July 2018, 2018, www.yadvashem.org/yv/en/education/newsletter/33/difficulties_involved.asp, Bogner, 293-4.
533 Rosenfeld, Bogner, 294.
534 Bogner, 294, Chalmers, *Betrayed: Child Sex Abuse in the Holocaust*, 178, Rosenfeld, Miri Merin-Freilich, "Sarah Shner-Nishmit," Jewish Women's Archive, 2009, accessed 9 February, 2021, https://jwa.org/encyclopedia/article/shner-nishmit-sarah.
535 Chalmers, *Betrayed: Child Sex Abuse in the Holocaust*, 178.
536 Bogner, 298.
537 Chalmers, *Betrayed: Child Sex Abuse in the Holocaust*, 157-60.
538 Anne Fox, and Eva Abraham-Podietz, *Ten Thousand Children: True Stories Told by Children Who Escaped the Holocaust on the Kindertransport* (New Jersey: Behrman House, Inc, 1999), 108.
539 Norton, 317-24.
540 Norton, 266.
541 Bogner, 271-2.
542 Bogner, 258, 337.
543 Irena Steinfeldt, "Rescuers-Rescued Relations - What Can and Cannot Be Found in the Files of the Righteous among Nations," in *Hiding, Sheltering, and Borrowing Identities: Avenues of Rescue during the Holocaust*, ed. Dan Michman (Jerusalem: Yad Vashem, 2017), 64.
544 Bogner, 276.
545 Nebenzahl, interview.
546 *Interview with Rabbi Alex Rosen, Part 1*, (2019 23 June), https://youtu.be/V8NR5Z0u_h8
547 Gruber, 3.
548 Medoff, 57-61.
549 Medoff, 23-7.
550 Gruber, 16-27.
551 Medoff, 64-66, Gruber, 25.
552 Gruber, 25-6.
553 Gruber, 79.
554 Gruber, 26-7.
555 Medoff, 263.
556 Gruber.
557 Lena Kuchler-Silberman, *My 100 Children* (London: Pan Books, 1961), 78.
558 Kuchler-Silberman, 75-6.
559 Kuchler-Silberman, 111.

560 Kuchler-Silberman, 116-7.
561 Rosen, 00-51-20.
562 Kuchler-Silberman, 88-89.
563 Kuchler-Silberman, 89-90.
564 Kuchler-Silberman, 106.
565 Kuchler-Silberman, 133.
566 Kuchler-Silberman, 121-5.
567 Kuchler-Silberman, 125.
568 Kuchler-Silberman, 129.
569 Kuchler-Silberman, 138.
570 Kuchler-Silberman, 145.
571 Kuchler-Silberman, 177-81.
572 Kuchler-Silberman, 185.
573 Kuchler-Silberman, 201.
574 Kuchler-Silberman, 202-3.
575 Coleman, 146.
576 Coleman, 146.
577 Coleman, 146-7.
578 Coleman, 148-9.
579 Coleman, 168-9.
580 Coleman, 168-9.
581 Coleman, 170.
582 Coleman, 174.
583 Coleman, 195.
584 Paldiel, *Saving One's Own: Jewish Rescuers during the Holocaust*, 236.
585 Coleman, 203.
586 Coleman, 208-10.
587 Zahra, 97.
588 Derek Taylor, *Solomon Schonfeld: A Purpose in Life* (London: Valentine Mitchell, 2009), 3.
589 Imperial War Museum, "Solomon Schonfeld, His Page in History," Imperial War Museum, 2021, accessed 15 January, 2021, https://www.iwm.org.uk/collections/item/object/1500103021, David Kranzler, *Holocaust Hero: Solomon Schonfeld* (Jersey City, New Jersey: KTAV Publishing House, 2004), 11.
590 Imperial War Museum, Kranzler, 10.
591 Imperial War Museum, Kranzler, 18.
592 Bogner, 253.
593 Tim Lewis, "From Nazi Camps to the Lake District: The Story of the Windermere Children," The Guardian, 2021, accessed 12 January, 2021, https://www.theguardian.com/tv-and-radio/2020/jan/05/windermere-children-arek-hersh-survivor-bbc-drama.
594 Lewis

595 Hemmendinger, and Krell, 27.

596 Zahra, 96.

597 Hemmendinger, and Krell, 55.

598 Henry, 169.

599 Pressman, 253.

600 Ingrid Lewis, *Women in European Holocaust Films: Perpetrators, Victims and Resisters* (Switzerland: Palgrave Macmillan, 2017), 235.

601 Coleman, 157.

602 Lewis, 236.

603 Lewis, 244.

604 Lewis, 245.

605 Lewis, 261-2.

606 Lewis, 261-2.

607 Harrison,

608 Anna Bikont, *The Crime and the Silence: Confronting the Massacre of Jews in Wartime Jedwabne* (New York: Farrar, Straus and giroux, 2004), Bikont, *Sendlerowa. W Ukryciu ('Sendler: In Hiding')17,*.

609 Brade, and Holmes 27.

610 *Lena: My 100 Children*, (Moonlight Productions, 1987).

611 Ira Zornberg, *Jews, Quakers and the Holocaust: The Struggle to Save the Lives of Twenty-Thousand Children* (USA: Unspecified, 2016), 305-6.

612 Blair Kramer, "Superman," Jewish Virtual Library, 2023, accessed 20 April, 2023, https://www.jewishvirtuallibrary.org/superman.

613 Primo Levi, *The Drowned and the Saved* (New York: Vintage International, 1989).

614 Lawrence Langer, *Versions of Survival: The Holocaust and the Human Spirit* (New York: State University of New York Press, 1982), 72.

615 Mazzeo, 140.

616 Chalmers, *Birth, Sex and Abuse: Women's Voices under Nazi Rule*, 90.

617 Szwajger.

618 Mercedes García-Arenal, Yonatan Glazer-Eytan, and Books Brill Online, *Forced Conversion in Christianity, Judaism and Islam: Coercion and Faith in Premodern Iberia and Beyond*, 1 ed., vol. 164, vol. Book, Whole (Leiden;Boston;: Brill, 2020), 1-13. https://go.exlibris.link/NWz6Fqzb.

619 García-Arenal, Glazer-Eytan, and Brill Online, 17-23.

620 Yad Vashem, "Where Was God during the Holocaust?," Yad Vashem, 2023, accessed 22 April, 2023, https://www.yadvashem.org/education/educational-materials/center-question/q7.html.

621 Father Patrick Desbois, *The Holocaust by Bullets:A Priest's Journey to Uncover the Truth Behind the Murder of 1.5 Million Jews* (New York: Palgrave, Macmillan, 2008), 67.

622 Chalmers, *Betrayed: Child Sex Abuse in the Holocaust*, 212.

623 Dov Lederman, *These Children Are Mine: A Story of Rescue and Survival* (Jerusalem: Feldheim, 2002).
624 Offer, 268-9.
625 Meed, 111-2.
626 Bikont, *Sendlerowa. W Ukryciu ('Sendler: In Hiding')17,.*
627 Jockel, 14-7.
628 Meed, 111.
629 Ciesielska.
630 Paldiel, *Saving One's Own: Jewish Rescuers during the Holocaust*, 274.
631 Bikont, *Sendlerowa. W Ukryciu ('Sendler: In Hiding')17,.*
632 Bikont, *Sendlerowa. W Ukryciu ('Sendler: In Hiding')17,.*
633 Szwajger.
634 Saidel
635 Ahavah
636 Paldiel, *Saving One's Own: Jewish Rescuers during the Holocaust*, 3-11.
637 Ritvo, and Plotkin, 181-2.
638 Pressman.
639 Paldiel, *Saving One's Own: Jewish Rescuers during the Holocaust*, 3-11.
640 Zucker.
641 Danty
642 Hájková, *Marie Schmolka, Who Inspired the Kindertransport.*
643 Arnon, "Jews Rescued Jews during the Holocaust."
644 Gromb, *Jews Who Rescued Jews during the Holocaust, Research and Documentation of Jewish Rescue XV: Jewish Women*, 65-7.
645 Gromb, *Jews Who Rescued Jews during the Holocaust, Research and Documentation of Jewish Rescue XV: Jewish Women*, 57, Paldiel, *Saving One's Own: Jewish Rescuers during the Holocaust*, 32-42.
646 Decoster.
647 Bronnen
648 Gromb, *Jews Who Rescued Jews during the Holocaust, Research and Documentation of Jewish Rescue XV: Jewish Women*, 68.
649 Gromb, *Jews Who Rescued Jews during the Holocaust, Research and Documentation of Jewish Rescue XV: Jewish Women*, 70.
650 Gromb, *Jews Who Rescued Jews during the Holocaust, Research and Documentation of Jewish Rescue XV: Jewish Women*, 71-2.
651 Holocaust Education and Archive Research Team
652 Holocaust Education and Archive Research Team
653 Paldiel, *Saving One's Own: Jewish Rescuers during the Holocaust*, 244-6.
654 Arnon, "Jews Rescued Jews during the Holocaust."
655 Lazare
656 Gromb, *Jews Who Rescued Jews during the Holocaust, Research and Documentation of Jewish Rescue XIII: Women Who Paid with Their Lives*, 88.

657 Rappaport, 32.

658 B'nai B'rith International

659 Gromb, *Jews Who Rescued Jews during the Holocaust, Research and Documentation of Jewish Rescue XV: Jewish Women*, 88-9.

660 Zullo, and Bovsun, 74-6.

661 Rappaport, 30.

662 Gromb, *Jews Who Rescued Jews during the Holocaust, Research and Documentation of Jewish Rescue XIII: Women Who Paid with Their Lives*, 83.

663 Gromb, *Jews Who Rescued Jews during the Holocaust, Research and Documentation of Jewish Rescue XIII: Women Who Paid with Their Lives*, 83.

664 Holocaust Education and Archive Research Team

665 Gromb, *Jews Who Rescued Jews during the Holocaust, Research and Documentation of Jewish Rescue XIII: Women Who Paid with Their Lives*, 83.

666 Gromb, *Jews Who Rescued Jews during the Holocaust, Research and Documentation of Jewish Rescue XV: Jewish Women*, 90.

667 Gromb, *Jews Who Rescued Jews during the Holocaust, Research and Documentation of Jewish Rescue XV: Jewish Women*, 92.

668 Gromb, *Jews Who Rescued Jews during the Holocaust, Research and Documentation of Jewish Rescue XIII: Women Who Paid with Their Lives*, 83.

669 Gromb, *Jews Who Rescued Jews during the Holocaust, Research and Documentation of Jewish Rescue XIII: Women Who Paid with Their Lives*, 83.

670 AJPN

671 Gromb, *Jews Who Rescued Jews during the Holocaust, Research and Documentation of Jewish Rescue XIII: Women Who Paid with Their Lives*, 83.

672 Gromb, *Jews Who Rescued Jews during the Holocaust, Research and Documentation of Jewish Rescue XIII: Women Who Paid with Their Lives*, 69-70.

673 Liphshiz

674 Holocaust Education and Archive Research Team

675 Gromb, *Jews Who Rescued Jews during the Holocaust, Research and Documentation of Jewish Rescue XIII: Women Who Paid with Their Lives*, 83.

676 Batalion, 407.

677 Coleman.

678 Gromb, *Jews Who Rescued Jews during the Holocaust, Research and Documentation of Jewish Rescue XIII: Women Who Paid with Their Lives*, 82-3.

679 Arnon, "Jews Rescued Jews during the Holocaust."

680 Paldiel, *Saving One's Own: Jewish Rescuers during the Holocaust*, 242-4.

681 Gromb, *Jews Who Rescued Jews during the Holocaust, Research and Documentation of Jewish Rescue XV: Jewish Women*, 119.

682 Paldiel, *Saving One's Own: Jewish Rescuers during the Holocaust*, 239-42.

683 Gromb, *Jews Who Rescued Jews during the Holocaust, Research and Documentation of Jewish Rescue XIII: Women Who Paid with Their Lives*, 83.

684 Lazare

685 Gromb, *Jews Who Rescued Jews during the Holocaust, Research and Documentation of Jewish Rescue XV: Jewish Women*, 127-8.

686 Decoster.

687 Gromb, *Jews Who Rescued Jews during the Holocaust, Research and Documentation of Jewish Rescue XV: Jewish Women*, 130.

688 Coleman, 39.

689 Rappaport, 28.

690 Coleman, 38.

691 Rappaport, 32.

692 Gromb, *Jews Who Rescued Jews during the Holocaust, Research and Documentation of Jewish Rescue XV: Jewish Women*, 132-3, Batalion, 428.

693 Gromb, *Jews Who Rescued Jews during the Holocaust, Research and Documentation of Jewish Rescue XV: Jewish Women*, 53.

694 Zullo, and Bovsun, 43.

695 Springer, in *Holocaust in Belorussia, 1941-1944*.

696 Springer, in *Holocaust in Belorussia, 1941-1944*.

697 Springer, in *Holocaust in Belorussia, 1941-1944*.

698 Springer, in *Holocaust in Belorussia, 1941-1944*.

699 Zullo, and Bovsun, 59.

700 Lazare, Paldiel, *Saving One's Own: Jewish Rescuers during the Holocaust*, 247-51.

701 Paldiel, *Saving One's Own: Jewish Rescuers during the Holocaust*, 246-7.

702 Paldiel, *Saving One's Own: Jewish Rescuers during the Holocaust*, 246-7.

703 Gromb, *Jews Who Rescued Jews during the Holocaust, Research and Documentation of Jewish Rescue XIII: Women Who Paid with Their Lives*, 64-5.

704 Gromb, *Jews Who Rescued Jews during the Holocaust, Research and Documentation of Jewish Rescue XIII: Women Who Paid with Their Lives*, 64-5.

705 Gromb, *Jews Who Rescued Jews during the Holocaust, Research and Documentation of Jewish Rescue XV: Jewish Women*, 95.
706 Gromb, *Jews Who Rescued Jews during the Holocaust, Research and Documentation of Jewish Rescue XV: Jewish Women*, 97-8.
707 Lazare, Paldiel, *Saving One's Own: Jewish Rescuers during the Holocaust*, 261.
708 Gromb, *Jews Who Rescued Jews during the Holocaust, Research and Documentation of Jewish Rescue XIII: Women Who Paid with Their Lives*, 84-5.
709 Arnon, "Jews Rescued Jews during the Holocaust."
710 Sklarew
711 Bartop, and Lakin, 82.
712 Wolff.
713 USHMM, "Studio Portrait of Hennie and Yehoshua Birnbaum and Their Baby Daughter Sonni."
714 Makarova
715 Belsen Online Archive
716 Loeb, in *Sisters in Sorrow: Voices of Care in the Holocaust*, 110.
717 Arnon, "Jews Rescued Jews during the Holocaust."
718 Rosensaft
719 Kerem.
720 Belsen Online Archive
721 Gromb, *Jews Who Rescued Jews during the Holocaust, Research and Documentation of Jewish Rescue XV: Jewish Women*, 48.
722 Gromb, *Jews Who Rescued Jews during the Holocaust, Research and Documentation of Jewish Rescue XV: Jewish Women*, 55.
723 Gromb, *Jews Who Rescued Jews during the Holocaust, Research and Documentation of Jewish Rescue XV: Jewish Women*, 76.
724 Clifford, 111.
725 Bogner, 260.
726 Gruber.
727 Gromb, *Jews Who Rescued Jews during the Holocaust, Research and Documentation of Jewish Rescue XV: Jewish Women*, 74-5.
728 Bogner, 309-10.
729 Bogner, 223, 92.
730 Lederman.
731 Kuchler-Silberman.

Bibliography

Ahavah. "Pleasure to Meet You." Ahavah. 2023. Accessed April 26, 2023. https://ahava-v.org.il/en/nice-to-meet-you/.

AJPN. "Rachel Lifchitz." AJPN.org. 2022. Accessed 26 July, 2022. https://www-ajpn-org.translate.goog/personne-Rachel-Lifchitz-9274.html?_x_tr_sch=http&_x_tr_sl=fr&_x_tr_tl=en&_x_tr_hl=en&_x_tr_pto=sc.

Allen, Simmy. "Family of Holocaust Survivor and Righteous among the Nations from Poland Visited Yad Vashem." *Yad Vashem*, 2 June, 2022.

Ariel, Yaakov. "Turning to Christianity: Hiding Jews and Conversions during the Holocaust." In *Hiding, Sheltering, and Borrowing Identities: Avenues of Rescue during the Holocaust*. Edited by Dan Michman. Jerusalem: Yad Vashem, 2017.

Arnon, Chana. "Jewish Rescuers Who Lived in Israel after the Shoah." World Federation of Jewish Child Survivors of the Holocaust & Descendants. 2021. Accessed 7 May, 2021. https://www.holocaustchild.org/jews-rescued-jews/jewish-rescuers-living-in-israel/.

Arnon, Chana. "Jews Rescued Jews during the Holocaust." Committee on Jews Rescued Jews. 2004. Accessed 5 May, 2021. https://www.holocaustchild.org/jews-rescued-jews/presentation-given-at-yad-vashem-conference-june-2004/.

B'nai B'rith International. "B'nai B'rith World Center and the Committee to Recognize Heroism of Jewish Rescuers during the Holocaust to Fete 20 Jewish Rescuers on Holocaust Martyrs' and Heroes' Remembrance Day." B'nai B'rith International. 2020. Accessed 13 June, 2022. https://www.bnaibrith.org/press-releases/april-20th-2020.

B'rith, B'nai. "B'nai B'rith World Center and Keren Kayemeth Leisrael Hold Unique Holocaust Day Ceremony Marking the Heroism of Jewish Rescuers." Centre Stage. 2016. Accessed 22 June, 2021.

Bartop, Paul, and Samantha Lakin. *Heroines of Vichy France: Rescuing French Jews during the Holocaust.* California, USA: Praeger, 2019.

Batalion, Judy. *The Light of Days: The Untold Story of Women's Resistance Fighters in Hitler's Ghettos.* USA: William Morrow, 2020.

Beit Lohamei Haghetaot. ""The Koordynacja": The Zionist Koordinatsia for the Redemption of Children in Poland." Beit Lohamei Haghetaot / Ghetto Fighters' House. 2002. Accessed 9 February, 2024. https://portal.ehri-project.eu/units/il-002806-kor_col.

Belsen Online Archive. "Luba Tryszynska - the Angel of Belsen." Belsen Online Archive. 1995. Accessed 5 November, 2023. https://www.belsen.co.uk/luba-tryszynska/.

Benhamon, Rebecca. "Jewish Children Hidden Twice over by the Church." Times of Israel. 2013. Accessed 15 May, 2019. www.timesofisrael.com/jewish-children-hidden-twice-over-by-the-church.

Berman, Kathryn. "Hidden Children in France during the Holocaust." Yad Vashem. 2023. Accessed 27 October, 2023. https://www.yadvashem.org/articles/general/hidden-children.html.

Bikont, Anna. *The Crime and the Silence: Confronting the Massacre of Jews in Wartime Jedwabne.* New York: Farrar, Straus and giroux, 2004.

Bikont, Anna. "Knowledge under Siege: Irena Sendler in Hiding." 2023. https://www.youtube.com/watch?v=yyqFiuWQLHQ.

Bikont, Anna. *Sendlerowa. W Ukryciu ('Sendler: In Hiding')17,.* Wołowiec Wydawnictwo Czarne, 2017.

Blum-Albert, Marie. *Le Recif De L'espoir: Souvenirs De Guerre Un Home D'ensfants Juifs.* Brussels: Presses interniversitaires, 1997.

Bogner, Nahum. *At the Mercy of Strangers: The Rescue of Jewish Children with Assumed Identities in Poland.* Jerusalem: Yad Vashem, 2009.

Brade, Laura E., and Rose Holmes. "Troublesome Sainthood: Nicholas Winton and the Contested History of Child Rescue in Prague,

1938–1940." *History & Memory* 29, no. 1 (2017): 3-40. https://marieschmolka.files.wordpress.com/2019/03/brade-holmes.pdf.

Bronnen, Oorlogs. "Rebecca Boas." Oorlogs Bronnen. 2023. Accessed April 24, 2023. https://www.oorlogsbronnen.nl/tijdlijn/Rebecca-Boas/27/43140.

Burg, Avraham. "The Righteous yet Unrecognized: The Muslims Who Saved Jewish Children during WWII." Haaretz. 2022. Accessed 28 March, 2022.

Centre, Simon Wiesenthal. *Marion Pritchard: Courage and Valor*. Vimeo, 2021. 6 mins 50 secs. C:\Users\Bev\AppData\Local\Microsoft\Windows\INetCache\Content.Outlook\70K2E5L6\email.mht.

Chalmers, Beverley. *Betrayed: Child Sex Abuse in the Holocaust*. UK: Grosvenor House Publishers, 2020.

Chalmers, Beverley. *Birth, Sex and Abuse: Women's Voices under Nazi Rule*. UK: Grosvenor House Publishers, 2015.

Chalmers, Beverley. *Child Sex Abuse: Power, Profit, Perversion*. UK: Grosvenor House Publishers 2022.

Ciesielska, Maria. "To Care for Children on Their Way and Beyond... History of Female Doctors from the Warsaw Ghetto Who Stood by Their Patients until the Very End." Paper presented at the Heroines of the Holocaust: Nurses and Doctors as Resistors in Genocide Conference, New York 2023.

Clifford, Rebecca. *Survivors: Children's Lives after the Holocaust*. New Haven, USA: Yale University Press, 2020.

Coleman, Fred. *The Marcel Network: How One French Couple Saved 527 Children from the Holocaust*. Washington: Potomac Books, 2013.

Danty, Michael. "Cecelia Razovsky." One Thousand Children. YIVO Institute for Jewish Research. 2021. Accessed 28 October, 2021. https://onethousandchildren.yivo.org/Cecilia-Razovsky.

Decoster, Charlotte. "Jewish Hidden Children in Belgium during the Holocaust: A Comparative Study of Their Hiding Places at Christian Establishments, Private Families and Jewish Orphanages." University of North Texas, 2006.

Dekel, Mikhal. *Tehran Children: A Holocaust Refugee Odyssey*. New York: WW Noton and Co., 2019.

Desbois, Father Patrick. *The Holocaust by Bullets:A Priest's Journey to Uncover the Truth Behind the Murder of 1.5 Million Jews*. New York: Palgrave, Macmillan, 2008.

Dwork, Deborah. *Children with a Star: Jewish Youth in Nazi Europe*. New Haven: Yale University Press, 1991.

Elsby, Liz. "Coping through Art - Friedl Dicker-Brandeis and the Children of Theresienstadt." Yad Vashem. 2021. Accessed 21 October, 2021. https://www.yadvashem.org/articles/general/coping-through-art-brandeis-theresienstadt.html.

Finn, Clodagh. *A Time to Risk All*. Dublin, Ireland: Gill Books, 2017.

Fogelman, Eva. *Conscience and Courage: The Rescuers of Jews during the Holocaust*. New York: Doubleday, 1994.

Fox, Anne, and Eva Abraham-Podietz. *Ten Thousand Children: True Stories Told by Children Who Escaped the Holocaust on the Kindertransport*. New Jersey: Behrman House, Inc, 1999.

Frears, Stephen. *Philomena*. 20th Century Fox 2013. 90 mins.

Friedman, Henry. *I'm No Hero: Journeys of a Holocaust Survivor*. Seattle, USA: University of Washington Press, 1999.

Gafny, Emunah Nachamy. *Dividing Hearts: The Removal of Jewish Children from Gentile Families in Poland in the Immediate Post Holocaust Years*. Jerusalem: Yad Vashem, 2009.

García-Arenal, Mercedes, Yonatan Glazer-Eytan, and Books Brill Online. *Forced Conversion in Christianity, Judaism and Islam: Coercion and Faith in Premodern Iberia and Beyond*. Vol. 164. 1 ed., vol. Book, Whole. Leiden;Boston;: Brill, 2020. https://go.exlibris.link/NWz6Fqzb.

Gilbert, Martin. *The Boys: The Story of 732 Young Concentration Camp Survivors*. New York: Henry Holt and Company, 1996.

Gillis-Carlebach, Miriam. *Each Child Is My Only One: Lotte Carlebach-Preuss, the Portrait of a Mother and Rabbi's Wife*. New York: Peter Lang, 2014.

Glassman, Les. *Interview with Rabbi Alex Rosen, Part 1*. 2019 23 June. https://youtu.be/V8NR5Z0u_h8

Goodman, Ernest, and Melissa Hacker. "Kindertransport." Encyclopaedia Britannica. 2020. Accessed 19 June, 2021. https://www.britannica.com/print/article/1983860.

Gromb, Moshe. *Jews Who Rescued Jews during the Holocaust, Research and Documentation of Jewish Rescue XIII: Women Who Paid with Their Lives*. Israel: Nadav Books, 2021.

Gromb, Moshe. *Jews Who Rescued Jews during the Holocaust, Research and Documentation of Jewish Rescue XV: Jewish Women*. Israel: Nadav Books, 2021.

Gruber, Ruth. *Haven: The Dramatic Story of 1,000 World War II Refugees and How They Came to America*. New York: Three Rivers Press, 2000.

Gushee, David. *The Righteous Gentiles of the Holocaust: A Christian Interpretation*. Minneapolis, Minnesota: Fortress Press, 1994.

Hájková, Anna. "Marie Schmolka Society." 2022. Accessed June 10, 2022. https://marieschmolka.org/.

Hájková, Anna. *Marie Schmolka, Who Inspired the Kindertransport*. UK: Jewish Voice for Labour, 2017. https://www.jewishvoiceforlabour. org.uk/article/marie-schmolka-inspired-kindertransport/.

Harris, Mark Jonathan, and Deborah Oppenheimer. *Into the Arms of Strangers: Stories of the Kindertransport*. London: Bloomsbury Publishing, 2000.

Harrison, John Kent. *The Courageous Heart of Irena Sendler*. Hallmark Hall of Fame Productions, 2009.

Heberer, Patricia. *Children during the Holocaust*. Lanham, USA: Rowman and Littlefield, 2011.

Heifetz, Julie. *Too Young to Remember*. Detroit: Wayne State University Press, 1989.

Hemmendinger, Judith, and Robert Krell. *The Children of Buchenwald: Child Survivors of the Holocaust and Their Post-War Lives*. Jerusalem: Geffen, 2000.

Henry, Patrick. *We Only Know Men*. Washington, DC: The Catholic University of America Press, 2007.

Herscho, Tsila, Patrick Henry, Mordecai Paldiel, Dalia Ofer, and Raymond Sun. "All Our Brothers and Sisters: Jews Saving Jews in the Holocaust." Israel, 2022.

Hilberg, Raul. *Perpetrators Victims Bystanders: The Jewish Catastrophe 1933-1945*. New York: Harper Collins Publishers, 1992.

Hogan, David, and David Aretha, eds., *The Holocaust Chronicle*. Illinois: Publications International, 2001.

Holocaust Education and Archive Research Team. "The Story of Walter Suskind." Holocaust Education and Archive Research Team. 2012. Accessed 9 February, 2021. http://www.holocaustresearchproject.org/survivor/suskind.html.

Imperial War Museum. "Solomon Schonfeld, His Page in History." Imperial War Museum. 2021. Accessed 15 January, 2021. https://www.iwm.org.uk/collections/item/object/1500103021.

Jakubowics, Jonathan. *Resistance*. Shout Factory, 2019. 121 mins.

Jockel, Helena. *We Sang in Hushed Voices*. Canada: The Azrieli Foundation, 2014.

Keneally, Thomas. *Schindler's List*. New York: Simon and Schuster, 1982.

Kerem, Yitzchak. "Greek Women as Resistors and Rescuers in the Holocaust." Paper presented at the Heroines of the Holocaust Symposium, New York, 16 June, 2022.

Kertzer, David I. *The Kidnapping of Edgardo Mortara*. New York: Vintage Books, 1998.

Klempner, Mark. *The Heart Has Reasons: Dutch Rescuers of Jewish Children during the Holocaust*. Amsterdam: Night Stand Books, 2012.

Klug, Etien G, Linda L Dahlberg, James A Merry, Anthony B Zwi, and Rafael Lozano. "Child Abuse and Neglect by Parents and Other Caregivers." In *World Report on Violence and Health*. Geneva: World Health Organization, 2002.

Kramer, Blair. "Superman." Jewish Virtual Library. 2023. Accessed 20 April, 2023. https://www.jewishvirtuallibrary.org/superman.

Kranzler, David. *Holocaust Hero: Solomon Schonfeld*. Jersey City, New Jersey: KTAV Publishing House, 2004.

Kuchler-Silberman, Lena. *My 100 Children*. London: Pan Books, 1961.

Lang, Berel. *The Future of the Holocaust: Between History and Memory*. Ithaca, New York: Cornell University Press, 1999.

Langer, Lawrence. *Versions of Survival: The Holocaust and the Human Spirit* New York: State University of New York Press, 1982.

Lazare, Lucien. "Resistance, Jewish Organizations in France: 1940-1944." Shalvi/Hyman Encyclopedia of Jewish Women. 2021. Accessed 26 April, 2022. https://jwa.org/encyclopedia/article/resistance-jewish-organizations-in-france-1940-1944.

Lederman, Dov. *These Children Are Mine: A Story of Rescue and Survival* Jerusalem: Feldheim, 2002.

Levi, Primo. *The Drowned and the Saved*. New York: Vintage International, 1989.

Lewis, Ingrid. *Women in European Holocaust Films: Perpetrators, Victims and Resisters*. Switzerland: Palgrave Macmillan, 2017.

Lewis, Tim. "From Nazi Camps to the Lake District: The Story of the Windermere Children." The Guardian. 2021. Accessed 12 January, 2021. https://www.theguardian.com/tv-and-radio/2020/jan/05/windermere-children-arek-hersh-survivor-bbc-drama.

Liphshiz, Cnaan. "Dutch-Jewish WWII Hero Betty Goudsmit-Oudkerk, Who Saved Hundreds of Children, Dies at 96." Global. 2020. Accessed April 24, 2023.

Loeb, Ellen. "Liebe Trude, Liebe Rudy [Dear Trudy, Dear Rudy]." In *Sisters in Sorrow: Voices of Care in the Holocaust*. Edited by Roger A Ritvo and Diane M Plotkin. College Station, USA: Texas A&M University Press, 1998.

Loftis, Larry. *The Watchmaker's Daughter*. New York: Harper Collins, 2023.

Makarova, Elena. "Friedl Dicker-Brandies 1898-1944." Jewish Women's Archive. 1999. Accessed 21 October, 2021. https://jwa.org/encyclopedia/article/dicker-brandeis-friedl.

March of the Living. "Uncovering Holocaust Perpetrators Where Few Have Looked." March of the Living. 2016. https://www.motl.org/uncovering-holocaust-perpetrators-where-few-have-looked/.

Marks, Jane. *The Hidden Children: The Secret Survivors of the Holocaust*. Great Britain: Bantam Books, 1995.

Marrus, Michael. "The Vatican and the Custody of Jewish Child Survivors after the Holocaust." *Holocaust and Genocide Studies* 21, no. 3 (2007): 378-403.

Mazzeo, Tilar. *Irena's Children: A True Story of Courage*. New York: Gallery Books, 2016.

Medoff, Rafael. *America and the Holocaust: A Documentary History*. Lincoln, Nebraska: University of Nebraska Press, 2022.

Meed, Vladka. *On Both Sides of the Wall*. Washington: Holocaust Library, 1993.

Merin-Freilich, Miri. "Sarah Shner-Nishmit." Jewish Women's Archive. 2009. Accessed 9 February, 2021. https://jwa.org/encyclopedia/article/shner-nishmit-sarah.

Michman, Dan, ed., *Hiding, Sheltering, and Borrowing Identities: Avenues of Rescue during the Holocaust*. Jerusalem: Yad Vashem, 2017.

Miller, Joe. "Rescuing Jewish Children: The Story of Lois Gunden." MCC. 2020. Accessed 12 January, 2021. https://mcccanada.ca/centennial/100-stories/rescuing-jewish-children-story-lois-gunden.

Momentum. "Recha Sternbuch: A Wartime Story of Selflessness and Courage." Momentum. 2021. Accessed 29 October, 2021. https://momentumunlimited.org/wov/recha-sternbuch-a-wartime-story-of-selflessness-and-courage/.

Nadeau, Barbie Latza. "Catholic Church to Beatify Polish Family, Including Newborn Baby, Killed by Nazis for Hiding Jews." CNN. 2023. Accessed 8 September, 2023. https://www.cnn.com/2023/09/06/world/ulma-family-beatify-nazis-intl-scli.

National Holocaust Centre and Museum. "Kindertransport." Unknown. Accessed 11 May 2022. https://www.holocaust.org.uk/kindertransport-overview.

Nebenzahl, Leah. "The Miraculous Story Hidden Child in a Monastary and with a Polish Family, Leah Nebenzahl." interview by Les Glassman. *Youtube*. February 14, 2023. Israel. https:/youtu.be/cMOKLZ4cHjk.

Nelson, Anne. *Suzanne's Children: A Daring Rescue in Nazi Paris*. New York: Simon and Schuster, 2017.

Nicholas, Lynn H. *Cruel World: The Children of Europe in the Nazi Web*. New York: Vintage Books, 2006.

Norton, Jennifer Craig-. *The Kindertransport: Contesting Memory*. Bloomington, Indiana: Indiana University Press, 2019.

Offer, Miriam. *White Coats in the Ghetto: Jewish Medicine in Poland during the Holocaust*. Israel: Yad Vashem, 2020.

Oliner, Samuel, and Pearl Oliner. *The Altruistic Personality: Rescuers of Jews in Nazi Europe*. New York: The Free Press, 1988.

Paldiel, Mordecai. "Jewish Women Rescuers of Jews." In *Women Defying Hitler*. Edited by Nathan Stoltzfus, Mordecai Paldiel, and Judy Baumel-Schwartz. London: Bloomsbury, 2021.

Paldiel, Mordecai. *Saving One's Own: Jewish Rescuers during the Holocaust*. Lincoln: University of Nebraska Press, 2017.

Palmer, Alun. "Renowned Mime Artist Marcel Marceau Saved Jewish Children from the Holocaust." The Mirror. 2020. Accessed 12 January,2021.https://www.mirror.co.uk/news/uk-news/renowned-mime-artist-marcel-marceau-22286631.

Polak, Joseph. *After the Holocaust the Bells Still Ring*. Jerusalem: Urim Publications, 2015.

Pressman, Steven. *50 Children: One Ordinary American Couple's Extraordinary Rescue Mission into the Heart of Nazi Germany* New York: HarperCollins Publishers, 2014.

Rappaport, Doreen. *Beyond Courage: The Untold Story of Jewish Resistance during the Holocaust*. Massachusetts, USA: Candlewick Press, 2012.

Ringelblum, Emanuel. *Ringelblumyoman Ve-Reshimot Mitkufat, Ha-Milhama [Diary and Notes from the Warsaw Ghetto: Sept 1939-December 1942]*. Jerusalem: Yad Vashem, September 1939-December 1942.

Ritvo, Roger A., and Diane M Plotkin. *Sisters in Sorrow: Voices of Care in the Holocaust*. College Station: Texas A & M University Press, 1998.

Rosen, Alan. *The Wonder of Their Voices: The 1946 Holocaust Interviews of David Boder*. Oxford, UK: Oxford University Press, 2010.

Rosen, R D. *Such Good Girls: The Journey of the Holocaust's Hidden Child Survivors*. New York: Harper Perenial, 2014.

Rosenberg, Maxine B. *Hiding to Survive: Stories of Jewish Children Rescued from the Holocaust*. New York: Clarion Books, 1994.

Rosenfeld, Sandra. "The Difficulties Involved in the Rescue of Children by Non-Jews - before and after Liberation." The International School for Holocaust Studies, Yad Vashem. 2018. Accessed 9 July 2018, 2018. www.yadvashem.org/yv/en/education/newsletter/33/difficulties_involved.asp.

Rosensaft, Menachem. "My Mother Was a Jewish Heroine of the Shoah." New York Jewish Weekly. 2022. Accessed 14 April, 2022. http://www.donate.jta.org/2016/12/20/default/my-mother-was-a-jewish-heroine-of-the-shoah-2.

Rubin, Susan Goldman. *Fireflies in the Dark: The Story of Friedl Dicker-Brandeis and the Children of Terezin*. New York: Holiday House, 2000.

Saidel, Rochelle. "Remembering a Hero of the Holocaust." Remember the Women Institute. 2022. Accessed 5 August, 2022. https://myemail.constantcontact.com/Remembering-a-Hero-of-the-Holocaust.html?soid=1111778380172&aid=v-iuIWkXC8I.

Samuel, Vivette. *Rescuing the Children: A Holocaust Memoir*. Madison, Wisconsin: The University of Wisconsin Press, 2002.

Samuels, Michael. *The Windermere Children*. Wall to Wall and Warner Bros, Germany 2020. 88 mins.

Schwartz, Judith Baumel. "Saving Jewish Children after the Holocaust." Research Gate. 2-13. Accessed 12 January, 2021. https://www.researchgate.net/publication/293439961_Saving_Jewish_Children_After_the_Holocaust.

Sherin, Ed. *Lena: My 100 Children*. Moonlight Productions, 1987. 95 minutes.

Shoah Resource Centre. "Jewish Army, France." Yad Vashem,. Accessed 8 February, 2024. https://www.yadvashem.org/odot_pdf/Microsoft%20Word%20-%206363.pdf.

Sixsmith, Martin. *Philomena: A Mother, Her Son and a Fifty-Year Search*. London: Pan Books, 2010.

Sklarew, Myra. "True History of an Unknown Hero of the French Jewish Resistance." Forward. 2013. Accessed 19 April, 2023. https://forward.com/culture/178027/true-history-of-an-unknown-hero-of-the-french-jewi/.

Sliwowska, Wiktoria, ed., *The Last Eyewitnesses: Children of the Holocaust Speak*. Translated by Julian and Fay Bussgang. Evanston, Illinois: Northwestern University Press, 1998.

Smith, Bradley E, and Agnes F Peterson. *Heinrich Himmler: Geheimreden 1933 Bis 1945* Frankfort, 1974.

Spielberg, Steven. *Schindler's List*. 1993. 3 hr.17 min.

Springer, Judith. "The Quest for Rescue in Occupied Territory." In *Holocaust in Belorussia, 1941-1944*. Edited by Leonid Smilovitsky. Vol. 2023 F. Tel Aviv: Yiskor Book, 2000.

Stein, Andre. *Hidden Children: Forgotten Survivors of the Holocaust*. Canada: Penguin Books, 1993.

Steinfeldt, Irena. "Rescuers-Rescued Relations - What Can and Cannot Be Found in the Files of the Righteous among Nations." In *Hiding, Sheltering, and Borrowing Identities: Avenues of Rescue during the Holocaust*. Edited by Dan Michman. Jerusalem: Yad Vashem, 2017.

Stoltzfus, Nathan, Mordecai Paldiel, and Judy Baumel-Schwartz. *Women Defying Hitler: Rescue and Resistance under the Nazis*. London: Bloomsbury Academic, 2021.

Sullivan, Rosemary. *The Betrayal of Anne Frank: A Cold Case Investigation*. USA: Harper, 2022.

Szwajger, Adina Blady. *I Remember Nothing More: The Warsaw Children's Hospital and Jewish Resistance*. New York: Simon and Schuster, 1988.

Taylor, Derek. *Solomon Schonfeld: A Purpose in Life*. London: Valentine Mitchell, 2009.

Tec, Nechama. *When Light Pierced the Darkness: Christian Rescue of Jews in Nazi Occupied Poland* New York: Oxford University Press, 1986.

Terezin Files. Friedl Dicker-Brandeis, Israel Beit Theresienstadt. *Convention on the Prevention and Punishment of the Crime of Genocide*, by United Nations. Geneva, 1948.

USHMM. "Alphabetical List of Children Found at Terezin's Children's Home, Hauptstrasse 14 in April 1945. (Id: 30781)." USHMM. 1945. Accessed 10 June, 2022. https://www.ushmm.org/online/hsv/source_view.php?SourceId=30781.

USHMM. "Beate Berger, Director of the Beith Ahawah Children's Home." USHMM. 2009. Accessed 13 June, 2022. https://collections.ushmm.org/search/catalog/pa1167888.

USHMM. "Eleanor and Gilbert Kraus." USHMM. 2021. Accessed 17 May, 2021. https://exhibitions.ushmm.org/americans-and-the-holocaust/personal-story/eleanor-gilbert-kraus?utm_source=mkto&utm_medium=email&utm_campaign=E20210509

MKTEMB&utm_term=read&utm_content=historical&mkt_tok =MTY1LUtZTy02MTYAAAF88GhWAtLWSeGARTpBZ5Lq5i 8KIXB1UpHPxa6l7V3UKAvgYd00QPdlIJrskBUqFT4xaIvLk YzvcwOG8RS0I3mfaWjd6RYUw-7JB99rhe4AyQ.

USHMM. *Holocaust Encyclopedia Kovno*. Washington, USA: United States Holocaust Memorial Museum, 2012. Accessed 29 October 2023. https://encyclopedia.ushmm.org/content/en/article/kovno.

USHMM. "Holocaust Encyclopedia: Bergen-Belsen." United States Holocaust Memorial Museum. 2023. Accessed 5 November, 2023. https://encyclopedia.ushmm.org/content/en/article/bergen-belsen.

USHMM. "Holocaust Encyclopedia:Le Chambon-Sur-Lignon." United States Holocaust Memorial Museum. Accessed 30 October, 2023. https://encyclopedia.ushmm.org/content/en/article/le-chambon-sur-lignon.

USHMM. "Jewish Aid and Rescue: Rescue of Children." USHMM. 2021. Accessed 12 January, 2021. https://encyclopedia.ushmm. org/content/en/article/jewish-aid-and-rescue.

USHMM. "Kindertransport, 1938-40." USHMM. 2021. Accessed 12 January, 2021. https://encyclopedia.ushmm.org/content/en/ article/kindertransport-1938-40?series=137.

USHMM. "Plight of Jewish Children." USHMM. Accessed 16 November, 2015. www.ushmm.org/wic/en/article.php? ModuleId=10006124.

USHMM. "The Rescue Mission of Gilbert and Eleanor Kraus." USHMM. 2021. Accessed 23 May 2022. https://encyclopedia. ushmm.org/content/en/article/the-rescue-mission-of-gilbert-and-eleanor-kraus.

USHMM. "Studio Portrait of Hennie and Yehoshua Birnbaum and Their Baby Daughter Sonni." USHMM. 2014. Accessed 13 June, 2022.

Von Zur Mühlen, Irmgard. *Liberation of Auschwitz: Child Survivors*. 1945. 1.12 mins. https://encyclopedia.ushmm.org/content/en/ film/liberation-of-auschwitz-child-survivors.

Vromen, Susanne. *Hidden Children of the Holocaust: Belgian Nuns and Their Daring Rescue of Young Jews from the Nazis*. New York: Oxford University Press, 2008.

Werber, Jack. *Saving Children: Diary of a Buchenwald Survivor and Rescuer*. New Brunswick, USA: Transaction Publishers, 2014.

Werner, Abraham. *Ordeal and Deliverance*. Translated by Shula Werner. Raanana, Israel: Docostory Publishing House Ltd., 2003.

Wikipedia. "Lejb Rotblat." Wikipedia. 2022. Accessed 7 June 2022. https://en.wikipedia.org/wiki/Lejb_Rotblat.

Wix, Linney. "Aesthetic Empathy in Teaching Art to Children: The Work of Friedl Dicker-Brandeis in Terezin." *Art Therapy: Journal of the American Art Therapy Association* 26, no. 4 (2009): 152-8.

Wolf, Diane. *Beyond Anne Frank: Hidden Children and Postwar Families in Holland*. Berkeley, California: University of California Press, 2007.

Wolf, Roni. "Saved in a Jewish Orphanage during the Holocaust My Story with Roni and Igor Wolf." interview by Les Glassman. Israel, 2023, Les Glassman. Youtube. https://www.youtube.com/watch?v=87mVNDQwq_8.

Wolff, Margo. *The Boys of Mon Respos: Rescue Operation "Sesame" from Vichy France*. New York: Townhouse Press, 1986.

Yad Vashem. "Irena Sendler." Yad Vashem. 2021. Accessed 12 January, 2021. https://www.yadvashem.org/yv/en/exhibitions/righteous-women/sendler.asp.

Yad Vashem. "Lois Gunden." Yad Vashem. 2021. Accessed 12 Janaury, 2021. https://www.yadvashem.org/yv/en/exhibitions/righteous-women/gunden.asp.

Yad Vashem. "Names of Righteous by Country." Yad Vashem. 2022. Accessed 29 April, 2022. https://www.yadvashem.org/righteous/statistics.html.

Yad Vashem. "Rescue by Jews during the Holocaust." *Yad Vashem Newsletter* 94, no. Winter 2021 (2021): 30-33. https://view.publitas.com/yad-vashem/yad-vashem-magazine-94/page/32-33.

Yad Vashem. "Rescue by Jews during the Holocaust Solidarity in a Disintegrating World: Unto Every Person There Is a Name." Yad Vashem. 2020. Accessed 3 April, 2024. embassies.gov.il/zagreb/NewsAndEvents/Documents/every-person.pdf.

Yad Vashem. "Rescue of Children." Yad Vashem. 2018. Accessed 9 July 2018, 2018. www.yadvashem.org/odot_pdf/Microsoft%20Word%20-%205820.pdf

Yad Vashem. "The Righteous among Nations Database." Yad Vashem. 2022. https://righteous.yadvashem.org/?search=Female&searchType=righteous_only&language=en.

Yad Vashem. "Suzanne Spaak." Yad Vashem. 2021. Accessed 12 January, 2021. https://www.yadvashem.org/yv/en/exhibitions/righteous-women/spaak.asp.

Yad Vashem. "Where Was God during the Holocaust?" Yad Vashem. 2023. Accessed 22 April, 2023. https://www.yadvashem.org/education/educational-materials/center-question/q7.html.

Yad Vashem. "Women of Valor: Stories of Women Who Rescued Jews during the Holocaust." Yad Vashem. 2021. Accessed 12 Janaury, 2021. https://www.yadvashem.org/yv/en/exhibitions/righteous-women/index.asp.

Yavneh Memorial and Education Centre. "Kindertransports from North Rhine-Westphalia: The Yavneh Kindertransports." Yavneh Memorial and Education Centre. 2021. Accessed 19 June, 2021. http://www.kindertransporte-nrw.eu/kindertransporte_jawne_e.html.

Young, Lauren. *Hitler's Girl*. Canada: Harper, 2022.

Zahra, Tara. *The Lost Children: Reconstructing Europe's Families after World War II*. Cambridge Massachusetts: Harvard University Press, 2011.

Ziemian, Joseph. *The Cigarette Sellers of Three Crosses Square: Searing Testament to Human Courage*. New York: Avon Publishers, 1975.

Zornberg, Ira. *Jews, Quakers and the Holocaust: The Struggle to Save the Lives of Twenty-Thousand Children* USA: Unspecified, 2016.

Zucker, Bat-Ami. "Cecilia Razovsky, the American Activist Who Rescued German Jewish Children (1933-1945)." *Women in Judaism: A Multidisciplinary e-Journal* 17, no. 2 (2020): 1-15.

Zullo, Allan, and Mara Bovsun. *Heroes of the Holocaust: The Stories of the Rescues of Teens*. New York: Scholastic, 2005.

Index

209

Yeshurun 63
Yiddish 31, 40, 54, 103
Youth Aliyah xii, 17, 39, 45, 46, 47,
    161, 162
Yvonne/Hava Jospa. *See* Hava
    (and Hertz) Jospa
Yvonne Nèvejearn 78

Z
Zakopane 139, 140

Żegota 32, 56, 76
Zionist xii, 46, 47, 48, 56, 57,
    60, 63, 65, 66, 76, 91,
    92, 94, 125, 127, 128,
    129, 130
Zivia Kapit 70, 163
ZOB 76
Zorah Warhaftig 57
Zosia Fener 137
Zyklon B 22

About the Authors

Dr. Beverley Chalmers

Dr. Chalmers has two doctoral degrees: the first in Humanities (PhD in Psychology) and the second, a senior doctorate, in Obstetrics (DSc (Med)). Currently an independent scholar, she has held Full Professorial positions in Departments of Psychology (University of the Witwatersrand, South Africa), Obstetrics and Gynaecology (Universities of Ottawa, Toronto, and Witwatersrand), Nursing, and Public Health Science (University of Toronto), and Epidemiology and Community Health (Queen's University, Canada). She currently serves on the Steering Committee of the Women in the Holocaust International Study Centre (WHISC), Israel.

Dr. Chalmers has over 300 publications including 58 book chapters, and 11 books to her credit. She has given over 470 conference presentations and addresses globally. She has undertaken over 140 international health promotion activities in more than 30 countries including in the Russian Federation, Tajikistan, Kyrgyzstan, Kazakhstan, Turkmenistan, Azerbaijan, Georgia, Armenia, Moldova, Belarus, Poland, Hungary, Ukraine, Czech Republic, Slovakia, Romania, Lithuania, Latvia, Estonia, Germany, Sweden, Norway, Greece, Switzerland, Italy, Sudan, Ethiopia, Singapore, China, Sri Lanka, Montevideo, South Africa and Canada.

Her work in both Canada and in South Africa was rewarded in Canada with two awards: a Canadian Women in Global Health Award (2018/2021), and a South African Women for Women Award (2000). In South Africa she was awarded the highest award offered by the

University of the Witwatersrand to Faculty members: a Council Research Fellowship for one year of international study. This was spent as the Acting Head of the WHO-Euro Maternal and Child Health unit (1991-2).

Dr. Chalmers' books on women's and children's experiences during the Holocaust have won 23 book awards. *Birth, Sex and Abuse: Women's Voices Under Nazi Rule* (2015) was awarded a USA National Jewish Book Award, a Canadian Vine Award, a Canadian Jewish Literary Award, and a CHOICE "Outstanding Academic Title" award, among others. Her more recent award-winning publications *Betrayed: Child Sex Abuse in the Holocaust* (2020) and *Child Sex Abuse: Power, Profit, Perversion* (2022) expose neglected subjects in both Holocaust and child abuse studies.

Dr. Dana Solomon

Dr. Dana Solomon is a researcher, artist, entrepreneur, and advocate for human rights and equity. Her academic, professional, and artistic work has been devoted to developing innovative and effective strategies to combat prejudice and champion the rights of all people to equity.

Dr. Solomon has both an MA and PhD in Interdisciplinary Studies and 15 years of experience developing innovative and effective strategies for reducing systemic inequities facing multiple communities in diverse settings. Her research includes the use of Theatre and ParaTheatre in the Holocaust, the ideologies of the Arab-Israeli conflict, the impact of weight bias and ableism, ideologies of genocide and conflict, and developing Ideologically Challenging Entertainment. She has 50 creative and academic publications, including her book, *Ideological Battlegrounds: Entertainment to Disarm Divisive Propaganda*.

Dr. Solomon has more than 25 years of experience as a multi-faceted theatre artist, including professional experience as a director, actor, and stage manager. She owns her own business, D-Editions &

Chalmers-Solomon Solutions, through which she provides research and publication support, and develops Ideologically Challenging Entertainment. Dr. Solomon is an independent scholar and serves as the Vice President of the Disability Affinity Group at the University of British Columbia.

Abuse, Birth & Children Series: Historical & Contemporary

Other books by Beverley Chalmers in the ABC Series.

Historical

- *Birth, Sex and Abuse: Women's Voices Under Nazi Rule*

- *Betrayed: Child Sex Abuse in the Holocaust*

- *African Birth: Childbirth in Cultural Transition*

Contemporary

- *Child Sex Abuse: Power, Profit, Perversion*

- *Abuse: Pregnancy, Birth, Postpartum* (Forthcoming)

- *Family-Centred Perinatal Care: Improving Pregnancy, Birth and Postpartum Care*

- *Humane Perinatal Care* (With Adik Levin)

- *Pregnancy and Parenthood: Heaven or Hell*

- *Female Genital Mutilation and Obstetric Care* (With Kowser Omer-Hashi)

Learn more or contact Dr. Chalmers at www.bevchalmers.com.

Praise for Related Books by These Authors

Birth, Sex and Abuse: Women's Voices Under Nazi Rule By Beverley Chalmers

"This book should be a 'must' for everybody dealing with the cruel chapters of the Holocaust, especially for those who are dealing with research about the subject of women and children, and medicine, during the Shoah."

(Prof. Dr. Miriam Gillis-Carlebach, Director, The Joseph Carlebach Institute, Bar-Ilan University, Israel)

"This book has an utterly unique, in-depth focus on all aspects of sexuality and reproduction during the Nazi regime; the author has written the first-ever, comprehensive tome on the treatment of women and infants that is essential for many disciplines."

(Prof. Caroline Pukall, PhD, Professor of Psychology, Director of SexLab and the Sex Therapy Service, Queen's University, Kingston, Canada)

"Overall, the text, while interdisciplinary in nature, is easy to comprehend [...]. This text would be an asset for anyone wishing to educate themselves on women's varying experiences during the Holocaust, as well as anyone wanting to know more about sexuality in ghettos, prisons, and concentration camps."

(Prof. Tamala Malerk, University of South Florida, Tampa, USA)

"Chalmers writing [...] reflects exhaustive research, clarity of thought, and unflinching engagement with complexities that have received inadequate prior attention. Essential, Upper division undergraduates and above."

(Prof. M.D. Lagerwey, Western Michigan University.
Review, Social and Behavioral Sciences)

"There are many Holocaust survival narratives and autobiographies that deal with brothels and forced sex in the camps. But *Birth, Sex and Abuse: Women's Voices under Nazi Rule* by Beverley Chalmers stands alone. [...] each word, each bit of information is precious and unlikely to be found elsewhere with such clarity and comprehensiveness [...]. It is a library within a library."

(Marcia Weiss Posner, Jewish Book Council USA Review)

"Chalmers [...] has published an encyclopedic work [...] it offers an accessible account of the experience of women's sexual and reproductive lives under Nazi rule. [...] will serve as an important reference volume [...] Chalmers has laid a superb foundation for what is hoped will lead to further research in this critical area of Holocaust studies."

(Prof. Michael Grodin, Boston University)

"A perspective that is both vast and specific at the same time. Chalmers does an impressive job negotiating and respecting the stories told by survivors in order to portray the brutality of the Nazis while also avoiding sensationalism or gratuitous violence. [...] Chalmers writing, research and attention to details shines. [...] meticulous record of events, stories and untold atrocities provides readers with access to a new understanding of the horrors of the Holocaust. [...] impressive bibliography and collection of notes. [...] an excellent addition to classes about Jewish history or Women and Judaism and for anyone interested in Holocaust studies."

(Prof. Rachel E. Silverman, Embry Riddle University,
Daytona Beach, Florida, USA)

Betrayed: Child Sex Abuse in the Holocaust By Beverley Chalmers

"With a rare combination of human empathy and scholarly criticism, Beverley Chalmers delves into a disturbingly difficult subject: the sexual abuse of children during World War II. Her research sheds light on the various forms of child abuse, and undermines conventional categorization patterns. For example, Chalmers shows that children were sexually abused not only by people related to the occupying forces or by hostile strangers, but also by others, including some of their very protectors. Chalmers puts the children and their suffering in the very centre and makes their voices – their cries – heard: by doing so, she creates a wider awareness of this dreadful phenomenon, awareness that is crucial to anyone who wishes to build a better world for our children."

(Noam Rachmilevitch, Ghetto Fighter's House, Israel)

"Sexual abuse is one of the many horrors that some children were forced to endure during the Holocaust. But their stories deserve to be told. *Betrayed* is a well written and researched, albeit difficult, read that gives these victims a voice to be heard."

(Dr. Tessa Chelouche M.D. Department of Bioethics and the Holocaust, Unesco Chair of Bioethics, Haifa, Israel)

"…the book fills a major knowledge gap […] it models the way that future academic investigations into this subject should go."

(Arthur B. Shostak, Prof. Emeritus of Sociology, Jewish Book Council Review)

"…proves to be an eye-opening account is also highly disturbing […]. This is a good detailed book that might greatly benefit historians and interested readers."

(Donna Ford, US Review of Books. Recommended by the US Review of Books.)

Ideological Battlegrounds: Entertainment to Disarm Divisive Propaganda By Dana Solomon

"In Ideological Battlegrounds, Dana L. Solomon opens up original and penetrating pathways toward understanding and possibly resolving what often appears to be an insolvable conflict. This book becomes more timely with the passing of each day. It is indispensable reading for anyone who hopes to even begin to comprehend the situation in the Middle East."

(Prof. David Patterson, The University of Texas at Dallas)

"In Ideological Battlegrounds, Solomon has developed a thoughtful and creative approach to engaging theater as a catalyst for critical discussions around the Arab-Israeli conflict. At the heart of this book rests her play, *Two Merchants*, which effectively subverts and disrupts, enabling audience members to rethink and reconsider these ongoing tensions. I strongly recommend this interdisciplinary and insightful book."

(Prof. George Belliveau, The University of British Columbia)

"The Department of Theatre and Film at UBC eagerly embraced the *Two Merchants* project in 2011 as it was a unique blend of practice and scholarship. Dana L. Solomon used a live theater event as the platform to test her belief that the theater could change minds and therefore change the world. Many of us have professed this for our entire professional lives, but Solomon tackled the belief head on and has provided analytic proof that we were right all along!"

(Prof. Stephen Heatley, University of British Columbia)

Milton Keynes UK
Ingram Content Group UK Ltd.
UKHW031946171124
451278UK00002B/106

9 781803 819815